O9-AIE-869

Aerospace Facts & Figures 2004/2005

Compiled by:
Aerospace Research Center
Aerospace Industries Association of America, Inc.

Director, Aerospace Research Center
David H. Napier

Manager, Electronic Data
Terry Ruby

Designed by:
MV Design

Published by:
Aerospace Industries Association of America, Inc.
1000 Wilson Boulevard #1700
Arlington, VA 22209-3928
703-358-1015
703-358-1115 Fax
AIA@AIA-aerospace.org

ACKNOWLEDGMENTS

Air BP Lubricants

Air Transport Association of America

The Boyd Company

Council of Economic Advisers

Export-Import Bank of the United States

Futron Corporation

General Aviation Manufacturers Association

Helicopter Association International

International Civil Aviation Organization

National Aeronautics and Space Administration

National Science Foundation

Office of Management and Budget

Office of Personnel Management

U.S. Department of Commerce (Bureau of Economic Analysis; Bureau of the Census; International Trade Administration)

U.S. Department of Defense (Air Force; Army; Comptroller; Information Technology Management Directorate; Missile Defense Agency; Navy)

U.S. Department of Labor (Bureau of Labor Statistics)

U.S. Department of Transportation (Federal Aviation Administration, Office of Airline Information)

CONTENTS

The Aerospace industry once again saw mixed fortunes in 2003, with business results varying widely depending on exactly where in the sector a company found itself. Once again the industry's two largest markets continued to move in opposite directions; defense decidedly positive, commercial a bit less so.

Defense orders increased for the sixth straight year as well as defense shipments for the last three. Civil orders, on the other hand, decreased for the third straight year–leading to a second year of declining civil shipments. Combined industry shipments declined, dragging aerospace employment to a post-World War II low.

As the aerospace workforce shrank due to decreased demand, the age of our workers increased. A large percentage of our experienced workers will retire this decade. Now an

expected turnaround in the commercial market will compound industry's shortage of skilled workers. AIA and industry are working with government, labor, and academia on a multi-pronged plan to address the looming workforce shortfall.

The industry's commercial customers, in particular scheduled air carriers, continued to post losses in aggregate. Airline traffic returned to pre-9/11 levels, but revenues remained depressed and costs–most notably fuel–remained high. Mindful that airlines are facing a profitless recovery, AIA is working hard to improve air traffic efficiency and safety to benefit those companies in the future. The top priority to that end is aiding the airlines in demanding the modernization of the global air traffic control, increasing system capacity, and improving aircraft efficiency.

President Bush's re-election cleared a level of uncertainty that hung over 2004 and we now expect to see a continuation of current policies and plans. We have clear visions for progress in all sectors of aerospace. In space, we have the national Vision for Space Exploration. In defense, we envision a continued financial commitment to keeping our nation safe and strong. In civil aviation, we look for investment in the Next-Generation Air Traffic Control System and other important improvements. We look forward to the president's second term to make progress on plans forged in his first term.

Aerospace is a global business. Free and fair trade is a cornerstone for global economic growth which our industry depends on. In addition, preserving our industry's position as the country's largest net exporter will require a fresh look at our antiquated export control system. AIA will renew its efforts to promote a level playing field and to modernize and right-size the scope of export licensing.

In 2004, AIA also marked the 85th anniversary of its founding in 1919. Despite a wave of consolidation among aerospace and defense companies, today AIA represents a record number of companies. This is a testament to our strength—industry working together with our government partners for mutual solutions. That first year AIA, originally known as the Aeronautical Chamber of Commerce, adopted a philosophy to promote aeronautics and "generally, to do every act and thing which may be necessary and proper for the advancement" of American aviation. We continue on that mission, tasked to us by visionaries with names like Wright and Curtiss, and trust the year ahead will bring advancement and success that would make them proud.

John W. Douglass
President and Chief Executive Officer
Aerospace Industries Association of America, Inc.

U.S. aerospace industry sales fell in 2003, ending a two-year rise. Despite a robust and growing domestic military market, reduced exports and sharply lower civil sales overwhelmed those gains. R&D funding, profits, and capital equipment investment, and overall orders improved while continuing losses for the world's airlines and record-low aerospace industry employment typify the divergent conditions the industry faced in 2003.

Highlights of the year in aerospace include:

SALES

Total aerospace industry sales declined—falling 2.9% or $4.5 billion—to $149 billion. DoD sales increased 11%, or $6.6 billion, to $64 billion, while sales to NASA and other civil agencies declined 5.3%, or $0.9 billion, to $15.5 billion. More than accounting for the overall decline, sales to other customers fell $9.4 billion, or 18%, to $44 billion.

Similarly, DoD-dominated product group sales (i.e., military aircraft, missiles, and space) grew in 2003. Substantial missile defense RDT&E funding helped raise missile sector sales to $13.5 billion which included a modest increase in procurement. Both the space sector and the military aircraft sector saw sales increases of $1.7 billion and $2.1 billion, respectively.

Aircraft sales—both military and civil combined—fell by $6.0 billion last year. Despite the above-mentioned military growth, the civil aircraft sector's 19% sales decline pulled overall sales down to $74 billion. Civil sales fell $8.2 billion to $34 billion.

For 2003, aerospace industry output accounted for 1.4% of the Gross Domestic Product and 3.7% of manufacturing sales.

EARNINGS

The aerospace industry generated $7.2 billion in net income after taxes (net profit) on $172 billion of corporate sales last year. 2003's net, while higher than profits posted before 1996, represented a decline of 29% from 1999's record-setting level. Net profit as a percentage of sales rose to 4.2%—the third lowest level since 1995—down from 6.5% in 1999 and 4.7% in 2000.

The corresponding profit margin for all manufacturing corporations in 2003 was 5.4%—up sharply from 2002's 3.3% and 2001's 0.8%, but the third worst showing since 1994. Similarly, the aerospace industry's net profit as a percentage of shareholders' equity rose to 12.3%. Profits as a percentage of assets, however, declined to

3.3%. For comparison, prior year aerospace returns on equity and assets were 11.7% and 3.7%; and the averages for all manufacturing corporations in 2003 were 12.2% and 4.7%, respectively.

ORDERS AND BACKLOG

New orders rose 1.6% to $117 billion in 2003. While military orders rose nicely from $66 billion to $74 billion, civil orders fell sharply—down $5.4 billion to $43 billion. Combined orders for aircraft, engines, and parts rose 3.1% to $62 billion with military orders rising $5.2 billion, or 18%, to $34 billion and civil orders falling $3.3 billion, or 11%, to $28 billion.

The industry's year-end backlog grew slightly to $223 billion. Growth in the military backlog continued for its fourth straight year after ending a three-year slide; and the civil backlog dropped $7.5 billion. The aircraft sector declined for a third year to $137 billion from an eight-year-high backlog of $156 billion for year-end 2000. Similarly after reaching record levels in 2000, unfilled orders for missiles, space, and rocket propulsion fell to $28 billion in 2003. On the other hand, unfilled orders for "Other Aerospace" rose $4.1 billion to $36 billion.

CIVIL AIRCRAFT

The civil aircraft manufacturing industry produced and delivered 35 more aircraft than in 2002—2,928 in all. The entirety of the increase came from helicopter shipments, whose production jumped from 318 to 517. General aviation aircraft shipments, on the other hand, dropped by 66 to 2,130. Transport aircraft production also fell in 2003 by 98 from 2002's 379. Domestic shipments fell 43% to 67 while transport exports fell 18% to 214.

According to Air BP's annual "Turbine-Engined Fleets of the World's Airlines," the world's airline fleet grew to 26,367 aircraft. There were more Boeing 737s in service than any other single type, with a total active fleet of 3,946. International Civil Aviation Organization statistics show that the world's airlines carried 18 million more passengers and flew slightly more passenger-miles in 2003. Load factors returned to historic high levels—filling planes, but still losing money in aggregate.

MILITARY AIRCRAFT PRODUCTION

Military aircraft production, as measured by acceptances, decreased on falling exports. Manufacturers delivered 337 aircraft of which 32% were destined to customers other than the U.S. government. The number of military aircraft exported declined for the sixth straight year—down 21 to 109—while those exported through the Foreign Military Sales program grew for a second year from the lowest level on record (29) in

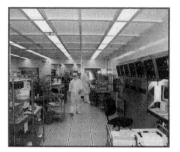

2001. Encouragingly, the value of military aircraft acceptances rose for a second straight year—rising 9% to $11 billion. U.S. military agencies accepted, for their own use, 228 aircraft in 2003—unchanged from 2002.

Three programs dominated new aircraft procurement in FY 2003: the Air Force's F-22 Raptor was the largest, big-ticket item with 21 fighters costing $4.5 billion, followed by 15 C-17 Globemaster III cargo aircraft worth $4.2 billion, and the Navy's 45 F/A-18E/F Super Hornet fighters for $3.2 billion. Eleven V-22 Osprey tiltrotor aircraft costing $1.2 billion logged a distant fourth. Scheduled for significant procurement funding increases in FY 2004 are the Air Force's C-130J variants and JPATS and the Navy's H-1 variants, MH-60, and T-45.

FOREIGN TRADE

Aerospace exports decreased by $4.3 billion to $53 billion. Civil exports decreased $3.3 billion on $2.2 billion fewer jetliner exports and military exports also decreased on fewer helicopter and fighter exports.

The aerospace industry continued to enjoy a trade surplus even as the manufacturing sector, as a whole, saw its trade deficit balloon to a record $535 billion. The aerospace trade surplus worsened by $2.4 billion to $27 billion despite a $1.8 billion decline in imports. Imports of aircraft engines dropped 33% to $2.5 billion as did transport and general aviation aircraft imports.

SPACE PROGRAMS

According to data compiled by the U.S. Census Bureau, sales of space vehicle systems fell $0.6 billion in 2003 to $7.4 billion. Both military and civil space sales declined—down $42 million to $3.8 billion and $0.5 billion to $3.6 billion, respectively.

NASA, on the other hand, estimated total federal spending for space activities increased in FY 2003 to $33 billion. DoD's space-related outlays, at $18.6 billion, topped NASA's $13.6 billion and rose sharply from $14.9 billion. Space spending at all other agencies increased a combined $41 million to a total of $1.2 billion.

Within the NASA budget, Science, Aeronautics, and Technology received $8.4 billion. Station and Shuttle budget items together accounted for 31% of NASA's $15.4 billion in total budget authority for 2003. NASA's FY 2004 budget should total $15.4 billion with Space Science receiving $4.0 billion; the Shuttle, $3.9 billion; and the ISS, $1.5 billion.

MISSILE PROGRAMS

Total DoD outlays for missile procurement rose slightly to $5.3 billion in FY 2003. Major programs include: MDA's Patriot with $756 million in funding; Air Force's JDAM, $752 million; Navy's Trident II, $573 million; and Army's Javelin, $222 million.

Ballistic Missile Defense continues to dominate missile RDT&E. Funding totaled $6.7 billion in FY 2003 and is scheduled to increase to $9.1 billion in 2005.

Also, net new orders jumped 13% to $9.9 billion in 2003. The year-end 2003 backlog of unfilled orders stood at $13 billion.

RESEARCH AND DEVELOPMENT

R&D spending by the federal government increased $13.5 billion—the third year of real growth—after languishing for six years at the same real-spending level. The DoD, with its $54 billion in outlays, continued to be the government's largest single spender on R&D, accounting for half of all federal funding. NASA's R&D totaled $7.7 billion and the Department of Energy invested $7.4 billion. Other agencies also saw healthy growth. Organizations such as the National Science Foundation, the National Institutes of Health, and the Transportation and Agriculture Departments collectively saw their R&D outlays rise 11% to $33 billion. Federally-funded R&D is scheduled to increase $13.6 billion to $115 billion in FY 2004.

In addition to the previously-mentioned Ballistic Missile Defense, other major RDT&E programs in FY 2003 include: the Joint Strike Fighter received $3.3 billion; F-22 Raptor, $909 million; RAH-66 Comanche, $866 million; Advanced EHF, $803 million; SBIRS-High, $775 million; and V-22 Osprey, $444 million.

EMPLOYMENT

Industry employment fell to its lowest level in at least 43 years to stand at 583,000. On an annual average basis, total employment declined by 35,000 in 2003. Production workers lost work at a slightly higher rate than other categories of employees. Most of the jobs losses were in the aircraft, engines, and parts manufacturing sector.

Despite the losses, however, experts agree that engineers and technical workers remain in demand. Most aerospace companies say they still need mechanical, structural, and aerodynamics engineers, as well as software engineers and information technology specialists.

Aerospace constituted 4.0% of all manufacturing employment and 6.5% of durable goods manufacturing employment. The aerospace share of manufacturing and durable goods employment has fallen from 6.3% and 10.4% in 1990, respectively.

STANDARD INDUSTRIAL CLASSIFICATIONS
APPLICABLE TO THE AEROSPACE INDUSTRY

3721 AIRCRAFT
- 37211 Military aircraft
- 37215 Civilian aircraft
- 37217 Modification, conversion, and overhaul of previously accepted aircraft
- 37218 Aeronautical services on complete aircraft, nec

3724 AIRCRAFT ENGINES AND ENGINE PARTS
- 37241 Aircraft engines for military aircraft
- 37242 Aircraft engines for civilian aircraft
- 37243 Aeronautical services on aircraft engines
- 37244 Aircraft engine parts and accessories

3728 AIRCRAFT PARTS AND AUXILIARY EQUIPMENT, NEC
- 37281 Aircraft parts and auxiliary equipment, nec
- 37282 Aircraft propellers and helicopter rotors
- 37283 Research and development on aircraft parts

3761 GUIDED MISSILES AND SPACE VEHICLES
- 37611 Complete guided missiles (excluding propulsion systems)
- 37612 Complete space vehicles (excluding propulsion systems)
- 37613 Research and development on complete guided missiles
- 37614 Research and development on complete space vehicles
- 37615 All other services on complete guided missiles and space vehicles

3663 RADIO AND TELEVISION COMMUNICATIONS EQUIPMENT
- 36631 Communication systems and equipment, except broadcast

3764 SPACE PROPULSION UNITS AND PARTS
- 37645 Complete missile or space vehicle engines and/or propulsion units
- 37646 Research and development on complete missile or space vehicle engines and/or propulsion units
- 37647 Services on complete guided missile or space vehicle engines and/or propulsion units, nec
- 37648 Missile and space vehicle engine and/or propulsion unit parts and accessories

3769 SPACE VEHICLE EQUIPMENT, NEC
- 37692 Missile and space vehicle components, parts and subassemblies, nec
- 37694 Research and development on missile and space vehicle parts and components, nec

3669 COMMUNICATIONS EQUIPMENT, NEC
- 36691 Alarm systems
- 36692 Traffic control equipment
- 36693 Intercommunication equipment

3812 SEARCH, DETECTION, NAVIGATION, GUIDANCE, AERONAUTICAL AND NAUTICAL SYSTEMS, INSTRUMENTS, AND EQUIPMENT
- 38121 Aeronautical, nautical, and navigational instruments, not sending or receiving radio signals
- 38122 Search, detection, navigation, and guidance systems and equipment

3829 MEASURING AND CONTROLLING DEVICES, NEC
- 38291 Aircraft engine instruments except flight

Source: Office of Management and Budget, "Standard Industrial Classification Manual, 1987."

NOTE: The Standard Industrial Classification (SIC) is a system developed by the U.S. Government to define the industrial composition of the economy, facilitating comparability of statistics. It is revised periodically to reflect the changing industrial composition of the economy.

NEC: Not elsewhere classified.

NORTH AMERICAN INDUSTRY CLASSIFICATION SYSTEM CODES APPLICABLE TO THE AEROSPACE INDUSTRY

33641	**Aerospace product & parts mfg**
336411	**Aircraft mfg**
3364111	Military aircraft
3364113	Civilian aircraft
3364115	Modification, conversion, and overhaul of previously accepted aircraft
3364117	Other aeronautical services on complete aircraft, nec
336411W	Aircraft manufacturing, nsk
336412	**Aircraft engine & engine parts mfg**
3364121	Military aircraft engines
3364123	Civilian aircraft engines
3364125	Aeronautical services on aircraft engines
3364127	Aircraft engine parts and accessories
336412W	Aircraft engines and engine parts manufacturing, nsk
336413	**Aircraft parts and auxiliary equipment mfg, nec**
3364131	Aircraft propellers and helicopter rotors
3364133	Research and development on aircraft parts (except engines)
3364135	Aircraft parts and auxiliary equipment, excluding hydraulic and pneumatic subassemblies and engines
336413W	Aircraft parts and auxiliary equipment, nec, nsk
336414	**Guided missile & space vehicle mfg**
3364141	Complete guided missiles
3364143	Research and development on complete guided missiles
3364145	Other services on complete guided missiles
3364147	Complete space vehicles (excluding propulsion systems)
3364149	Research and development on complete space vehicles
336414A	All other services on complete space vehicles
336414W	Guided missile and space vehicle manufacturing, nsk
336415	**Guided missile & space vehicle propulsion unit & parts mfg**
3364151	Complete missile or space vehicle engines and/or propulsion units
3364153	Research and development on complete missile or space vehicle engines and/or propulsion units
3364155	Other services on complete missile or space vehicle engines and/or propulsion units

3364157	Missile and space vehicle engine and/or propulsion parts and accessories
336415W	Space propulsion units and parts, nsk
336419	**Other guided missile & space vehicle parts & auxiliary equip mfg**
3327221	**Aircraft (including aerospace) fasteners other than plastics (meet specifications for flying vehicles)**
3345191	**Aircraft engine instruments mfg, except flight**
332912	**Fluid power valve and hose fitting mfg**
3329121	Aerospace type hydraulic fluid power valves
3329123	Aerospace type pneumatic fluid power valves
332912F	Aerospace type hydraulic and pneumatic fluid power hose or tube end fittings and assemblies
33399	**All other general purpose machinery mfg**
3339957	Aerospace type fluid power cylinders and actuators, hydraulic and pneumatic
3339967	Aerospace type fluid power pumps and motors
3339996	Filters for hydraulic and pneumatic fluid power systems, aerospace
3342201	**Communication systems and equipment, except broadcast, but including microwave equipment, and space satellites**
334290	**Alarm systems, traffic control equipment, and intercommunication and paging systems mfg**
334511	**Search, detection, navigation, guidance, aeronautical, and nautical systems and instruments mfg**
3345111	Aeronautical, nautical, and navigational instruments, not sending or receiving radio signals, except engine instruments
3345113	Search, detection, navigation, and guidance systems and equipment
334511W	Search, detection, navigation, guidance, aeronautical, and nautical systems and instruments, nsk

Source: Office of Management and Budget, "North American Industry Classification System, United States, 1997."

11

AEROSPACE INDUSTRY SALES BY PRODUCT GROUP
Calendar Years 1989-2003
(Millions of Dollars)

Year	TOTAL	Aircraft			Missiles	Space	Related Products & Services
		TOTAL	Civil	Military			

CURRENT DOLLARS

Year	TOTAL	TOTAL	Civil	Military	Missiles	Space	Related Products & Services
1989	$120,534	$61,550	$21,903	$39,646	$13,622	$25,274	$20,089
1990	134,375	71,353	31,262	40,091	14,180	26,446	22,396
1991	139,248	75,918	37,443	38,475	10,970	29,152	23,208
1992	138,591	73,905	39,897	34,008	11,757	29,831	23,099
1993	123,183	65,829	33,116	32,713	8,451	28,372	20,531
1994	110,558	57,648	25,596	32,052	7,563	26,921	18,426
1995	107,782	55,048	23,965	31,082	7,386	27,385	17,964
1996	116,812	60,296	26,869	33,427	8,008	29,040	19,469
1997	131,582	70,804	37,428	33,376	8,037	30,811	21,930
1998	147,991	83,951	49,676	34,275	7,730	31,646	24,665
1999	153,707	88,731	52,931	35,800	8,825	30,533	25,618
2000	144,741	81,612	47,580	34,032	9,298	29,708	24,123
2001 r	151,632	86,470	51,256	35,215	10,391	29,499	25,272
2002 r	153,409	80,438	42,291	38,147	12,847	34,556	25,568
2003	148,928	74,392	34,122	40,270	13,489	36,226	24,821

CONSTANT DOLLARS[ar]

Year	TOTAL	TOTAL	Civil	Military	Missiles	Space	Related Products & Services
1989	$114,359	$58,397	$20,781	$37,615	$12,924	$23,979	$19,060
1990	123,506	65,582	28,733	36,848	13,033	24,307	20,585
1991	124,886	68,088	33,581	34,507	9,839	26,145	20,814
1992	118,454	63,167	34,100	29,067	10,049	25,497	19,743
1993	102,311	54,675	27,505	27,170	7,019	23,565	17,052
1994	89,666	46,754	20,759	25,995	6,134	21,834	14,944
1995	86,088	43,968	19,141	24,826	5,899	21,873	14,348
1996	91,761	47,365	21,107	26,258	6,291	22,812	15,294
1997	102,478	55,143	29,150	25,994	6,259	23,996	17,079
1998	114,544	64,978	38,449	26,529	5,983	24,494	19,091
1999	118,236	68,255	40,716	27,538	6,788	23,487	19,706
2000	108,177	60,996	35,561	25,435	6,949	22,203	18,029
2001	110,600	63,071	37,386	25,686	7,579	21,516	18,433
2002	110,208	57,786	30,381	27,404	9,229	24,825	18,368
2003	104,073	51,986	23,845	28,141	9,426	25,315	17,345

Source: Aerospace Industries Association.
NOTE: See Glossary for explanation of "Aerospace Industry", "Aerospace Sales", "Other Customers", and "Related Products and Services".
a Based on AIA's aerospace composite deflator 1987=100.

AEROSPACE INDUSTRY SALES BY CUSTOMER
Calendar Years 1989-2003
(Millions of Dollars)

Year	TOTAL	Aerospace Products and Services				Related Products and Services
		TOTAL	U.S. Government		Other Customers	
			Dept. of Defense	NASA and Other Agencies		

CURRENT DOLLARS

Year	TOTAL	TOTAL	Dept. of Defense	NASA and Other Agencies	Other Customers	Related Products and Services
1989	$120,534	$100,445	$61,199	$ 9,601	$29,645	$20,089
1990	134,375	111,979	60,502	11,097	40,379	22,396
1991	139,248	116,040	55,922	11,739	48,379	23,208
1992	138,591	115,493	52,202	12,408	50,882	23,099
1993	123,183	102,653	47,017	12,255	43,380	20,531
1994	110,558	92,132	43,795	11,932	36,405	18,426
1995	107,782	89,818	42,401	11,413	36,004	17,964
1996	116,812	97,344	42,535	12,391	42,418	19,469
1997	131,582	109,651	43,702	12,753	53,196	21,930
1998	147,991	123,326	42,937	13,343	67,047	24,665
1999	153,707	128,089	45,703	13,400	68,986	25,618
2000	144,741	120,617	47,505	13,382	59,730	24,123
2001[r]	151,632	126,360	50,118	14,481	61,761	25,272
2002[r]	153,409	127,841	57,701	16,384	53,756	25,568
2003	148,928	124,106	64,251	15,519	44,337	24,821

CONSTANT DOLLARS[ar]

Year	TOTAL	TOTAL	Dept. of Defense	NASA and Other Agencies	Other Customers	Related Products and Services
1989	$114,359	$ 95,299	$58,064	$ 9,109	$28,126	$19,060
1990	123,506	102,922	55,608	10,199	37,113	20,585
1991	124,886	104,072	50,154	10,528	43,389	20,814
1992	118,454	98,712	44,617	10,605	43,489	19,743
1993	102,311	85,260	39,051	10,179	36,030	17,052
1994	89,666	74,722	35,519	9,677	29,526	14,944
1995	86,088	71,740	33,867	9,116	28,757	14,348
1996	91,761	76,468	33,413	9,734	33,321	15,294
1997	102,478	85,398	34,036	9,932	41,430	17,079
1998	114,544	95,454	33,233	10,327	51,894	19,091
1999	118,236	98,530	35,156	10,308	53,066	19,706
2000	108,177	90,147	35,504	10,001	44,641	18,029
2001	110,600	92,166	36,556	10,562	45,048	18,433
2002	110,208	91,840	41,452	11,770	38,618	18,368
2003	104,073	86,727	44,899	10,845	30,983	17,345

Source: Aerospace Industries Association.
NOTE: See Glossary for explanation of "Aerospace Industry", "Aerospace Sales", "Other Customers", and "Related Products and Services".
a   Based on AIA's aerospace composite deflator 1987=100.

13

SALES OF MAJOR AEROSPACE COMPANIES
AS REPORTED BY THE BUREAU OF THE CENSUS
Calendar Years 1989-2003
(Millions of Dollars)

Year	GRAND TOTAL	TOTAL		Aircraft, Engines, & Parts		Missiles, Space, & Rocket Propulsion	Other Aerospace		Non-Aerospace
		Military	Non-Mil.	Military	Non-Mil.		Military	Non-Mil.	

CURRENT DOLLARS

Year	GRAND TOTAL	Military	Non-Mil.	Military	Non-Mil.	Propulsion	Military	Non-Mil.	Non-Aerospace
1989	$122,148	$71,647	$50,501	$24,287	$29,538	$22,643	$16,908	$3,605	$25,167
1990	136,646	73,616	63,030	27,667	38,622	22,040	15,773	4,342	28,202
1991	123,862	67,089	56,773	25,385	43,155	23,311	13,472	4,281	14,258
1992	118,736	61,410	57,326	23,509	44,160	21,349	12,153	3,377	14,188
1993	109,926	56,102	53,824	20,099	40,987	18,134	11,936	3,592	15,178
1994	104,296	58,012	46,284	23,652	30,901	18,406	11,981	4,417	14,939
1995	102,797	52,476	50,321	22,944	32,085	18,366	11,921	4,462	13,019
1996	103,115	53,153	49,962	24,804	32,722	18,506	12,171	4,624	10,287
1997	114,946	50,648	64,298	23,944	42,614	21,354	12,320	3,922	10,792
1998	119,258	45,110	74,148	23,795	52,708	16,109	7,818	5,035	13,796
1999	124,181	49,690	74,491	26,043	56,406	15,661	9,062	4,472	12,535
2000	109,311	43,256	66,055	23,196	46,477	15,603	6,035	4,785	13,215
2001	117,088	47,232	69,856	22,133	52,504	15,512	8,187	5,732	13,020
2002[r]	115,202	55,422	59,781	25,249	43,435	15,636	11,030	5,251	14,601
2003	116,154	65,712	50,442	26,098	36,786	16,010	14,659	4,397	18,204

CONSTANT DOLLARS[ar]

Year	GRAND TOTAL	Military	Non-Mil.	Military	Non-Mil.	Propulsion	Military	Non-Mil.	Non-Aerospace
1989	$115,890	$67,976	$47,914	$23,043	$28,025	$21,483	$16,042	$3,420	$23,878
1990	125,594	67,662	57,932	25,429	35,498	20,257	14,497	3,991	25,921
1991	111,087	60,170	50,917	22,767	38,704	20,907	12,083	3,839	12,787
1992	101,484	52,487	48,997	20,093	37,744	18,247	10,387	2,886	12,126
1993	91,301	46,596	44,704	16,694	34,042	15,061	9,914	2,983	12,606
1994	84,587	47,049	37,538	19,182	25,062	14,928	9,717	3,582	12,116
1995	82,106	41,914	40,192	18,326	25,627	14,669	9,522	3,564	10,399
1996	81,002	41,754	39,247	19,485	25,705	14,537	9,561	3,632	8,081
1997	89,522	39,445	50,076	18,648	33,188	16,631	9,595	3,055	8,405
1998	92,305	34,915	57,390	18,417	40,796	12,468	6,051	3,879	10,678
1999	95,524	38,223	57,301	20,033	43,389	12,047	6,971	3,440	9,642
2000	81,697	32,329	49,368	17,336	34,736	11,661	4,510	3,576	9,877
2001	85,403	34,451	50,953	16,144	38,296	11,314	5,972	4,181	9,497
2002	82,760	39,815	42,946	18,139	31,203	11,233	7,924	3,772	10,489
2003	81,170	45,920	35,249	18,238	25,706	11,188	10,244	3,073	12,721

Source: Bureau of the Census, "Aerospace Industry (Orders, Sales, and Backlog)" (Annually).
   a Based on AIA's aerospace composite price deflator, 1987=100.

ORDERS AND BACKLOG OF MAJOR AEROSPACE COMPANIES
AS REPORTED BY THE BUREAU OF THE CENSUS
Calendar Years 1989-2003
(Millions of Dollars)

Year	GRAND TOTAL	TOTAL		Aircraft, Engines, & Parts		Missiles, Space, & Rocket Propulsion	Other Aerospace		Non-Aerospace
		Military	Non-Mil.	Military	Non-Mil.		Military	Non-Mil.	
NET NEW ORDERS									
1989	$173,635	$79,992	$93,643	$28,818	$67,773	$26,820	$17,814	$3,945	$28,465
1990	145,965	56,405	89,560	17,735	64,651	20,207	12,945	3,556	26,871
1991	122,485	63,017	59,468	26,675	40,815	24,955	11,329	4,360	14,351
1992	100,306	57,383	42,923	19,631	30,110	22,849	11,201	3,256	13,259
1993	79,770	49,541	30,229	19,518	16,090	14,919	11,121	4,629	13,493
1994	88,706	53,268	35,438	23,352	20,166	13,705	12,924	5,395	13,164
1995	109,109	49,350	59,759	19,854	36,467	19,181	13,716	5,261	14,630
1996	126,267	62,127	64,140	25,343	45,281	27,067	12,136	5,070	11,370
1997	118,993	47,802	71,192	21,424	49,676	21,326	12,348	4,125	10,096
1998	109,993	38,678	71,314	16,870	47,613	19,699	7,628	4,468	13,715
1999	115,257	49,696	65,561	25,009	48,018	18,824	10,261	4,152	8,992
2000	140,086	54,525	85,165	31,396	65,459	18,368	7,046	3,900	13,917
2001	122,206	63,619	58,587	21,762	40,731	12,727	25,659	5,876	15,451
2002[r]	114,830	66,437	48,393	28,498	31,482	17,288	11,156	4,985	21,420
2003	116,693	73,744	42,949	33,667	28,145	10,111	17,690	5,617	21,465
BACKLOG AS OF DECEMBER 31									
1989	$252,401	$114,070	$138,331	$44,026	$115,124	$33,771	$24,186	$7,652	$27,642
1990	250,079	88,471	161,608	33,788	139,152	31,648	18,501	4,999	21,991
1991	245,241	89,517	155,724	39,149	134,527	32,657	17,213	4,907	16,788
1992	236,076	92,139	143,937	44,255	124,322	32,933	14,886	4,859	14,821
1993	211,814	91,751	120,063	46,177	96,228	29,511	16,668	7,958	15,272
1994	192,561	84,445	108,116	44,624	85,305	24,746	15,599	8,043	14,244
1995	202,638	82,309	120,329	44,642	92,239	27,113	17,534	8,214	12,906
1996	229,871	89,500	140,371	47,635	106,341	35,440	16,176	9,339	14,940
1997	218,951	78,870	140,082	43,615	111,931	34,585	12,125	4,754	11,942
1998	200,288	69,962	130,326	37,530	106,166	31,174	9,665	3,488	12,264
1999	188,409	68,379	120,029	36,565	96,596	33,880	9,904	3,051	8,413
2000	214,966	73,741	141,225	41,250	115,241	36,283	10,028	4,081	8,083
2001[r]	223,189	88,863	134,326	39,623	107,124	32,139	27,922	3,631	12,748
2002[r]	222,453	99,948	122,505	42,811	95,100	33,851	28,118	3,376	19,198
2003	222,917	107,884	115,027	50,383	86,460	27,937	31,045	4,595	22,490

Source: Bureau of the Census, "Aerospace Industry (Orders, Sales, and Backlog)" (Annually).

AEROSPACE SALES AND THE NATIONAL ECONOMY
Calendar Years 1989-2003
(Billions of Dollars)

Year	Gross Domestic Product[r]	Industry Sales			Aerospace Sales as Percent of		
		Manufac-turing[r]	Durable Goods[r]	Aero-space	GDP	Manufac-turing	Durable Goods
CURRENT DOLLARS							
1989	$ 5,484.4	$2,837.8	$1,475.9	$120.5	2.2%	4.2%	8.2%
1990	5,803.1	2,909.0	1,483.1	134.4	2.3	4.6	9.1
1991	5,995.9	2,878.8	1,453.2	139.2	2.3	4.8	9.6
1992	6,337.7	2,898.7	1,517.3	138.6	2.2	4.8	9.1
1993	6,657.4	3,019.9	1,603.7	123.2	1.9	4.1	7.7
1994	7,072.2	3,241.1	1,766.1	110.6	1.6	3.4	6.3
1995	7,397.7	3,481.4	1,903.2	107.8	1.5	3.1	5.7
1996	7,816.9	3,589.0	1,973.6	116.8	1.5	3.3[r]	5.9
1997	8,304.3	3,836.0	2,148.1	131.6	1.6	3.4	6.1
1998	8,747.0	3,898.5	2,229.4	148.0	1.7	3.8	6.6
1999	9,268.4	4,032.0	2,326.8	153.7	1.7	3.8	6.6
2000	9,817.0	4,202.5	2,370.6	144.7	1.5	3.4	6.1
2001[r]	10,128.0	3,974.7	2,177.0	151.6	1.5	3.8	7.0
2002	10,487.0	3,897.1	2,136.1	153.4	1.5	3.9	7.2
2003	11,004.0	3,997.5	2,148.0	148.9	1.4	3.7	6.9

Year	Gross Domestic Product[r]	Industry Sales			Real Annual Growth[br]			
		Manufac-turing[r]	Durable Goods[r]	Aero-space	GDP	Mfg.	Durs.	Aero.
CONSTANT DOLLARS[ar]								
1989	$ 6,543.6	$3,385.9	$1,761.0	$114.4	3.3%	1.3%	(0.1)%	1.3%
1990	6,677.8	3,347.5	1,706.6	123.5	2.1	(1.1)	(3.1)	8.0
1991	6,670.8	3,202.8	1,616.8	124.9	(0.1)	(4.3)	(5.3)	1.1
1992	6,887.8	3,150.4	1,649.0	118.5	3.3	(1.6)	2.0	(5.2)
1993	7,071.6	3,207.8	1,703.4	102.3	2.7	1.8	3.3	(13.6)
1994	7,354.1	3,370.3	1,836.5	89.7	4.0	5.1	7.8	(12.4)
1995	7,542.3	3,549.5	1,940.4	86.1	2.6	5.3	5.7	(4.0)
1996	7,816.9	3,589.0	1,973.6	91.8	3.6	1.1	1.7	6.6
1997	8,173.7	3,775.7	2,114.3	102.5	4.6	5.2	7.1	11.7
1998	8,511.3	3,793.5	2,169.3	114.5	4.1	0.5	2.6	11.8
1999	8,889.7	3,867.2	2,231.8	118.2	4.4	1.9	2.9	3.2
2000	9,218.2	3,946.1	2,226.0	108.2	3.7	2.0	(0.3)	(8.5)
2001[r]	9,287.3	3,644.7	1,996.3	110.6	0.7	(7.6)	(10.3)	2.2
2002	9,459.5	3,515.3	1,926.8	110.2	1.9	(3.6)	(3.5)	(0.4)
2003	9,747.9	3,541.2	1,902.8	104.1	3.0	0.7	(1.2)	(5.6)

Source: Council of Economic Advisers, "Economic Indicators" (Monthly); Bureau of Census; and Aerospace Industries Association.
  a Aerospace industry constant dollar sales based on AIA's aerospace composite price deflator, 1987=100. Others based on GDP deflator, 2000=100.
  b Parentheses indicate negative real annual growth.

GROSS DOMESTIC PRODUCT, FEDERAL BUDGET, AND DEFENSE BUDGET
Fiscal Years 1972-2005
(Billions of Dollars)

Year	Fiscal Year GDP [r]	Federal Budget Outlays		Defense Outlays as Percent of	
		Net Total[a]	National Defense[b]	GDP	Federal Budget
1972	$ 1,176.9	$ 230.7	$ 79.2	6.7%	34.3%
1973	1,311.0	245.7	76.7	5.8 [r]	31.2
1974	1,438.9	269.4	79.3	5.5	29.5
1975	1,560.8	332.3	86.5	5.5	26.0
1976	1,738.8	371.8	89.6	5.2	24.1
Tr.Qtr.	459.6	96.0	22.3	4.8 [r]	23.2
1977	1,974.4	409.2	97.2	4.9	23.8
1978	2,218.3	458.7	104.5	4.7	22.8
1979	2,502.4	504.0	116.3	4.6	23.1
1980	2,725.6	590.9	134.0	4.9	22.7
1981	3,058.6	678.2	157.5	5.1	23.2
1982	3,225.5	745.7 [r]	185.3	5.7	24.8
1983	3,442.7	808.4	209.9	6.1	26.0
1984	3,846.7	851.9	227.4	5.9	26.7
1985	4,148.9	946.4	252.7 [b]	6.1	26.7
1986	4,406.7	990.4 [r]	273.4	6.2	27.6
1987	4,654.4	1,004.1	282.0	6.1	28.1
1988	5,011.9	1,064.5	290.4	5.8	27.3
1989	5,401.7	1,143.6 [r]	303.6	5.6	26.5
1990	5,737.0	1,253.2	299.3	5.2	23.9
1991	5,934.2	1,324.4	273.3 [c]	4.6	20.6
1992	6,240.6	1,381.7	298.4 [c]	4.8	21.6
1993	6,578.4	1,409.5	291.1 [c]	4.4	20.7
1994	6,964.2	1,461.9	281.6	4.0 [r]	19.3
1995	7,325.1	1,515.8	272.1	3.7	17.9
1996	7,697.4	1,560.5	265.8	3.5	17.0
1997	8,186.6	1,601.3	270.5	3.3	16.9
1998	8,626.3	1,652.6	268.5	3.1	16.2
1999	9,127.0	1,701.9	274.9	3.0	16.2
2000	9,708.4	1,788.8	294.5	3.0	16.5
2001	10,040.7	1,863.8 [r]	305.5	3.0	16.4
2002	10,373.4	2,011.0	348.6	3.4	17.3
2003	10,828.3	2,157.6	404.9	3.7	18.8
2004 [E]	11,466.0	2,318.8	453.7	4.0	19.6
2005 [E]	12,042.4	2,399.8	450.6	3.7	18.8

Source: Office of Management and Budget, "The Budget of the United States Government" (Annually).
  a "Net Total" is government-wide total less intragovenmental transactions.
  b "National Defense" includes the military budget of DoD and other defense-related activities. Beginning in 1985, the Federal Budget reflects establishment of a military retirement trust fund. Data for prior years adjusted for comparable treatment of the military retired pay.
  c 1991-1993 reflects transfers from the Defense Cooperation Account funded by foreign government and private cash contributions reducing total U.S.-funded military outlays.

FEDERAL OUTLAYS FOR DEFENSE, NASA, AND AEROSPACE PRODUCTS AND SERVICES
Fiscal Years 1976-2005
(Millions of Dollars)

Year	Total National Defense	Total NASA	Federal Outlays for Aerospace Products and Services			Aero-space as Percent of Total National Defense and NASA
			TOTAL	DoD[a]	NASA	
1976	$ 89,619	$ 3,669	$12,364	$ 8,816	$ 3,548	13.3%
Tr.Qtr.	22,269	951	2,855	1,959	926	12.3
1977	97,241	3,945	13,229	9,389	3,840	13.1
1978	104,495	3,983	13,926	10,067	3,859	12.8
1979	116,342	4,197	16,686	12,622	4,064	13.8
1980	133,995	4,852	20,269	15,558	4,711	14.6
1981	157,513	5,421	24,276	19,002	5,274	14.9
1982	185,309	6,035	29,501	23,575	5,926	15.4
1983	209,903	6,664	35,364	28,808	6,556	16.3
1984	227,413	7,048	39,663	32,723	6,940	16.9
1985	252,748	7,318	44,483	37,335	7,148	17.1
1986	273,375	7,404	49,773	42,558	7,215	17.7
1987	281,999	7,591	51,871	44,429	7,442	17.9
1988	290,361	9,092	48,848	39,922	8,926	16.3
1989	303,559	11,036	52,933	42,072	10,861	16.8
1990	299,331	12,429	53,194	40,992	12,202	17.1
1991[b]	273,292	13,878	53,630	40,089	13,541	18.7
1992[b]	298,350	13,961	50,569	37,085	13,484	16.2
1993[b]	291,086	14,305	45,496	31,763	13,733	14.9
1994	281,642	13,695	41,082	27,774	13,308	13.9
1995	272,066	13,378	36,696	23,638	13,058	12.9
1996	265,753	13,881	32,947	20,530	12,417	11.8
1997	270,505	14,360	32,808	19,888	12,920	11.5
1998	268,456	14,206	33,184	20,380	12,804	11.7
1999	274,873	13,664	32,968	20,564	12,404	11.4
2000	294,495	13,442	34,617	22,222	12,395	11.2
2001	305,500	14,095	36,721	23,420	13,301	11.5
2002	348,555	14,430	39,223	25,776	13,447	10.8
2003	404,920	14,552	39,399	26,542	12,857	9.4
2004[E]	453,684	14,604	42,226	28,674	13,552	9.0
2005[E]	450,586	16,386	45,487	30,131	15,356	9.7

Source: Office of Management and Budget, "The Budget of the United States Government" (Annually).
NOTE: "National Defense" includes the military budget of the Department of Defense and other defense-related activities. "Total NASA" includes all categories of the NASA budget; NASA construction is not included in "Aerospace Products and Services." See additional explanation with following table.
  a Outlays for aircraft and missile procurement. Does not include RDT&E, which DoD has not reported by product group since 1977, and which, for comparability, has been subtracted from data previously reported in this table for earlier years. Also included are revisions to missile procurement data.
  b 1991–1993 reflects transfers from the Defense Cooperation Account funded by foreign government and private cash contributions reducing total U.S.-funded military outlays.

FEDERAL OUTLAYS FOR AEROSPACE PRODUCTS AND SERVICES
Fiscal Years 1972-2005
(Millions of Dollars)

Year	TOTAL	Department of Defense[a]			NASA[b]
		TOTAL	Aircraft	Missiles	
1972	$12,309	$ 8,936	$ 5,927	$ 3,009	$ 3,373
1973	11,360	8,089	5,066	3,023	3,271
1974	11,168	7,987	5,006	2,981	3,181
1975	11,554	8,373	5,484	2,889	3,181
1976	12,364	8,816	6,520	2,296	3,548
Tr.Qtr.	2,885	1,959	1,557	402	926
1977	13,229	9,389	6,608	2,781	3,840
1978	13,926	10,067	6,971	3,096	3,859
1979	16,686	12,622	8,836	3,786	4,064
1980	20,269	15,558	11,124	4,434	4,711
1981	24,276	19,002	13,193	5,809	5,274
1982	29,501	23,575	16,793	6,782	5,926
1983	35,364	28,808	21,013	7,795	6,556
1984	39,663	32,723	23,196	9,527	6,940
1985	44,483	37,335	26,586	10,749	7,148
1986	49,773	42,558	30,828	11,730	7,215
1987	51,871	44,429	32,956	11,473[c]	7,442
1988	48,848	39,922	28,246	11,676	8,926
1989	52,933	42,072	27,569	14,503	10,861
1990	53,194	40,992	26,142	14,851	12,202
1991	53,630	40,089	25,689	14,400	13,541
1992	50,569	37,085	23,581	13,504	13,484
1993	45,496	31,763	20,359	11,404	13,733
1994	41,082	27,774	18,840	8,934	13,308
1995	36,696	23,638	16,125	7,513	13,058
1996	32,947	20,530	14,331	6,199	12,417
1997	32,808	19,888	14,663	5,225	12,920
1998	33,184	20,380	15,473	4,907	12,804
1999	32,968	20,564	16,484	4,080	12,404
2000	34,617	22,222	17,991	4,231	12,395
2001	36,721	23,420	17,979	5,441	13,301
2002	39,223	25,776	20,546	5,230	13,447
2003	39,399	26,542	21,280	5,262	12,857
2004[E]	42,226	28,674	22,403	6,271	13,552
2005[E]	45,487	30,131	23,187	6,944	15,356

Source: Office of Management and Budget, "The Budget of the United States Government" (Annually).

a Outlays for aircraft and missile procurement. Does not include RDT&E, which DoD has not reported by product group since 1977, and which for comparability, has been subtracted from data previously reported in this table for earlier years.

b Excludes Construction of Facilities, Office of Inspector General, and Air Transportation.

c Beginning in 1978, DoD combined Navy Missile Procurement with torpedoes and other related products into Navy Weapons Procurement, of which missiles comprise approximately 80 percent.

DEPARTMENT OF DEFENSE
MILITARY OUTLAYS BY FUNCTIONAL TITLE[a]
Fiscal Years 1996-2005
(Millions of Dollars)

	1996	1997	1998	1999
TOTAL....................................	$253,187	$258,311	$256,122	$261,380
Procurement—TOTAL................	$ 48,913	$ 47,690	$ 48,206	$ 48,826
Aircraft......................................	14,331	14,663	15,473	16,484
Missiles[b]...................................	6,199	5,225	4,907	4,080
Ships...	7,346	7,085	6,784	6,697
Weapons[b]..................................	1,788	1,918	1,824	1,885
Ammunition................................	1,232	1,615	1,761	1,998
Other[c]......................................	18,017	17,184	17,457	17,682
Military Personnel—TOTAL........	66,669	69,724	68,976	69,503
Active Forces............................	57,843	60,371	59,793	59,718
Reserve Forces.........................	8,826	9,353	9,183	9,785
RDT&E.....................................	36,494	37,015	37,420	37,363
Operations & Maintenance........	88,759	92,461	93,473	96,418
Military Construction................	6,683	6,187	6,044	5,521
Family Housing.........................	3,828	4,003	3,871	3,692
Other.......................................	1,841	1,231	(1,868)	57

(Continued on next page)

DEPARTMENT OF DEFENSE
MILITARY OUTLAYS BY FUNCTIONAL TITLE[a]
Fiscal Years 1996-2005, continued
(Millions of Dollars)

2000	2001	2002	2003	2004[E]	2005[E]
$281,223	$291,015	$331,951	$387,319	$434,777	$429,554
$ 51,696	$ 54,986	$ 62,515	$ 67,926	$ 77,687	$ 78,232
17,991	17,979	20,546	21,280	22,403	23,187
4,231	5,441	5,230	5,262	6,271	6,944
6,679	7,115	8,287	9,455	10,579	11,739
1,756	1,856	2,343	2,672	2,631	2,417
1,836	2,153	2,587	2,571	4,034	3,727
19,203	20,442	23,522	26,686	31,769	30,218
75,950	73,977	86,799	106,744	117,352	108,883
65,535	63,109	75,179	93,235	102,503	92,468
10,415	10,868	11,620	13,509	14,849	16,415
37,606	40,459	44,389	53,098	60,593	66,207
105,870	112,015	130,005	151,408	165,719	163,869
5,109	4,977	5,052	5,851	6,165	6,003
3,413	3,516	3,736	3,784	3,897	3,976
1,579	1,085	(545)	(1,492)	3,364	2,384

Source: Office of Management and Budget, "The Budget of the United States Government" (Annually).
NOTE: Data in parentheses are credit items.
a Includes all items in the DoD military budget; excludes the DoD civil budget for the Army Corps of Engineers and other non-defense related activities.
b Beginning in 1978, DoD combined Navy Missiles Procurement with torpedoes and other related products into Navy Weapons Procurement. Missiles comprise approximately 80 percent of the value of this category.
c Includes Communications and Electronics.

FEDERAL PRICE DEFLATORS FOR GDP, DEFENSE, PPI, AND CPI
Calendar/Fiscal Years 1974-2005

| Year | GDP [r] | | Federal Government Defense Purchases[r] | | PPI, Capital Equip-ment | CPI, (Urban) All Items |
| | FY GDP | CY GDP | Goods & Services | Equipment Investment | | |
	(FY 2000 =100)	(CY 2000 =100)	(CY 2000 =100)	(CY 2000 =100)	(CY 1982 =100)	(CY 82-84 =100)
1974	33.3	34.7	33.2	59.6	50.5	49.3
1975	36.7	38.0	36.5	62.7	58.2	53.8
1976	39.4	40.2	39.1	68.0	62.1	56.9
1977	42.3	42.8	42.1	72.6	66.1	60.6
1978	45.2	45.8	45.0	78.0	71.3	65.2
1979	48.8	49.6	48.6	80.6	77.5	72.6
1980	53.1	54.1	53.9	85.3	85.8	82.4
1981	58.3	59.1	59.2	92.5	94.6	90.9
1982	62.3	62.7	63.4	99.0	100.0	96.5
1983	65.0	65.2	65.6	101.8	102.8	99.6
1984	67.4	67.7	70.3	103.1	105.2	103.9
1985	69.6	69.7	71.6	100.5	107.5	107.6
1986	71.3	71.3	71.6	95.5	109.7	109.6
1987	73.1	73.2	72.3	91.4	111.7	113.6
1988	75.4	75.7	73.6	90.6	114.3	118.3
1989	78.3	78.7	75.5	91.5	118.8	124.0
1990	81.3	81.6	78.0	93.2	122.9	130.7
1991	84.3	84.4	80.8	95.1	126.7	136.2
1992	86.4	86.4	83.6	95.9	129.1	140.3
1993	88.4	88.4	85.3	98.1	131.4	144.5
1994	90.3	90.3	87.4	101.0	134.1	148.2
1995	92.2	92.1	89.6	103.3	136.7	152.4
1996	94.0	93.9	92.4	103.5	138.3	156.9
1997	95.6	95.4	93.7	100.9	138.2	160.5
1998	96.8	96.5	94.6	99.5	137.6	163.0
1999	98.0	97.9	96.9	100.6	137.6	166.6
2000	100.0	100.0	100.0	100.0	138.8	172.2
2001	102.3	102.4	102.0	98.2	139.7	177.1
2002	104.2	104.1	105.5	97.2	139.1	179.9
2003	105.9	106.0	109.9	97.0	139.5	184.0
2004 [E]	107.2	106.8	NA	NA	NA	186.6
2005 [E]	108.6	108.2	NA	NA	NA	189.4

Source: Bureau of Economic Analysis, Price Measurement Branch; Bureau of Labor Statistics; and Office of Management and Budget, "The Budget of the United States Government" (Annually).

Key: PPI = Producer Price Index for Capital Equipment.
CPI = Consumer Price Index, All Items, All Urban Consumers for 1978 and subsequent years. Previous years, All Urban Wage Earners.
GDP = Gross Domestic Product.

PRICE DEFLATORS FOR AEROSPACE INDUSTRY [r]
Calendar Years 1974-2003

Year	Aerospace Deflators (1987 = 100)					
	Composite	SIC 3721	SIC 3724	SIC 3728	SIC 3761	SIC 3764,9
1972	33.7	39.9	30.1	36.6	39.7	34.4
1973	37.7	41.2	30.9	38.1	39.4	35.6
1974	41.5	44.8	34.9	44.0	41.6	40.5
1975	46.6	48.3	42.3	51.6	45.2	49.2
1976	51.0	52.8	45.9	56.5	50.4	53.8
1977	54.6	56.2	49.1	58.7	55.6	58.2
1978	57.5	59.3	54.6	55.2	60.7	63.6
1979	63.5	65.3	60.9	58.9	69.7	70.0
1980	70.6	72.9	66.3	65.3	78.9	78.5
1981	79.5	80.8	77.0	74.9	87.1	89.5
1982	87.9	89.8	85.2	84.3	93.4	97.2
1983	92.2	94.4	89.5	87.9	98.6	101.5
1984	99.8	105.9	98.1	93.6	100.7	102.9
1985 [a]	98.7	100.7	99.2	94.5	102.4	103.2
1986	99.8	100.7	99.3	98.0	103.5	102.4
1987	100.0	100.0	100.0	100.0	100.0	100.0
1988	101.5	102.3	103.0	103.5	98.6	95.7
1989	105.4	111.0	105.8	106.8	97.0	97.1
1990	108.8	116.8	111.7	109.8	94.3	97.9
1991	111.5	121.3	117.0	113.6	91.1	101.6
1992	117.0	125.2	122.7	118.0	89.7	103.3
1993	120.4	129.5	124.7	120.9	92.6	109.1
1994	123.3	133.9	128.0	123.5	91.5	109.7
1995	125.2	138.3	129.9	124.4	88.5	106.7
1996	127.3	141.5	132.4	128.8	85.8	105.6
1997	128.4	143.4	133.7	131.4	81.6	105.3
1998	129.2	143.8	134.7	133.0	82.6	104.5
1999	130.0	145.1	135.7	134.3	80.0	105.0
2000	133.8	151.6	138.6	135.4	80.0	105.1
2001	137.1	156.9	142.9	138.5	78.0	104.5
2002	139.2	160.0	144.6	139.9	77.2	107.0
2003	143.1	165.5	151.8	139.4	78.6	107.9

Source: Aerospace Industries Association, based on data from: Bureau of Labor Statistics, Producer Price Indexes; Bureau of Economic Analysis, Chain-Type Price Indexes and Implicit Price Deflators; and International Trade Administration.

a   The International Trade Administration has discontinued its reporting of the Aerospace Deflators with 1986. Subsequent composite deflators computed by AIA and deflators for 1985 and 1986 revised for consistency.

Key: SIC = Standard Industrial Classification, SIC 3721 = Aircraft; SIC 3724 = Aircraft Engines and Engine Parts; SIC 3728 = Aircraft Parts; SIC 3761 = Missiles and Space Vehicles; SIC 3764 = Space Propulsion; SIC 3769 = Space Equipment not elsewhere classified.

Sales of new aircraft, engines, and parts fell $5.8 billion from 2002's level to $63 billion, led by declines in the civil sector. Data compiled by the U.S. Census Bureau showed military sales grew by $0.8 billion to $26 billion, while civil sales fell sharply again—down 15% to $37 billion. Hidden in the aircraft sector's overall decline was continuing growth in sales of military engines and parts—up for its fifth straight year in 2003.

Military aircraft production, as measured by acceptances, decreased on falling exports. Manufacturers delivered 337 aircraft of which 32% were destined to customers other than the U.S. government. The number of military aircraft exported declined for the sixth straight year—down 21 to 109—while those exported through the FMS program grew for a second year from their lowest level on record (29) in 2001. Encouragingly, the value of military aircraft acceptances in total rose for a second straight year.

Aircraft acceptances (including FMS) increased by nine to 293. The fighter/attack and trainer categories showed gains whereas helicopter acceptances declined. The overall flyaway

costs also increased—rising 9% to $11 billion. Despite fewer transport/tanker acceptances, their corresponding flyaway costs increased.

The civil aircraft industry produced and delivered 35 more aircraft in 2003 than it had in 2002. Production of civil helicopters jumped from 318 to 517—accounting for the entirety of that increase. Transport and general aviation aircraft shipments, on the other hand, posted declines. The majority of the decline came from transport aircraft, whose production fell by 98, or 26%, to 281. General aviation aircraft shipments declined by 66 to 2,130. Likewise, domestic shipments dropped by 50 whereas exports rose by 85. For example, Boeing shipped 43% fewer jetliners domestically than last year and only 31% of what it did overseas—exporting 214 versus delivering 67 transports domestically.

Net new orders in 2003 rose by $1.8 billion from year-earlier levels. Military orders grew $5.2 billion—meaning that civil orders declined $3.3 billion or 11%. Similarly, the aircraft sector's unfilled order backlog declined $1.1 billion to $137 billion. While the military backlog grew $7.6 billion, civil registered falling backlogs—down $8.6 billion.

Three programs dominated new aircraft procurement in FY 2003: the Air Force's F-22 Raptor was the largest, big-ticket item with 21 fighters costing $4.5 billion, followed by 15 C-17 Globemaster III cargo aircraft worth $4.2 billion, and the Navy's 45 F/A-18E/F Super Hornet fighters for $3.2 billion. Eleven V-22 Osprey tiltrotor aircraft costing $1.2 billion logged a distant fourth. Scheduled for significant procurement funding increases in FY 2004 are the Air Force's C-130J variants and JPATS and the Navy's H-1 variants, MH-60, and T-45.

SALES OF AIRCRAFT, ENGINES, AND PARTS
Calendar Years 1989-2003
(Millions of Dollars)

Year	GRAND TOTAL	TOTAL		Complete Aircraft & Parts		Aircraft Engines & Parts	
		Mili-tary	Non-Mil.	Mili-tary	Non-Mil.	Mili-tary	Non-Mil.
CURRENT DOLLARS							
1989	$53,825	$24,287	$29,538	$18,256	$20,140	$6,031	$ 9,398
1990	66,289	27,667	38,622	22,023	27,872	5,644	10,750
1991	68,540	25,385	43,155	19,710	33,215	5,675	9,940
1992	67,669	23,509	44,160	18,411	35,595	5,098	8,565
1993	61,086	20,099	40,987	16,118	32,780	3,981	8,207
1994	54,553	23,652	30,901	20,127	23,176	3,525	7,725
1995	55,029	22,944	32,085	19,596	22,897	3,348	9,188
1996	57,526	24,804	32,722	20,822	20,993	3,982	11,729
1997	66,558	23,944	42,614	21,297	33,206	2,647	9,408
1998	76,503	23,795	52,708	21,154	42,541	2,641	10,167
1999	82,449	26,043	56,406	22,917	45,107	3,126	11,299
2000	69,673	23,196	46,477	19,650	37,538	3,546	8,939
2001	74,637	22,133	52,504	18,176	40,548	3,957	11,956
2002 r	68,683	25,249	43,435	19,579	34,278	5,670	9,157
2003	62,883	26,098	36,786	20,355	28,666	5,743	8,120
CONSTANT DOLLARS[ar]							
1989	$51,067	$23,043	$28,025	$17,321	$19,108	$5,722	$ 8,917
1990	60,927	25,429	35,498	20,242	25,618	5,188	9,881
1991	61,471	22,767	38,704	17,677	29,789	5,090	8,915
1992	57,837	20,093	37,744	15,736	30,423	4,357	7,321
1993	50,736	16,694	34,042	13,387	27,226	3,306	6,816
1994	44,244	19,182	25,062	16,324	18,796	2,859	6,265
1995	43,953	18,326	25,627	15,652	18,288	2,674	7,339
1996	45,189	19,485	25,705	16,357	16,491	3,128	9,214
1997	51,836	18,648	33,188	16,586	25,861	2,062	7,327
1998	59,213	18,417	40,796	16,373	32,926	2,044	7,869
1999	63,422	20,033	43,387	17,628	34,698	2,405	8,692
2000	52,072	17,336	34,736	14,686	28,055	2,650	6,681
2001	54,440	16,144	38,296	13,257	29,575	2,886	8,721
2002	49,341	18,139	31,203	14,065	24,625	4,073	6,578
2003	43,943	18,238	25,706	14,224	20,032	4,013	5,674

Source: Bureau of the Census, "Aerospace Industry (Orders, Sales, and Backlog)" (Annually).
a Based on AIA's aerospace composite price deflator, 1987=100.

ORDERS AND BACKLOG OF AIRCRAFT, ENGINES, AND PARTS
Calendar Years 1989-2003
(Millions of Dollars)

Year	GRAND TOTAL	TOTAL		Complete Aircraft & Parts		Aircraft Engines & Parts	
		Mili-tary	Non-Mil.	Mili-tary	Non-Mil.	Mili-tary	Non-Mil.
NET NEW ORDERS							
1989	$96,591	$28,818	$67,773	$23,569	$52,619	$5,249	$15,154
1990	82,386	17,735	64,651	12,766	52,371	4,969	12,280
1991	67,490	26,675	40,815	22,140	30,745	4,535	10,070
1992	49,741	19,631	30,110	16,391	20,548	3,240	9,562
1993	35,608	19,518	16,090	15,853	11,238	3,665	4,852
1994	43,518	23,352	20,166	19,806	12,854	3,546	7,312
1995	56,321	19,854	36,467	16,248	27,156	3,606	9,311
1996	70,624	25,343	45,281	21,755	33,802	3,588	11,479
1997	71,100	21,424	49,676	19,102	41,439	2,322	8,237
1998	64,483	16,870	47,613	14,051	37,362	2,819	10,251
1999	73,027	25,009	48,018	21,422	35,529	3,587	12,489
2000	96,855	31,396	65,459	27,440	54,335	3,956	11,124
2001	62,493	21,762	40,731	18,144	27,525	3,618	13,206
2002 r	59,979	28,498	31,482	20,946	25,333	7,552	6,149
2003	61,812	33,667	28,145	27,878	21,590	5,789	6,555
BACKLOG AS OF DECEMBER 31							
1989	$159,150	$44,026	$115,124	$36,888	$ 95,108	$7,138	$20,016
1990	172,940	33,788	139,152	27,259	119,123	6,529	20,029
1991	173,676	39,149	134,527	32,795	116,139	6,354	18,388
1992	168,577	44,255	124,322	39,748	107,686	4,507	16,636
1993	142,405	46,177	96,228	41,732	82,772	4,445	13,456
1994	129,929	44,624	85,305	40,206	72,295	4,418	13,010
1995	136,871	44,642	92,229	39,673	77,802	4,969	14,427
1996	153,976	47,635	106,341	42,788	91,851	4,847	14,490
1997	155,546	43,615	111,931	40,562	100,022	3,053	11,909
1998	143,696	37,530	106,166	34,866	94,161	2,664	12,005
1999	133,161	36,565	96,596	33,374	83,412	3,191	13,184
2000	156,491	41,250	115,241	37,650	99,942	3,600	15,299
2001 r	146,747	39,623	107,124	36,456	90,370	3,167	16,754
2002 r	137,910	42,811	95,100	37,761	81,417	5,050	13,683
2003	136,844	50,383	86,460	45,286	74,338	5,097	12,122

Source: Bureau of the Census, "Aerospace Industry (Orders, Sales, and Backlog)" (Annually).

U.S. AIRCRAFT PRODUCTION—CIVIL
Calendar Years 1969-2003
(Number of Aircraft)

Year	TOTAL	Domestic Shipments			Export Shipments		
		Trans-ports	Heli-copters	General Aviation	Trans-ports	Heli-copters	General Aviation
1969	13,505	332	282	9,996	182	252	2,461
1970	8,076	127	150	5,246	184	332	2,037
1971	8,158	50	171	5,900	173	298	1,566
1972	10,576	79	319	7,702	148	256	2,072
1973	14,709	143	342	10,482	151	428	3,163
1974	15,326	91	433	9,903	241	395	4,263
1975	15,251	127	528	10,804	188	336	3,268
1976	16,429	64 [a]	442	12,232	158	315	3,218
1977	17,913	54	527	13,441	101	321	3,469
1978	18,962	130	536	14,346	111	368	3,471
1979	18,460	176	570	13,177	200	459	3,878
1980	13,634	150	841	8,703	237	525	3,178
1981	10,916	132	619	6,840	255	453	2,617
1982	5,085	111	333	3,326	121	254	940
1983	3,356	133	187	2,172	129	216	519
1984	2,999	102	143	2,013	83	233	425
1985	2,691	126	247	1,545	152	137	484
1986	2,156	171	120	1,031	159	210	464
1987	1,800	187	116	598	170	242	487
1988	1,949	206	103	500	217	280	643
1989	2,448	138	221	225	260	294	1,310
1990	2,268	215	254	335	306	349	809
1991	2,181	204	253	487	385	318	534
1992	1,790	180	112	541	387	212	358
1993	1,630	130	83	631	278	175	333
1994	1,545	87	154	543	222	154	385
1995	1,625	119	82	714	137	210	363
1996	1,662	97	64	732	172	214	383
1997	2,269	122	87	1,140	252	259	409
1998	3,115	184	125	1,794	375	238	399
1999	3,456	279	180	1,972	341	181	503
2000	3,780	217	189	2,391	268	304	411
2001	3,559	273	106	2,172	253	309	446
2002	2,893 [r]	117	24	1,875 [r]	262	294	321
2003	2,928	67	118	1,781	214	399	349

Source: Aerospace Industries Association, based on company reports; General Aviation Manufacturers Association; and Department of Commerce, International Trade Administration.
a Prior to 1976, includes the C-130 military transport.

U.S. AIRCRAFT PRODUCTION—MILITARY
Calendar Years 1969-2003
(Number of Aircraft)

Year	TOTAL	U.S. Military Agencies	Exports		
			TOTAL	FMS[a]	Direct[b]
1969	4,290	3,644	646	NA	NA
1970	3,720	3,085	635	NA	NA
1971	2,914	2,232	682	NA	NA
1972	2,530	1,993	537	124	413
1973	1,821	1,243	578	129	449
1974	1,513	799	714	365	349
1975	1,779	844	935	525	410
1976	1,318	625	693	518	175
1977	1,134	454	680	408	272
1978	996	467	529	256	273
1979	837	531	306	203	103
1980	1,047	625	422	194	228
1981	1,062	703	359	215	144
1982	1,159	690	469	68	401
1983	1,053	766	287	70	217
1984	936	561	375	71	304
1985	919	643	276	134	142
1986	1,107	708	399	110	289
1987	1,210	725	485	133	352
1988	1,305	687	618	138	480
1989	1,261	614	647	92	555
1990	1,053	664	387	99	290
1991	911	556	355	94	261
1992	753	422	331	122	209
1993	955[c]	437	518	146	372[c]
1994	764	418	346	69	277
1995	811[d]	354	457	108	349
1996	558	242	316	106	210
1997	488	151	337	181	156
1998	418	149	269	175	94
1999	359	133	226	114	112
2000	333	138	195	42	153
2001	345	196	149	29	120
2002	358[r]	228[r]	130	56	74
2003	337	228	109	65	44

Source: Aerospace Industries Association, based on USAF, USA, and USN survey responses and Department of Commerce, International Trade Administration.
a Also includes acceptances of NATO AWACS aircraft.
b Military aircraft exported via commercial contracts, directly from manufacturers to foreign governments.
c The number of small (450 kg–2000 kg), new aircraft exported doubled in 1993 to 340 worth $18 million.
d Includes 358 small (450 kg–2000 kg), new aircraft worth $14.7 million.

CIVIL AIRCRAFT SHIPMENTS
Calendar Years 1989-2003

Year	TOTAL	Transport Aircraft[a]	Helicopters	General Aviation
NUMBER OF AIRCRAFT SHIPPED				
1989	2,448	398	515	1,535
1990	2,268	521	603	1,144
1991	2,181	589	571	1,021
1992	1,790	567	324	899
1993	1,630	408	258	964
1994	1,545	309	308	928
1995	1,625	256	292	1,077
1996	1,662	269 [a]	278	1,115
1997	2,269	374	346	1,549
1998	3,115	559	363	2,193
1999	3,456	620	361	2,475
2000	3,780	485	493	2,802
2001	3,559	526	415	2,618
2002	2,893 [r]	379	318	2,196 [r]
2003	2,928	281	517	2,130
VALUE (Millions of Dollars)				
1989	$17,129	$15,074	$251	$1,804
1990	24,477	22,215	254	2,008
1991	29,035	26,856	211	1,968
1992	30,728	28,750	142	1,836
1993	26,389	24,133	113	2,144
1994	20,666	18,124 [E]	185	2,357
1995	18,299	15,263 [E]	194	2,842
1996	20,805	17,564 [E]	193	3,048
1997	31,753	26,929	231	4,593
1998	41,449	35,663	252	5,534
1999	45,161	38,171	187	6,803
2000	38,637	30,327	270	8,040
2001	42,399	34,155	247	7,997
2002	35,000 [r]	27,574	157	7,269 [r]
2003	27,523	21,033	366	6,124

Source: Aerospace Industries Association, based on company reports and General Aviation Manufacturers' Association.
    a U.S.-manufactured fixed-wing aircraft over 33,000 pounds empty weight, including all jet transports plus the four-engine turboprop-powered Lockheed L-100.

SHIPMENTS OF CIVIL TRANSPORT AIRCRAFT[a]
Calendar Years 1999-2003

Company and Model	1999	2000	2001	2002	2003
TOTAL					
Number of Aircraft	620	485	526	379	281
Value (Millions of Dollars).............	$38,171	$30,327	$34,155	$27,547	$21,033
Boeing—TOTAL	561	446	475	359	269
B-737	320	278	298	221	173
B-747	47	24	31	27	19
B-757	67	45	45	29	14
B-767	44	44	40	35	24
B-777	83	55	61	47	39
Douglas[b] —TOTAL......................	59	39	51	20	12
MD-11	8	4	2	—	—
MD-80	26	—	—	—	—
MD-90	13	3	—	—	—
MD-95 (B-717)	12	32	49	20	12

Source: Aerospace Industries Association, based on company reports.
  a U.S.-manufactured fixed-wing aircraft over 33,000 lbs.
  b Formerly reported as McDonnell Douglas.

SPECIFICATIONS OF U.S. CIVIL JET TRANSPORT AIRCRAFT[a]
On Order or in Production as of 2003

Number of Engines and Crew, and Model Designation[b]	Initial Service	Standard Mixed Class	Operating Empty Weight (000's lbs)	Maximum Takeoff Gross Weight (000's lbs)	Range (Nautical Miles)[c]	Engine Manufacturer[d] and Model
FOUR ENGINES/CREW OF 2						
747-400*	1989	416-524	399	875	7,260	GE CF6-80C2, P&W PW4000, or RR RB211-524
747-400ER*	2002	416-524	407	910	7,670	GE GE CF6-80C2 or P&W PW4000
TWO ENGINES/CREW OF 2						
MD-95 (717)	1999	106	69	121	2,060	RR BR715
737-600	1998	110-132	81	144	3,050	CFMI CFM56-7B
737-700	1997	126-149	84	155	3,260	CFMI CFM56-7B
737-800	1998	162-189	92	174	2,940	CFMI CFM56-7B
737-900	2001	177-189	95	174	2,745	CFMI CFM56-7B
757-200	1983	200-228	130	255	3,900	RR RB211-535 or P&W PW2000
757-300	1999	243-280	142	273	3,395	RR RB211-535 or P&W PW2000
767-200ER*	1984	181-255	187	395	6,600	P&W PW4000 or GE CF6-80C2
767-300ER*	1997	218-351	200	412	6,105	P&W PW4000, GE CF6-80C2, or RR RB211-524
777-200*	1995	305-440	302	545	5,210	RR Trent, GE GE90, or P&W PW4000
777-200ER*	1997	301-440	320	656	7,730	RR Trent, GE GE90, or P&W PW4000
777-200LR*	2003	301	344	766	9,280	GE GE90
777-300*	1998	368-550	343	660	5,955	RR Trent, GE GE90, or P&W PW4000
777-300ER*	2003	365	372	760	7,705	GE GE90

Source: Aerospace Industries Association, based on company reports.
a All jet-powered passenger transport aircraft 33,000 pounds or more empty weight.
b The Boeing Company manufactures models: 737, 747, 757, 767, & 777 and its Douglas Products Division manufactures MD-95 (renamed the 717).
c Full passenger load and baggage.
d P&W = Pratt & Whitney; GE = General Electric; RR = Rolls-Royce; CFMI = General Electric/Snecma.
TBD To be determined.
* Wide-body aircraft.

CIVIL TRANSPORT AIRCRAFT BACKLOG[a]
As of December 31, 1989-2003

Company and Model	1999	2000	2001	2002	2003
TOTAL AIRCRAFT ON ORDER[b]					
Number of Aircraft	1,512	1,612	1,357	1,152	1,108
Value (Millions of Dollars)...........	$72,972	$89,780	$75,850	$68,159	$63,929
Boeing—TOTAL	1,385	1,503	1,313	1,112	1,072
B-737	916	1,016	902	798	829
B-747	77	77	62	52	37
B-757	81	79	57	28	13
B-767	122	84	76	39	25
B-777	189	247	216	195	168
Douglas[c]—TOTAL.....................	127	109	44	40	36
MD-11	6	2	—	—	—
MD-80/90	3	—	—	—	—
MD-95 (B-717)	118	107	44	40	36
TOTAL FOREIGN ORDERS					
Number of Aircraft	493	477	444	440	476
Value[E] (Millions of Dollars)	$29,939	$38,972	$34,891	$34,079	$34,439
Boeing—TOTAL	458	450	423	426	460
B-737	258	227	229	249	303
B-747	65	64	47	41	34
B-757	15	9	8	5	8
B-767	14	19	21	16	20
B-777	106	131	118	115	95
Douglas[c]—TOTAL.....................	35	27	21	26	16
MD-11	6	2	—	—	—
MD-80/90	3	—	—	—	—
MD-95 (B-717)	26	25	21	26	16

Source: Aerospace Industries Association, based on company reports.

    a Unfilled announced orders excluding options for U.S.-manufactured transport aircraft over 33,000 pounds. Includes new transports contracted for lease from the manufacturer.

    b Includes 84 unidentified orders in 1999, 64 in 2000, 156 in 2001, 69 in 2002, and 33 in 2003.

    c Formerly reported as McDonnell Douglas.

SPECIFICATIONS OF U.S. CIVIL HELICOPTERS
In Production as of 2003

Company	Commercial Model	Number of Places	Useful Load (Lbs.)	Range with Useful Load (N. Miles)	External Cargo Payload (Lbs.)
Bell/Agusta Aerospace	BA609	10-11	5,500	750	—
Brantly International	B-2B	2	620	174	—
Enstrom Helicopter	F-28 Series	3	1,030	241	1,000
	280 Series	3	1,015	260	1,000
	480 Series	5	1,305	375	1,000
MD Helicopters	500 Series	5	1,519 ^{r}	264 ^{r}	2,069
	520 Series	5	1,764	182 ^{r}	2,364
	530F	5	1,509	202 ^{r}	2,159
	600 Series	8	2,000	330 ^{r}	3,000
	900 Series	8	2,875	255 ^{r}	3,525
Robinson Helicopter	R22	2	515	180	—
	R44	4	980-994 ^{r}	348-365	—
Schweizer Aircraft	300C	3	950	201	1,050
	300CB	2–3	662	NA	—
	330/333	4	1,300	310	—
Sikorsky Aircraft	S-76C	14	4,721 ^{r}	439	3,300
	S-92	21	10,250	544 ^{r}	10,000

Source: Helicopter Association International, "2004 Helicopter Annual" (Annually).

CIVIL HELICOPTER SHIPMENTS[a]
Calendar Years 1999-2003

Company and Model	1999	2000	2001	2002	2003
CIVIL SHIPMENTS					
Number of Aircraft	361	493	415	318	517
Value (Millions of Dollars)	$187	$270	$247	$157	$366
Brantly—TOTAL	—	6	2	1	1
B-2B	—	6	2	1	1
Enstrom—TOTAL	8	7	8	12	17
F-28/280 series	5	2	4	4	7
480 series...........................	3	5	4	8	10
Hiller—TOTAL	—	1	2	—	—
UH12E	—	1	2	—	—
Kaman—TOTAL	—	3	6	—	—
K-1200	—	3	6	—	—
MD Helicopters[b]—TOTAL.....	33	41	28	12	16
500 series...........................	5	11	4	5	3
520N series	5	4	2	3	1
530 series...........................	6	4	—	—	3
600 series...........................	6	8	2	—	1
900 series...........................	11	14	20	4	8
Robinson—TOTAL..............	278	390	328	255	422
R22...................................	128	126	134	107	128
R44...................................	150	264	194	148	294
Schweizer—TOTAL	35	36	33	32	38
300C..................................	23	13	17	13	20
300CB/300CBi.....................	11	17	12	17	15
330/333	1	6	4	2	3
Sikorsky—TOTAL	7	9	8	6	23
S-70	—	2	—	—	—
S-76	7	7	8	6	23

Source: Aerospace Industries Association, based on company reports.
NOTE: All data exclude production by foreign licensees.
   a Domestic and export helicopter shipments for non-military use. Helicopters in military configuration exported to foreign governments and purchased under commercial contract are reported elsewhere. Please note that shipments from Bell Helicopter's Canadian facilities are excluded as are other foreign-produced helicopters, but reported separately below for information purposes only.
   b Formerly reported as McDonnell Douglas.

Bell—TOTAL	146	143	122	92	105
206B	28	14	14	10	10
206L/LT	12	27	10	12	6
407	62	62	47	33	46
412	26	24	22	25	29
427	—	5	15	5	7
430	18	11	14	7	7

GENERAL AVIATION AIRCRAFT SHIPMENTS
BY SELECTED MANUFACTURERS
Calendar Years 1999-2003

	1999	2000	2001	2002	2003
NUMBER OF AIRCRAFT SHIPPED	2,475	2,802	2,618	2,196 r	2,130
Single-Engine, Piston	1,634	1,810	1,581	1,366	1,519
Multi-Engine, Piston.....................	114	103	147	130	71
Turboprop......................................	239	315	306	187	163
Turbojet	488	574	584	513 r	377
VALUE[a] OF SHIPMENTS					
(Millions of Dollars)......................	$6,803	$8,040	$7,997	$7,269 r	$6,124
Piston	$ 385	$ 446	$ 471	$ 389 r	$ 440
Turboprop.....................................	658	934 r	742	487	411
Turbojet	5,760	6,659	6,784	6,394 r	5,273
Number of Aircraft Shipped by					
Selected Manufacturer					
American Champion	91	96	56	53	63
Aviat...	83	91	57	38	47
Bellanca.......................................	1	1	1	—	—
Cessna	1,202	1,256	1,202	944	841
Cirrus Design...............................	9	95	183	397	469
Commander...................................	13	20	11	7	—
Gulfstream	70	71	71	61	50
Lancair..	—	5	27	24	51
Learjet..	99	133	109	53 r	31
Maule..	69	57	57	46	32
Micco	—	6	10	—	—
Mooney...	97	100	29	10	36
Piper	341	395	441	290	229
Raytheon[b]..................................	400	476	364	259	263
Tiger...	—	—	—	14	18

Source: General Aviation Manufacturers' Association.
    a   Manufacturers' net billing price.
    b   Formerly reported as Beech.

DIRECT EXPORT SHIPMENTS OF MILITARY HELICOPTERS[a]
Calendar Years 1999-2003

Manufacturer and Model	1999	2000	2001	2002	2003
TOTAL					
Number of Aircraft.............................	28	39	10	10	2
Value (Millions of Dollars)	$484	$699	$164[b]	$300[b]	$25[b]
Boeing AH-64[c]	6	1	—	—	—
Boeing Vertol CH-47/414/352.............	10	7	—	—	—
Sikorsky S-70C	12	31	10	10	2

Source: Aerospace Industries Association, company reports.
    a Shipments of helicopters in military configuration exported directly from U.S. manufacturers to foreign governments.
       Military helicopters exported via Foreign Military Sales (FMS) are reported with Dept. of Defense (DoD) aircraft
       acceptance data elsewhere in this chapter. Some models reported on this page may be shipped in either military or
       civil configuration; see Civil Helicopter Shipments table for additional data.
    b Estimated by AIA using trade statistics.
    c Formerly reported as McDonnell Douglas.

SPECIFICATIONS OF U.S. MILITARY AIRCRAFT
On Order or in Production as of 2003

Primary Mission, DoD Designation, & Popular Name	Manufacturer	U.S. Military Service	Crew	Empty Weight (000's lbs.)	Engines	Performance Typical for Primary Mission	Remarks
FIGHTER/ATTACK							
F-15E Strike Eagle	Boeing	USAF	2	37	2xP&W F100	Mach 2.5 class	Dual role fighter/long range interdiction
F-16C/D Fighting Falcon	LM	USAF	1-2	19	1xP&W F100/ 1xGE F110	Mach 2+ class	Multirole fighter
F/A-18E/F Hornet	Boeing/NGC	USN	1-2	31	2xGE F414	Mach 1.6+ class	Multi-mission strike fighter
F/A-22A Raptor	LM/Boeing	USAF	1	NA	2xP&W F119	Mach 2+ class	Air superiority with near-precision ground attack
BOMBER/COMMAND/CONTROL/PATROL							
E-2C Hawkeye 2000	NGC	USN	5	40	2xRR T56	6+ hr. mission duration	AEW command & control; active & passive detection
E-8C Joint STARS	NGC	USAF/Army	21+	171	4xP&W JT3D	11-20+ hr. loiter	Ground surveillance/battle mgmt.
RC-12 P/Q	Raytheon	Army	2	9	2xP&W PT6A	4 hr. loiter	Electronic intercept
YAL-1A Airborne Laser	Boeing	USAF	6	TBD	4xGE CF6	TBD	Airborne high-energy chemical laser system
CARGO-TRANSPORT/TANKER							
C-12R	Raytheon	Army	2	8	2xP&W PT6A	268 mph; 788 n.m.	Utility/transport
C-17A Globemaster III	Boeing	USAF	3	277	4xP&W F117	Mach 0.77; 2,400 n.m.	102 troops or 170,000 lbs.
C-20F/G/H	Gulfstream	All	3-5	42-43	2xRR Tay	Mach 0.80; 4,200 n.m.	Versions of Gulfstream IV
C-37A/B	Gulfstream	All	3-5	48	2xBR 710	Mach 0.80; 6,750 n.m.	Version of Gulfstream V
C-40A	Boeing	USN	3-7	92	2xCFM 56-7	Mach 0.79; 3,000 n.m.	Navy Unique Fleet Essential Aircraft
C-40B	Boeing	USAF	3-7	92	2xCFM 56-7	Mach 0.79; 5,000 n.m.	Special air mission aircraft
C/EC/WC-130J	LM	USAF/ANG	3	97	4xRR AE2100	396 mph; 3,260 mi.	41,000 lbs.
KC-130J	LM	USMC	3	97	4xRR AE2100	12,100 gals.	Tanker
MV/CV-22 Osprey	Bell/Boeing	USMC/USAF	2-3	33	2xRR AE1107C	Max 257 mph	With internal fuel tanks, engine nacelles tilt for STOL
UC-35B/D	Cessna	Army/USMC	2	10	2xP&W 535A	Mach 0.75; 1,700 n.m.	Utility/transport
TRAINER							
T-1A Jayhawk	Raytheon	USAF	2	10	2xP&W JT-15D	Max 538 mph	Tanker/transport trainer
T-6A Texan II	Raytheon	USN/USAF	2	5	1xP&W PT6A-68	Max 368 mph	Primary trainer
T-45C Goshawk	Boeing/BAe	USN	2	11	1xRR F405	Mach 0.85, 675 mph	Next generation trainer
TH-57 Sea Ranger	Bell	USN	1	2	1xRR 250	Max 135 mph; 405 mi.	Rotary wing trainer
TH-67 Creek	Bell	Army	1	2	1xRR 250	Max 135 mph; 405 mi.	Rotary wing trainer
HELICOPTER							
AH-1Z	Bell	USMC	2	12	2xGE T700	Max 255 mph; 475 mi.	Attack helicopter
AH-64D Apache	Boeing	Army	2	11	2xGE T700	Max 226 mph; 445 mi.	Attack helicopter
CH-47F Chinook	Boeing	Army	3	23	2xHI T55	Max 165 mph; 266 mi.	Transport
CH-53E	Sikorsky	USN	3-8	33-36	3xGE T64	Max 196 mph; 710 mi.	55 passengers, aux. tanks/ minesweeping
HH/SH-60 Seahawk	Sikorsky	USN	4-12	14	2xGE T700	Max 184 mph; 500 mi.	Combat search and rescue, SOF
HH/MH-60G Pave Hawk	Sikorsky	USAF	3	12	2xGE T700	Max 184 mph; 1,380 mi.	11 troops; combat; search; rescue
MH-60S	Sikorsky	USN	4	11	2xGE T700	Max 184 mph; 373 mi.	Vertical replenishment
RAH-66 Comanche	Boeing/Sikorsky	Army	2	9	2xLHTEC T801	Max 201 mph; 400 mi.	Program cancelled in 2004
UH-1Y	Bell	USMC	2	12	2xGE T700	Max 219 mph; 400 mi.	Utility assault helicopter
UH-60L Black Hawk	Sikorsky	Army	3	11	2xGE T700	Max 184 mph; 373 mi.	Utility assault helicopter

Source: Aerospace Industries Association, based on company reports.
KEY: BAe = BAE Systems; BR = BMW-Rolls Royce; GE = General Electric; HI = Honeywell;
LHTEC = Light Helicopter Turbine Engine Co.;LM = Lockheed Martin; NGC = Northrop Grumman;
P&W = Pratt & Whitney; RR = Rolls-Royce.
TBD To be determined.

MILITARY AIRCRAFT PROGRAM PROCUREMENT[a]
Fiscal Years 2003, 2004, and 2005
(Costs in Millions of Dollars)

Agency and Model	2003		2004[E]		2005[E]	
	No.	Cost	No.	Cost	No.	Cost
AIR FORCE						
B-2 Stealth Bomber.................	—	$ 91.7	—	$ 122.3	—	$ 96.0
C-17 Globemaster III..............	15	4,187.7	11	3,408.8	14	3,839.9
C-130J Hercules	—	427.0	4	660.3	11	1,029.6
Civil Air Patrol Aircraft.............	27	5.2	27	8.5	27	2.3
E-8C JSTARS.........................	1	280.7	—	38.9	—	45.3
F-15E Eagle	—	274.0	—	200.3	—	181.6
F-16 Falcon	—	274.9	—	307.3	—	336.3
F-22 Raptor	21	4,461.0	22	4,114.6	24	4,157.0
JPATS[b]..................................	39	232.3	54	297.7	53	309.6
Unmanned Aerial Vehicles[c].....	37	463.3	28	535.1	17	609.3
ARMY						
AH-64 Apache Mods..............	74	$ 889.0	64	$ 763.2	19	$ 554.8
C-XX Medium Range Aircraft...	1	8.2	2	42.7	1	12.0
CH-47 Mods...........................	—	728.0	—	510.2	—	542.7
OH-58D Kiowa Warrior	—	41.3	—	50.9	—	33.8
TH-67 Creek	6	9.8	—	—	—	—
UH-60 Black Hawk.................	19	290.1	17	254.7	8	124.5
NAVY						
C-37	—	$ —	1	$ 54.6	1	$ 53.3
C-40A....................................	1	61.6	1	63.5	1	65.2
E-2C Hawkeye	5	286.6	2	226.8	2	248.0
EA-6B Prowler	—	314.2	—	334.8	—	165.7
F-5...	4	2.0	4	2.0	9	4.5
F/A-18E/F Hornet...................	45	3,197.0	42	3,044.1	42	2,985.8
KC-130J	4	307.9	—	78.6	4	324.2
MH-60R.................................	—	117.2	6	385.6	8	409.1
MH-60S.................................	15	352.5	13	408.5	15	400.8
T-48/T-39 replacement...........	—	—	1	21.9	1	52.4
T-45 Goshawk.......................	8	218.2	14	336.7	8	253.6
UC-35....................................	1	8.1	4	30.9	—	—
UH-1Y/AH-1Z.........................	—	—	9	308.5	9	241.8
V-22 Osprey[b].........................	11	1,166.4	11	1,203.3	11	1,361.1

Source: Department of Defense Budget, "Program Acquisition Costs by Weapon System" (Annually) and "Procurement
Programs (P-1)" (Annually).

NOTE: See Research and Development Chapter for aircraft program RDT&E authorization data.

a Total Obligational Authority for procurement, excluding initial spares and mods (except where noted).

b Air Force and Navy funding.

c Air Force, Army, and Navy funding.

DEPARTMENT OF DEFENSE OUTLAYS FOR AIRCRAFT PROCUREMENT BY AGENCY

Fiscal Years 1969–2005
(Millions of Dollars)

Year	TOTAL	Air Force	Army	Navy
1969	$ 9,177	$ 5,230	$1,126	$ 2,821
1970	7,948	4,623	2,488	837
1971	6,631	3,960	546	2,125
1972	5,927	3,191	389	2,347
1973	5,066	2,396	113	2,557
1974	5,006	2,078	122	2,806
1975	5,484	2,211	136	3,137
1976	6,520	3,323	136	3,061
Tr.Qtr.	1,557	859	26	672
1977	6,608	3,586	301	2,721
1978	6,971	3,989	380	2,602
1979	8,836	5,138	558	3,140
1980	11,124	6,647	787	3,689
1981	13,193	7,941	855	4,397
1982	16,793	9,624	1,297	5,872
1983	21,013	11,799	1,724	7,490
1984	23,196	12,992	2,165	8,040
1985	26,586	15,619	2,705	8,263
1986	30,828	18,919	2,987	8,922
1987	32,956	20,036	3,306	9,614
1988	28,246	15,961	2,878	9,407
1989	27,569	14,662	2,834	10,073
1990	26,142	14,303	2,808	9,031
1991	25,689	13,794	2,840	9,055
1992	23,581	13,154	2,520	7,907
1993	20,359	11,438	1,675	7,246
1994	18,840	10,303	1,711	6,826
1995	16,125	8,891	1,549	5,685
1996	14,331	7,862	1,435	5,034
1997	14,663	7,799	1,542	5,322
1998	15,473	8,236	1,392	5,845
1999	16,484	8,928	1,532	6,024
2000	17,991	8,979	1,268	7,744
2001	17,979	8,217	1,358	8,404
2002	20,546	10,424	1,633	8,489
2003	21,280	11,303	1,781	8,196
2004 [E]	22,403	11,710	2,078	8,615
2005 [E]	23,187	12,317	2,073	8,797

Source: Office of Management and Budget, "Budget of the United States Government" (Annually).

MILITARY AIRCRAFT ACCEPTED BY U.S. MILITARY AGENCIES
Calendar Years 1989–2003

Year	TOTAL	Bomber/ Patrol/ Command/ Control	Fighter/ Attack	Trans- port/ Tanker	Trainer	Heli- copter	Other
NUMBER OF AIRCRAFT							
1989	706	24	408	21	—	253	—
1990	763	24	454	25	—	260	—
1991	650	17	395	23	—	215	—
1992	544	10	312	30	37	155	—
1993	583	11	293	25	56	198	—
1994	487	6	167	40	114	157	3
1995	462	4	133	32	102	176	15
1996	348	4	116	28	54	146	—
1997	332	4	202	19	26	81	—
1998	324	10	188	30	33	63	—
1999	247	6	153	45	12	31	—
2000	180	2	82	30	33	33	—
2001	225	3	77	36	52	48	9
2002ʳ	284	4	83	34	55	90	18
2003	293	3	110	31	65	68	16
FLYAWAY VALUE (Millions of Dollars)							
1989	$11,968	$1,423	$7,735	$ 743	$ —	$2,067	$ —
1990	13,036	1,499	8,731	605	—	2,201	—
1991	11,754	1,023	8,517	437	—	1,777	—
1992	11,482	613	7,673	1,346	267	1,583	—
1993	12,101	1,530	6,400	1,553	484	2,134	—
1994	13,000	3,861	3,661	3,298	477	1,686	17
1995	12,369	3,585	3,547	2,759	460	1,922	98
1996	11,383	3,596	3,524	2,350	337	1,576	—
1997	10,945	1,921	5,653	2,336	270	766	—
1998	15,099	4,831	6,240	2,890	319	835	—
1999	10,731	415	6,164	3,588	219	345	—
2000	8,366	140	3,810	3,651	356	409	—
2001	8,334	218	4,026	2,962	376	691	61
2002ʳ	10,075	295	3,918	3,972	407	1,278	205
2003	10,970	188	5,457	4,075	374	749	127

Source: Aerospace Industries Association, based on USAF, USA, and USN survey responses.

NOTE: Data represent new U.S.-manufactured aircraft, excluding gliders and targets. Values include spares, spare parts, and support equipment that are procured with the aircraft. Includes aircraft accepted for shipment to foreign governments for military assistance programs and foreign military sales.

MILITARY AIRCRAFT ACCEPTANCES BY UNITED STATES AIR FORCE[a]
Calendar Years 2002–2003
(Costs in Millions of Dollars)

Type and Model	Number of Aircraft		Flyaway Cost[b]		Weapon System Cost[c]	
	2002	2003	2002	2003	2002	2003
TOTAL	101[r]	76	$4,791[r]	$5,001	$5,912[r]	$6,970
Fighter/Attack—TOTAL	20[r]	13	$ 893[r]	$1,463	$1,296[r]	$2,615
F-15	2[r]	4	141[r]	173	142[r]	304
F-16	13	—	280	—	491	—
F/A -22	5	9	472	1,290	663	2,311
Transports/Tankers—TOTAL	22[r]	20	3,586[r]	3,343	4,245	4,108
C-17	16	16	3,150	3,134	3,761	3,885
C-37	—	3[d]	—	132[E]	—	138[E]
C-130 variants....................	6[r]	1	436[r]	77	484[r]	85
Trainers—TOTAL	41	27	107	68	166	106
T-6	41	27	107	68	166	106
Other—TOTAL	18	16	205[Er]	127	205[Er]	141
Predator	18	15	205	90	205	90
RQ-4A Global Hawk...........	—	1	—	37	—	51

Source: Aerospace Industries Association, based on USAF survey responses.
  a Air Force acceptances for own use; excludes FMS/MAP shipments.
  b Flyaway Cost includes airframe, engines, electronics, communications, armament, other installed equipment, and non-recurring costs associated with the manufacture of aircraft.
  c Weapon System Cost includes flyaway costs, peculiar ground equipment, training equipment, and technical data.
  d Under lease.

MILITARY AIRCRAFT ACCEPTANCES BY UNITED STATES ARMY[a]
Calendar Years 2002–2003
(Costs in Millions of Dollars)

Type and Model	Number of Aircraft		Flyaway Cost[b]		Weapon System Cost[c]	
	2002	2003	2002	2003	2002	2003
TOTAL	32	40	$258[r]	$265	$323[r]	$372
Transports/Tankers—TOTAL	2	=	$ 52[r]	$ =	$ 52[r]	$ =
C-37	1	—	45[r]	—	45[r]	—
UC-35	1	—	7	—	7	—
Helicopters—TOTAL	30	40	207	265	271[r]	372
TH-67	10	20	13	32	14	32
UH-60L	20	20	193[r]	233	257[r]	339

Source: Aerospace Industries Association, based on USA survey responses.
a Army acceptances for own use; excludes FMS/MAP shipments.
b Flyaway Cost includes airframes, engines, electronics, communications, armament and other installed equipment.
c Weapon System Cost includes flyaway cost, initial spares, ground equipment, training equipment and other support items.

MILITARY AIRCRAFT ACCEPTANCES BY UNITED STATES NAVY[a]
Calendar Years 2002–2003
(Costs in Millions of Dollars)

Type and Model	Number of Aircraft		Flyaway Cost[b]		Weapon System Cost[c]	
	2002	2003	2002	2003	2002	2003
TOTAL	95[r]	112	$3,970[r]	$3,887	$5,079[r]	$4,554
Patrol—TOTAL	4	3	$ 295	$ 188	$ 513	$ 204
E-2..	4	3	295[r]	188	513[r]	204
Fighter/Attack—TOTAL	55	44	2,814	2,397	3,560	2,721
AV-8B	15	—	311	—	383	—
F/A-18	40	44	2,503	2,397	3,176	2,721
Transports/Tankers—TOTAL	6	9	312[r]	716	350[r]	880
C-37	1	—	43	—	50	—
C-40	2	—	109[r]	—	114[r]	—
KC-130................................	1	3	65	199	77	238
UC-35	1	—	7	—	8	—
V-22	1	6	88	517	101	642
Trainers—TOTAL	14[r]	38	300[r]	306	357[r]	369
T-6..	2	26	5	68	9	100
T-45A	12[r]	2	295[r]	238	348[r]	269
Helicopters—TOTAL	16	18	249	280	299	380
MH-60S	16	18	249	280	299	380

Source: Aerospace Industries Association, based on USN survey responses.
a Navy acceptances for own use; excludes FMS shipments.
b Flyaway Cost includes airframe, engines, electronics, communications, armament, other installed equipment, non-recurring costs, and ancillary equipment.
c Weapons System Cost (Investment Cost) includes flyaway cost, initial spares, ground equipment, training equipment, and other support items.

MILITARY AIRCRAFT ACCEPTANCES FOR REIMBURSABLE PROGRAMS[a]
Calendar Years 2002–2003
(Costs in Millions of Dollars)

Accepting Agency, Type, and Model	Number of Aircraft		Flyaway Cost[b]	
	2002	2003	2002	2003
TOTAL...............................	56	65	$1,055	$1,817
AIR FORCE—TOTAL	8	53	$ 211	$1,597
Fighter/Attack—TOTAL	8	53	211	1,597
F-16	8	53	211	1,597
ARMY—TOTAL	48	11	$ 844	$ 210
Helicopters—TOTAL	44	9	822	194
AH-64	14	—	300	—
CH-47	7	7	280	175
UH-60	23	2	242	19
Transports/Tankers—TOTAL	4	2	22	16
B200 (C-12).........................	4	2	22	16
NAVY—TOTAL	—	1	$ —	$ 10
Helicopters—TOTAL	—	1	—	10
CH-53...................................	—	1	—	10

Source: Aerospace Industries Association, based on USAF, USA, and USN survey responses.
 a Foreign government aircraft purchases through the Department of Defense Foreign Military Sales program.
 b Flyaway Cost includes airframes, engines, electronics, communications, armament, other installed equipment, and non-recurring costs associated with the manufacture of the aircraft.

Sales of missile systems and parts reached an 11-year high in 2003, coming in at $8.1 billion. The U.S. Census Bureau also reported that new orders grew 13%. The year-end 2003 backlog of unfilled orders stood at $12.8 billion.

DoD outlays for missile procurement rose in FY 2003. Despite the second highest level in seven years at $5.3 billion, procurement spending remained much lower than in the late 1980s and early 1990s. Ballistic Missile Defense continued to dominate missile RDT&E. Funding totaled $6.7 billion in FY 2003 and is scheduled to increase to $9.1 billion in 2005.

The services funded procurement in excess of $200 million for a few programs. For instance, the Air Force's largest program was the Joint Direct Attack Munition (JDAM) with $752 million in combined USAF/USN funding. The joint procurement totaled 35,620 units, which use a low-cost Global Positioning System unit and some additional fins to turn a simple gravity bomb into a precision-guided munition. The Navy's Trident II, with $573 million of funding for 12 submarine-launched ballistic missiles, constituted its largest missile procurement program. Javelin, a surface-to-surface anti-armor missile, was the Army's largest program with $222 million of FY 2003 funding. Finally, the Missile Defense Agency (MDA) funded the purchase of 122 Patriots with joint MDA/Army money totaling $756 million. Other "large" programs were Air Force's Minuteman III with

$583 million in funding and Navy's 350 Tomahawks totaling $437 million in FY 2003.

Procurement of several smaller programs continued. The Air Force had six other missile procurements underway in FY 2003: 234 Advanced Medium Range Air-to-Air Missiles (AMRAAM) costing $135 million; 310 Sensor-Fused Weapons (SFW), $124 million; 570 AIM-9X air-to-air missiles, $108 million; 3,262 Wind-Corrected Munitions Dispensers (WCMD), $95 million; 100 Joint Air-to-Surface Stand-off Missiles (JASSM), $54 million; and 137 Predator Hellfires, $10 million. The Navy had five other programs in active procurement including: 554 joint Air Force/Navy Joint Stand-Off Weapons (JSOW) costing $172 million; 93 Standard missiles, $151 million; 120 Sea-Launched Attack Missile-Extended Range (SLAM-ER), $83 million; 106 Rolling Airframe Missiles (RAM), $59 million; and 23 Evolved SeaSparrow Missiles (ESSM) for $42 million. The Army bought: 156 Army TACtical Missile Systems (ATACMS) for $138 million; 822 HIgh Mobility Artillery Rocket System/Guided Multiple Launch Rocket System (HIMARS/GMLRS) rockets, $131 million; and 139 Stingers, $25 million.

In FY 2004, two programs begin or return to unit procurement: 76 Army Line-Of-Sight Anti-Tank (LOSAT) weapons with $43 million in funding and 200 Army Tube-launched, Optically-tracked, Wire-guided (TOW 2) anti-armor weapons costing $26 million.

ORDERS, SALES, AND BACKLOG OF MISSILE SYSTEMS AND PARTS[a]
Calendar Years 1989-2003
(Millions of Dollars)

Year	SALES—Current Dollars	SALES—Constant Dollars[br]
1989	$9,283	$ 8,807
1990	9,102	8,366
1991	8,989	8,062
1992	9,032	7,720
1993	7,713	6,406
1994	5,294	4,294
1995	4,688	3,744
1996	4,792	3,764
1997	4,024	3,134
1998	4,356	3,372
1999	4,521	3,478
2000	5,567	4,161
2001	6,241	4,552
2002[r]	7,218	5,185
2003	8,083	5,648

Year	NET NEW ORDERS	BACKLOG AS OF DECEMBER 31
1989	$8,998	$14,005
1990	7,917	12,956
1991	8,072	12,571
1992	9,234	11,814
1993	4,775	9,305
1994	2,785	5,823
1995	3,164	4,833
1996	8,672	6,563
1997	4,239	5,828
1998	4,884	6,539
1999	3,753	5,342
2000	9,738	9,389
2001	5,215	9,547
2002[r]	8,742	11,072
2003	9,855	12,823

Source: Bureau of the Census, "Aerospace Industry (Orders, Sales, and Backlog)" (Annually).
   a Excludes engines and propulsion units where separable.
   b Based on AIA's aerospace composite price deflator, 1987=100.

DEPARTMENT OF DEFENSE OUTLAYS FOR MISSILE PROCUREMENT
BY AGENCY
Fiscal Years 1969–2005
(Millions of Dollars)

Year	TOTAL	Air Force	Army	Navy
1969	$ 2,509	$1,382	$ 593	$ 534
1970	2,912	1,467	743	702
1971	3,140	1,497	852	791
1972	3,009	1,334	844	831
1973	3,023	1,454	941	628
1974	2,981	1,537	903	541
1975	2,889	1,602	672	615
1976	2,296	1,549	163	584
Tr.Qtr.	402	347	(93)	148
1977	2,781	1,501	374	905
1978	3,096[a]	1,376	418	1,302[a]
1979	3,786	1,537	547	1,702
1980	4,434	1,810	651	1,973
1981	5,809	2,366	1,146	2,297
1982	6,782	3,069	1,269	2,444
1983	7,795	3,383	1,600	2,812
1984	9,527	4,640	2,079	2,809
1985	10,749	5,409	2,399	2,941
1986	11,731	6,473	2,478	2,780
1987	11,473	6,002	2,314	3,157
1988	11,676	6,046	2,239	3,392
1989	14,503	7,349	2,709	4,445
1990	14,851	7,951	2,453	4,446
1991	14,400	6,906	2,540	4,954
1992	13,504	6,409	2,401	4,694
1993	11,404	5,424	2,187	3,794
1994	8,934	4,312	1,384	3,238
1995	7,513	3,845	974	2,694
1996	6,199	3,235	919	2,045
1997	5,225	2,743	936	1,546
1998	4,907	2,543	964	1,400
1999	4,080	2,299	783	998
2000	4,231	2,243	926	1,062
2001	5,441	2,982	1,248	1,211
2002	5,230	2,719	1,256	1,255
2003	5,262	2,802	1,273	1,187
2004[E]	6,271	3,559	1,175	1,537
2005[E]	6,944	4,121	1,294	1,529

Source: Office of Management and Budget, "The Budget of the United States Government" (Annually).
a Beginning 1978, DoD combined Navy Missile Procurement with torpedoes and other related products into Navy Weapons Procurement. Missiles comprise approximately 80 percent of the value of this category.

MAJOR MISSILE PROGRAMS
IN RESEARCH, DEVELOPMENT, OR PRODUCTION
As of 2003

Program	Agency	Status	Systems Contractor	Propulsion Manufacturer	Guidance Manufacturer
AIR-TO-AIR					
AMRAAM-120C	USAF/USN	P	Raytheon	ATK	Ray/NGC/BAE
Sidewinder-9M	USN/USAF	P	NASC	ATK	Raytheon
Sidewinder-9X	USN/USAF	P	Raytheon	ATK	Raytheon/BAE
AIR-TO-SURFACE					
AGM-142	USAF	P	LM/Rafael	Rafael	NGC/BAE
EGBU 15	USAF	P	Raytheon	—	Honeywell
GATS/GAM	USAF	P	NGC	—	Honeywell
HARM-88A/B/C	USN/USAF	P	Raytheon	ATK	Raytheon
*Harpoon-84A/C/ D/G	USN	P	Boeing	TCM/ATK	Ray/Kearfott/HI
*Harpoon-84L	USN	P	Boeing	TCM/ATK	HI/Ray/Kearfott
JASSM	USN/USAF	P	LM	TCM	HI/BAE
JCM	Army	D	LM	Aerojet	LM
JDAM	USAF/USN	P	Boeing	—	HI/Boeing
JSOW-154	USN/USAF	D	Raytheon	—	HI/Kearfott
Maverick-65D/G/H/K	USAF	P	Raytheon	ATK	Raytheon
Maverick-65F	USN	P	Raytheon	ATK	Raytheon
Maverick-65J	USN/USMC	D	Raytheon	ATK	Raytheon
Paveway-Enhanced	USN/USAF	P	Raytheon	—	Ray/HI/BAE
SLAM-ER-84H/K	USN	P	Boeing	TCM	Boeing/Ray/HI
Small Diameter Bomb	USAF	D	Boeing	—	Honeywell
WCMD	USAF	P	LM	—	LM/BAE/HI
ANTI-SUBMARINE					
VLA-44A	USN	P	LM	ATK	LM
BATTLEFIELD SUPPORT AND ANTIARMOR					
ATACMS	Army	P	LM	Aerojet	Honeywell
Excalibur	Army	D	Raytheon	—	HI/L-3/BAE
ERGM	USN	D	Raytheon	ATK	BAE/L-3
GMLRS	Army	D	LM	Aerojet	Honeywell
HELLFIRE II-114K	Army/USMC	P	LM	ATK	LM
Longbow HELLFIRE 114L	Army	P	LM/NGC	ATK	LM/NGC/BAE
HELLFIRE-114M	USN/USMC	P	LM	ATK	LM
LOSAT	Army	D	LM	ATK	HI/Aerojet
Javelin	Army/USMC	P	Ray/LM	Aerojet	LM/Ray/BAE
MLRS-26	Army	P	LM	Aerojet	—
Predator	USMC	P	LM	ATK	LM
TOW2A-71E	Army	P	Raytheon	ATK	Raytheon/BAE
TOW2B-71F	Army	P	Raytheon	ATK	Raytheon/BAE

* Also Surface-to-Surface   (Continued on next page)

MAJOR MISSILE PROGRAMS
IN RESEARCH, DEVELOPMENT, OR PRODUCTION
As of 2003, continued

Program	Agency	Status	Systems Contractor	Propulsion Manufacturer	Guidance Manufacturer
SURFACE-TO-AIR					
PAC-3	Army	P	LM	Aerojet	LM/HI/Boeing
RAM-RIM 116B	USN	P	Raytheon	Aerojet	Ray/RAMSYS
SeaSparrow-7M	USN	P	Raytheon	ATK	Raytheon/BAE
SeaSparrow-Evolved	USN	D	Raytheon	ATK/Raufoss	Ray/HI/BAE
Standard 2 MR	USN	P	Raytheon	Aerojet	Raytheon/HI
Standard 2-IV	USN	P	Raytheon	Aerojet/UTC	Raytheon/HI
Standard 3	USN	D	Raytheon	Aerojet/UTC/ATK	Raytheon/HI
Stinger-92D/E	All	P	Raytheon	Aerojet	Raytheon/HI
THAAD	Army	D	LM	Boeing/Aerojet	LM/Honeywell
SURFACE-TO-SURFACE					
*Harpoon-84A/C/D	USN	P	Boeing	TCM/ATK	Ray/IBM/LSI/HI/Kearfott
*Harpoon-84L	USN	D	Boeing	TCM/ATK	HI/IBM/LSI/Ray/Kearfott
Minuteman III	USAF	P	NGC	ATK/UTC/Aerojet	Boeing
NLOS-LS	Army	D	LM/Raytheon	Aerojet	LM/Raytheon
NLOS-LAM	Army	D	LM	Aerojet	LM
NLOS-PAM	Army	D	Raytheon	Aerojet	Raytheon
Tomahawk Tactical	USN	P	Raytheon	WI/Aerojet	Raytheon/HI

Source: Aerospace Industries Association, based on company reports.
Status: R-Research; D-Development; P-Production.
  * Also Air-to-Surface

Abb:					
ATK	— Alliant Techsystems	LM	— Lockheed Martin	TCM	— Teledyne Continental Motors
BAE	— BAE Systems	NASC	— Naval Air Systems Command	UTC	— United Technologies
HI	— Honeywell	NGC	— Northrop Grumman	WI	— Williams International
LSI	— Lear Siegler	Ray	— Raytheon		

MISSILE PROGRAM PROCUREMENT[a]
Fiscal Years 2003, 2004, and 2005
(Costs in Millions of Dollars)

Agency and Model	2003		2004[E]		2005[E]	
	No.	Cost	No.	Cost	No.	Cost
AIR FORCE						
AIM-9X[b]	570	$107.9	355	$ 78.8	405	$ 87.8
AMRAAM[b]	234	135.4	243	141.9	248	141.3
JASSM	100	53.8	240	100.9	360	148.2
JDAM[b]	35,620	752.3	32,570	699.9	29,757	673.0
Minuteman III	—	583.1	—	594.9	—	640.8
Predator Hellfire	137	9.9	100	14.8	235	20.0
SDB	—	—	—	—	158	29.3
SFW	310	124.1	320	117.0	315	117.0
WCMD	3,262	94.6	3,715	71.9	2,507	58.7
ARMY						
ATACMS	156	$137.5	60	$ 57.4	56	$ 61.5
HIMARS/GMLRS	822	130.5	786	107.0	1,026	112.3
Javelin	1,478	221.7	901	139.7	1,038	117.8
Longbow Hellfire	—	181.2	—	24.9	—	15.6
LOSAT	—	—	76	42.9	158	86.3
Stinger	139	25.4	—	2.9	—	—
TOW 2	—	—	200	26.4	500	26.3
MDA						
Patriot[f]	122	$755.7	135	$818.0	108	$577.2
NAVY						
ESSM	23	$ 42.0	82	$102.0	71	$ 80.3
JSOW[b]	554	171.8	635	197.0	389	139.4
RAM	106	59.2	90	48.0	90	47.4
SLAM-ER	120	82.6	77	50.8	—	—
Standard	93	151.4	75	147.2	75	150.1
Tomahawk	350	437.1	350	352.6	293	256.2
Trident II	12	573.0	12	645.4	5	768.6

Source: Department of Defense, "Program Acquisition Costs by Weapon System" (Annually) and "Procurement Programs (P-1)" (Annually).
a   Total Obligational Authority excluding initial spares and RDT&E.
b   Navy and Air Force funding.
c   Army and Navy funding.
d   Army and Marine Corps funding.
f   Army and MDA funding.

MISSILE PROGRAMS RESEARCH, DEVELOPMENT, TEST, AND EVALUATION[a] BY AGENCY AND MODEL
Fiscal Years 2003, 2004, and 2005
(Millions of Dollars)

Agency and Model	2003	2004[E]	2005[E]
AIR FORCE			
ACM/ALCM	$ 22.0	$ 42.7	$ 19.6
AMRAAM[b]	47.0	41.2	42.4
ICBM	176.4	232.8	164.2
JASSM[b]	64.7	46.4	72.8
SDB[b]	56.3	125.4	86.5
WCMD	3.4	17.5	28.0
ARMY			
AAWS-M	$ 0.5	$ 0.9	$ 0.9
BAT (ATACMS)	55.9	9.9	0.0
Common Missile	28.1	93.7	152.4
HIMARS/MRLS	94.6	83.9	97.4
LOSAT	10.6	30.5	22.6
MEADS	—	249.4	264.5
Patriot	39.3	202.9	95.9
MDA			
BMD	$6,687.0	$7,625.5	$9,146.7
NAVY			
AIM-9X Sidewinder[b]	$ 5.6	$ 2.6	$ 9.7
HARM	58.8	51.6	163.4
JDAM[b]	63.9	35.2	—
JSOW	16.7	5.0	9.5
Standard	24.2	81.0	99.0
Tomahawk	97.3	76.5	28.8
Trident II	38.1	65.5	108.8
Tri-Service Standoff Attack Missile	16.1	20.9	27.0

Source: Department of Defense Budget, "Program Acquisition Costs by Weapon System" (Annually) and "RDT&E Programs (R-1)" (Annually).
a Total Obligational Authority.
b Navy and Air Force funding.

Missile Program Acronyms:

AAWS-M	—Advanced Anti-tank Weapon System-Medium	ACM/ALCM	—Advanced & Air Launched Cruise Missile
AIM	—Air Intercept Missile	AMRAAM	—Advanced Medium Range Air-to-Air Missile
ATACMS	—Army TACtical Missile System	BAT	—Brilliant Anti-Tank submunition
BMD	—Ballistic Missile Defense	HARM	—High-speed Anti-Radiation Missile
HIMARS	—HIgh Mobility Artillery Rocket System	ICBM	—Inter-Continental Ballistic Missile
JASSM	—Joint Air-to-Surface Stand-off Missile	JDAM	—Joint Direct Attack Munition
JSOW	—Joint Stand-Off Weapon	LOSAT	—Line Of Sight Anti-Tank
MEADS	—Medium Extended Air Defense System	MRLS	—Multiple Launch Rocket Systems
SDB	—Small Diameter Bomb	SFW	—Sensor-Fused Weapon
WCMD	—Wind-Corrected Munitions Dispenser		

BALLISTIC MISSILE DEFENSE FUNDING
Fiscal Years 2001-2005
(Millions of Dollars)

Category and Title	Program Element	2001	2002	2003	2004^E	2005^E
TOTAL		$5,888	$7,775	$7,411	$7,734	$10,193
BMDO/MDA Programs—TOTAL		$4,755	$7,775	$7,411	$7,712	$ 9,169
Procurement—TOTAL		$ 444	$ 737	$ 492	$ —	$ —
TMD BMC3..............................	0208864C	4	—	—	—	—
PAC-3	0208865C	365	737	492	—	—
National Missile Defense	0208871C	75	—	—	—	—
Military Construction—TOTAL		104	8	23	22	22
National Missile Defense	0603871C	104	—	—	—	—
BMD System	0603880C	—	8	—	—	—
Terminal	0603881C	—	1	23	—	—
BMD Midcourse Defense Segment	0603882C	—	—	—	20	20
BMD Test & Targets	0603888C	—	—	—	2	3
RDT&E—TOTAL		4,207	7,030	6,896	7,712	9,147
TMD—TOTAL..........................		1,653	1,101	1,211	—	—
Navy Theater Wide...............	0603868C	463	—	—	—	—
MEADS	0603869C	53	—	118	—	—
Family of Systems E&I	0603873C	231	—	—	—	—
THAAD System	0604861C	550	872	912	—	—
PAC-3	0604865C	81	129	181	—	—
Navy Area.............................	0604867C	274	100	—	—	—

(Continued on next page)

BALLISTIC MISSILE DEFENSE FUNDING
Fiscal Years 2001-2005, continued
(Millions of Dollars)

Category and Title	Program Element	2001	2002	2003	2004^E	2005^E
RDT&E (continued)						
Support Technology/Applied Research	0602173C	$ 40	$ —	$ —	$ —	$ —
Support Technology/Advanced Development	0603173C	122	—	—	—	—
Support Technology/Space Based Laser	0603174C	75	—	—	—	—
BMD Technology	0603175C	—	141	155	229	204
NMD	0603871C	1,875	—	—	—	—
BMD Technical Operations	0603874C	291	—	—	—	—
International Cooperative Programs	0603875C	125	—	—	—	—
Threat and Countermeasures	0603876C	23	—	—	—	—
Advanced Concepts Evaluation & Systems	0603879C	—	—	—	152	256
BMD System Segment	0603880C	—	819	1,073	—	—
Terminal Defense Segment	0603881C	—	203	140	884	938
Midcourse Defense Segment	0603882C	—	3,821	3,186	3,795	4,385
Boost Defense Segment	0603883C	—	609	737	624	493
Sensors Segment	0603884C	—	341	359	430	592
BMD System Interceptors	0603886C	—	—	—	119	511
BMD Test & Targets	0603888C	—	—	—	613	714
BMD Products	0603889C	—	—	—	309	419
BMD System Core	0603890C	—	—	—	450	480
Pentagon Reservation Maintenance Fund	0901585C	5	7	7	14	14
Headquarters Management	0901598C	—	28	28	93	142
BMD-Related Programs—TOTAL		$1,133	$ —	$ —	$1,012	$1,024
Air Force SBIRS-High	0604441F	$ 569	$ —	$ —	$ —	$ —
Air Force SBIRS-Low	0604442F	241	—	—	—	—
Air Force ABL	0603319F	234	—	—	—	—
Air Force SBL	0603876F	73	—	—	—	—
Army Missile Defense Improvement	0203801A	—	—	—	—	32
Army THEL	0602307A	16	—	—	—	—
Army MEADS	0603869A	—	—	—	(a)	265
Army PAC-3	0604865A	—	—	—	622 [a]	641
JTAMDO	0605126J	—	—	—	—	86

Source: Missile Defense Agency.
a Funds combined by appropriators.

Sales of space vehicle systems (including propulsion units) fell $0.6 billion in 2003 to $7.4 billion, according to figures compiled by the U.S. Census Bureau. Both military and civil sales declined—down $42 million and $0.5 billion, respectively.

Net new orders plummeted on an apparent cancellation of military orders in 2003. Civil orders also declined—down $1 billion to $1.8 billion. The resulting backlog of unfilled orders dropped 35% to $14 billion with a lopsided 10/90 split between military and civil work.

Federal outlays on space programs totaled $33 billion in FY 2003, with DoD accounting for $18.6 billion and NASA $13.6 billion. The federal government's space spending by all other agencies increased a combined $41 million to a total of $1.2 billion.

A variety of unclassified military space programs received funding in FY 2003. The Air Force led the majority of major DoD space programs, including: Advanced EHF, $803 million; SBIRS-High, $775 million; NAVSTAR GPS, $614 million; Defense Space Recon, $321 million; NPOESS, $232 million; EELV, $231 million; Titan Launch Vehicles, $254 million; and Wideband Gapfiller, $201 million. The Army's DSCS received $105 million and the Navy's

Sat Comm Systems/Mobile User Objective System (MOUS) programs received a combined $269 million. Of the above-mentioned programs, NPOESS, EELV, Sat Comm Systems/MOUS, and DSCS are scheduled to receive increased funding in FY 2004.

Operating the Space Shuttle and building the International Space Station (ISS) dominated NASA's FY 2003 budget, accounting for 31% of NASA's $15.4 billion in budget authority for the year. The Station accounted for $1.5 billion, while operating the Shuttle cost $3.3 billion, according to NASA budget summaries. Space science funding totaled $3.5 billion and aeronautics technology received $1.0 billion. NASA's FY 2004 budget decreased slightly to a total of $15.4 billion. However, the Space Shuttle is budgeted for a $0.6 billion increase; Space Science, up $0.4 billion; and the ISS, up $36 million.

While the pace of launching decreased from 2002 overall, U.S. flights rebounded and China became the third country to successfully launch manned spacecraft into orbit.

Orders for commercial geosynchronous (GEO) satellites doubled in 2003, according to figures supplied by the Futron Corporation. The world's manufacturers received orders for 21 satellites worth $2.1 billion in 2003—up from ten costing $1.0 billion in 2002. The unfilled order backlog was estimated at 89 commercial GEO s   lites worth $9.7 billion.

ORDERS, SALES, AND BACKLOG OF SPACE VEHICLE SYSTEMS[a]
Calendar Years 1989–2003
(Millions of Dollars)

Year	SALES—Current Dollars			SALES—Constant Dollars[br]		
	TOTAL	Military	Non-Military	TOTAL	Military	Non-Military
1989	$ 9,758	$6,457	$ 3,301	$ 9,258	$ 6,126	$ 3,132
1990	9,691	6,556	3,135	8,907	6,026	2,881
1991	10,515	6,770	3,745	9,430	6,072	3,359
1992	9,266	5,887	3,379	7,920	5,032	2,888
1993	7,317	4,175	3,142	6,077	3,468	2,610
1994	10,594	5,707	4,887	8,592	4,629	3,964
1995	11,314	4,782	6,532	9,037	3,819	5,217
1996	11,698	5,613	6,085	9,189	4,409	4,780
1997	14,643	4,919	9,724	11,404	3,831	7,573
1998	9,491	4,227	5,264	7,346	3,272	4,074
1999	9,022	5,107	3,915	6,940	3,928	3,012
2000	8,164	3,723	4,441	6,102	2,783	3,319
2001[c]	9,032	4,413	4,619	6,588	3,219	3,369
2002[cr]	7,946	3,824	4,121	5,708	2,747	2,960
2003[c]	7,392	3,782	3,610	5,166	2,643	2,523

Year	NET NEW ORDERS			BACKLOG AS OF DECEMBER 31		
	TOTAL	Military	Non-Military	TOTAL	Military	Non-Military
1989	$11,709	$8,107	$ 3,602	$13,356	$ 9,192	$ 4,164
1990	9,598	6,256	3,342	12,462	8,130	4,332
1991	11,222	5,468	5,754	11,664	6,221	5,443
1992	10,491	6,773	3,718	12,809	7,622	5,187
1993	8,436	5,106	3,330	13,663	7,384	6,279
1994	9,041	4,896	4,145	12,888	6,732	6,156
1995	13,212	4,679	8,533	15,650	5,872	9,778
1996	16,527	8,888	7,639	23,004	9,125	13,879
1997	15,078	4,584	10,494	23,189	8,848	14,341
1998	12,420	4,563	7,857	20,372	7,970	12,402
1999	11,175	7,912	3,263	22,356	10,666	11,690
2000	7,205	2,310	4,895	21,395	8,942	12,453
2001[c]	7,267	3,719	3,548	21,886[r]	5,767[r]	16,121[r]
2002[cr]	7,968	5,176	2,793	21,968	7,178	14,789
2003[c]	(217)	(2,008)	1,790	14,365	1,388	12,977

Source: Bureau of the Census, "Aerospace Industry (Orders, Sales, and Backlog)" (Annually).
   a Excludes engines and propulsion units where separable.
   b Based on AIA's aerospace composite price deflator, 1987=100.
   c Due to disclosure limitations, space propulsion units combined with space vehicle systems.

ORDERS, SALES, AND BACKLOG OF ENGINES AND PROPULSION UNITS FOR MISSILES AND SPACE VEHICLES
Calendar Years 1989–2003
(Millions of Dollars)

Year	SALES—Current Dollars			SALES—Constant Dollars[ar]		
	TOTAL	Military	Non-Military	TOTAL	Military	Non-Military
1989	$3,602	$1,771	$1,831	$3,417	$1,680	$1,737
1990	3,247	1,911	1,336	2,984	1,756	1,228
1991	3,807	1,869	1,938	3,414	1,676	1,738
1992	3,051	1,577	1,474	2,608	1,348	1,260
1993	3,104	1,619	1,485	2,578	1,345	1,233
1994	2,518	1,123	1,395	2,042	911	1,131
1995	2,364	1,035	1,329	1,888	827	1,062
1996	2,016	635	1,381	1,584	499	1,085
1997	2,687	558	2,129	2,093	435	1,658
1998	2,262	496	1,766	1,751	384	1,367
1999	2,118	525	1,593	1,629	404	1,225
2000	1,872	683	1,189	1,399	510	889
2001[b]	239	239	—	174	174	—
2002[br]	472	472	—	339	339	—
2003[b]	535	535	—	374	374	—

Year	NET NEW ORDERS			BACKLOG AS OF DECEMBER 31		
	TOTAL	Military	Non-Military	TOTAL	Military	Non-Military
1989	$6,113	$2,475	$3,638	$6,410	$2,595	$3,815
1990	2,692	1,891	801	6,230	2,887	3,343
1991	5,661	1,087	4,574	8,422	2,327	6,095
1992	3,124	2,097	1,027	8,310	2,729	5,581
1993	1,708	710	998	6,543	1,903	4,640
1994	1,879	484	1,395	6,035	1,390	4,645
1995	2,805	444	2,361	6,630	1,065	5,565
1996	1,868	745	1,123	5,873	1,108	4,765
1997	2,009	477	1,532	5,568	1,023	4,545
1998	2,395	655	1,740	4,263	1,102	3,161
1999	3,896	687	3,209	6,182	1,017	5,165
2000	1,425	493	932	5,499	816	4,683
2001[b]	245	245	—	486	486	—
2002[br]	578	578	—	811	811	—
2003[b]	473	473	—	749	749	—

Source: Bureau of the Census, "Aerospace Industry (Orders, Sales, and Backlog)" (Annually).
  a Based on AIA's aerospace composite price deflator, 1987=100.
  b Due to disclosure limitations, space propulsion units combined with space vehicle systems. See page 58.

WORLDWIDE SPACE LAUNCHINGS[a]
WHICH ATTAINED EARTH ORBIT OR BEYOND
Calendar Years 1957–2003

Country	Total 1957-2003	1999	2000	2001	2002	2003[c]
TOTAL	5,302	74	82	66	62	43
U.S.S.R./C.I.S	3,702	29	36	31	23	14
United States	1,279	30	29	25	18	21
European Space Agency	154	10	12	8	12	4
People's Republic of China	70	4	5	1	4	1
Japan	59	—	—	—	3	2
India	14	1	—	1	1	1
Israel	4	—	—	—	1	—
Other[b]	20	—	—	—	—	—

Source: NASA, "Aeronautics and Space Report of the President" (Annually).
   a   Number of launchings rather than spacecraft; some launches orbited multiple spacecraft.
   b   Includes 10 by France, 8 by Italy (5 were U.S. spacecraft), 1 by Australia, and 1 by the United Kingdom.
   c   Through September 30.

U.S. GOVERNMENT SPACECRAFT RECORD[a]
Calendar Years 1957–2003

Year	Earth Orbit[b] Success	Earth Orbit[b] Failure	Earth Escape[b] Success	Earth Escape[b] Failure	Year	Earth Orbit[b] Success	Earth Orbit[b] Failure	Earth Escape[b] Success	Earth Escape[b] Failure
1957	—	1	—	—	1982	21	—	—	—
1958	5	8	—	4	1983	31	—	—	—
1959	9	9	1	2	1984	35	3	—	—
1960	16	12	1	2	1985	37	1	—	—
1961	35	12	—	2	1986	11	4	—	—
1962	55	12	4	1	1987	9	1	—	—
1963	62	11	—	—	1988	16	1	—	—
1964	69	8	4	—	1989	24	—	2	—
1965	93	7	4	1	1990	40	—	1	—
1966	94	12	7	1[c]	1991	32[d]	—	—	—
1967	78	4	10	—	1992	26[d]	—	1	—
1968	61	15	3	—	1993	28[d]	1	1	—
1969	58	1	8	1	1994	31[d]	1	1	—
1970	36	1	3	—	1995	24[d]	2	1	—
1971	45	2	8	1	1996	30[d]	1	3	—
1972	33	2	8	—	1997	22	—	1	—
1973	23	2	3	—	1998	23	—	2	—
1974	27	2	1	—	1999	35	4	2	—
1975	30	4	4	—	2000	31	—	—	—
1976	33	—	1	—	2001	23	—	3	—
1977	27	2	2	—	2002	18	—	—	1[c]
1978	34	2	7	—	2003[f]	24	—	2	—
1979	18	—	—	—					
1980	16	4	—	—	**TOTAL**	1,548	153	99	16
1981	20	1	—	—					

Source: NASA, "Aeronautics and Space Report of the President" (Annually).
a Payloads, rather than launchings; some launches account for multiple spacecraft. Includes spacecraft from cooperating countries launched on U.S. launch vehicles.
b The criterion of success is attainment of Earth orbit or Earth escape rather than judgement of mission success. "Escape" flights include all that were intended to go at least an altitude equal to the lunar distance from the Earth.
c This Earth-escape failure did attain Earth orbit and therefore is included in the Earth-orbit success totals.
d Excludes commercial satellites.
f Through September 30.

U.S. SPACE LAUNCH VEHICLES
As of 2003

Vehicle and Initial Launch & First Launch of This Modification	Stages	Thrust (Kilo-newtons)	Maximum Payload (Kg)[a]		
			185-Km Orbit	Geo-synch.-Transfer Orbit	Circular Sun-synch. Orbit
Athena (1995)	1. Athena*	1,450.0	520	245	—
Atlas E (1958; 1968)	1. Atlas MA-3	1,739.5	820[b] 1,860[bc]	—	910[c]
Atlas I (1966; 1990)	1. Atlas MA-5 2. 2 Centaur I	1,952.0 146.8	—	2,255	—
Atlas II (1966; 1991)	1. Atlas MA-5A 2. 2 Centaur II	2,110.0 146.8	6,580 5,510[b]	2,810	4,300
Atlas IIA (1966; 1992)	1. Atlas MA-5A 2. 2 Centaur II	2,110.0 185.1	6,828 6,170[b]	3,062	4,750
Atlas IIAS (1966; 1993)	1. Atlas MA-5A plus 4 Castor IV* 2. 2 Centaur II	2,110.0 1,734.4 185.1	8,640 7,300[b]	3,606	5,800
Delta II 7900 Series (1960; 1990)	1. RS-270/A plus 9 Hercules GEM* 2. AJ10-118K 3. Star 48B*	1,043.0 4,388.4 42.4 66.4	5,089 3,890[b]	1,842[d]	3,175
Delta III (1998)[f]	1. RS-27 plus 9 Alliant GEM* 2. RL-10B 3. Star 48B*	1,043.0 5,479.2 110.0 66.4	8,292	3,810	6,768
Pegasus (1990)	1. Orion 50S* 2. Orion 50* 3. Orion 38*	484.9 118.2 31.9	380 280[b]	—	210
Pegasus XL (1994)[f]	1. Orion 50S-XL* 2. Orion 50-XL* 3. Orion 38*	743.3 201.5 31.9	460 350[b]	—	335
Space Shuttle (reusable) (1981)	0. 3 main engines (SSMEs) fire in parallel with solid-fueled rocket boosters (SRBs) 1. 2 SRBs mounted on external tank (ET) fire in parallel with SSMEs 2. 2 OMS	5,006.1 23,580.0 53.4	24,900[g]	5,900[h]	—
Taurus (1994)	0. Castor 120* 1. Orion 50S* 2. Orion 50* 3. Orion 38*	1,687.7 580.5 138.6 31.9	1,400 1,080[b]	255	1,020

(Continued on next page)

U.S. SPACE LAUNCH VEHICLES
As of 2003, continued

Vehicle and Initial Launch & First Launch of This Modification	Stages	Thrust (Kilo-newtons)	Maximum Payload (Kg)[a]		
			185-Km Orbit	Geo-synch.-Transfer Orbit	Circular Sun-synch. Orbit
Titan II (1964; 1988)	1. 2 LR-87 2. LR-91	2,090.0 440.0	1,905[b]	—	—
Titan III (1964; 1989)	0. 2 5 1/2-segment, 3.05-m. dia* 1. 2 LR-87 2. LR-91	12,420.0 2,429.0 462.8	14,515	5,000[i]	—
Titan IV (1989)	0. 2 7-segment, 3.05-m. dia* 1. 2 LR-87 2. LR-91	14,000.0 2,429.0 462.8	17,700 14,110[b]	6,350[i]	—
Titan IV/Centaur (1994)	0. 2 7-segment, 4.3-m. dia* 1. 2 LR-87 2. LR-91 3. Centaur 4. SRMU	14,000.0 2,429.0 462.5 73.4 7,690.0	—	5,760	—

Source: NASA, "Aeronautics and Space Report of the President" (Annually).
* Solid propellant; all others are liquid.
a Due east launch except as indicated.
b Polar launch.
c With TE-M-364-4 upper stage.
d With Star 48B.
f First launch was a failure.
g In full performance configuration (280–420 km orbit).
h With IUS or TOS.
i With appropriate upper stage.

FEDERAL SPACE ACTIVITIES BUDGET AUTHORITY
Fiscal Years 1966-2005
(Millions of Dollars)

Year	TOTAL	NASA[a]	DoD	Commerce	Energy	Other[b]
1966	$ 6,968	$ 5,065	$ 1,689	$ 27	$187	$ —
1967	6,707	4,830	1,664	29	184	—
1968	6,526	4,430	1,922	28	145	1
1969	6,005	3,822	2,013	20	118	32
1970	5,366	3,547	1,678	8	103	30
1971	4,775	3,101	1,512	27	95	40
1972	4,611	3,071	1,407	31	55	47
1973	4,863	3,093	1,623	40	54	53
1974	4,683	2,759	1,766	60	42	56
1975	4,965	2,915	1,892	64	30	64
1976	5,376	3,225	1,983	72	23	73
Tr.Qtr.	1,352	849	460	22	5	16
1977	6,046	3,440	2,412	91	22	81
1978	6,587	3,623	2,738	103	34	89
1979	7,314	4,030	3,036	98	59	91
1980	8,759	4,680	3,848	93	40	98
1981	10,054	4,992	4,828	87	41	106
1982	12,520	5,528	6,679	145	61	107
1983	15,674	6,328	9,019	178	39	110
1984	17,448	6,858	10,195	236	34	125
1985	20,277	6,925	12,768	423	34	127
1986	21,768	7,165	14,126	309	35	133
1987	26,562	9,809	16,287	278	48	140
1988	26,742	8,322	17,679	352	241	148
1989	28,563	10,097	17,906	301	97	162
1990	27,582	11,460	15,616	243	79	184
1991	27,999	13,046	14,181	251	251	270
1992	29,020	13,199	15,023	327	223	248
1993	27,901	13,064	14,106	324	165	242
1994	26,820	13,022	13,166	312	74	246
1995	23,946	12,543	10,644	352	60	347
1996	24,911	12,569	11,514	472	46	310
1997	24,973	12,457	11,727	448	35	306
1998	25,519	12,321	12,359	435	103	301
1999	26,644	12,459	13,203	575	105	302
2000	26,518	12,521	12,941	575	164	317
2001	28,692	13,304	14,326	577	145	340
2002[r]	30,807	13,871	15,740	644	169	383
2003	35,053	14,360	19,388	649	191	465
2004[E]	35,797	14,317	20,019	761	198	502
2005[E]	38,493	15,297	21,677	829	195	495

Source: NASA, "Aeronautics and Space Report of the President" (Annually).
   a Excludes amounts for air transportation.
   b Departments of Interior, Transportation, and Agriculture, the National Science Foundation, and the Environmental Protection Agency.

FEDERAL SPACE ACTIVITIES OUTLAYS
Fiscal Years 1965-2003
(Millions of Dollars)

Year	TOTAL	NASA[a]	DoD	Commerce	Energy	Other[b]
1965	$ 6,886	$ 5,035	$ 1,592	$ 24	$232	$ 3
1966	7,719	5,858	1,637	28	188	7
1967	7,237	5,337	1,673	39	184	5
1968	6,667	4,595	1,890	29	147	6
1969	6,326	4,078	2,095	31	118	5
1970	5,453	3,565	1,756	24	103	5
1971	4,999	3,171	1,693	30	97	8
1972	4,772	3,195	1,470	37	60	10
1973	4,719	3,069	1,557	29	51	13
1974	4,854	2,960	1,777	64	39	14
1975	4,891	2,951	1,831	64	34	11
1976	5,314	3,336	1,864	71	26	16
Tr.Qtr.	1,361	869	458	23	8	4
1977	5,559	3,600	1,833	87	22	18
1978	6,188	3,582	2,457	101	29	20
1979	6,808	3,744	2,892	97	55	21
1980	7,734	4,340	3,162	89	49	94
1981	9,238	4,877	4,131	81	47	102
1982	10,542	5,463	4,772	142	60	106
1983	12,668	6,101	6,247	178	40	103
1984	14,813	6,461	8,000	209	33	109
1985	17,353	6,607	10,441	155	34	115
1986	18,683	6,756	11,449	317	35	127
1987	21,948	7,254	14,264	262	37	130
1988	23,521	8,451	14,397	334	199	140
1989	25,255	10,195	14,504	306	97	153
1990	25,788	12,292	12,962	279	79	177
1991	28,484	13,351	14,432	266	251	184
1992	27,998	12,838	14,437	298	223	202
1993	27,537	13,092	13,779	295	165	206
1994	23,929	12,363	10,973	297	83	213
1995	24,700	12,593	11,494	330	70	213
1996	24,675	12,694	11,353	354	46	228
1997	25,620	13,055	11,959	336	37	233
1998	25,827	12,866	12,230	326	97	308
1999	25,771	12,466	12,453	431	103	318
2000	26,633	12,427	13,207	517	165	317
2001	27,226	13,197	13,046	525	143	315
2002[r]	29,465	13,449	14,906	579	170	361
2003	33,316	13,556	18,612	579	191	381

Source: NASA, "Aeronautics and Space Report of the President" (Annually).
   a Excludes amounts for air transportation.
   b Departments of Interior, Transportation, and Agriculture, the National Science Foundation, and the Environmental Protection Agency.

NATIONAL AERONAUTICS AND SPACE ADMINISTRATION
BUDGET AUTHORITY
Fiscal Years 1977-2005
(Millions of Dollars)

Year	TOTAL	Research and Development	Space Flight Control and Data Communications[a]	Contruction of Facilities	Research & Program Management[b]
1977	$ 3,819	$2,856	$ —	$ 118	$ 845
1978	4,064	3,012	—	162	890
1979	4,559	3,477	—	148	934
1980	5,243	4,088	—	159	996
1981	5,522	4,334	—	117	1,071
1982	6,020	4,772	—	114	1,134
1983	6,875	5,539	—	139	1,197
1984	7,316	2,064[a]	3,772	223	1,256
1985	7,573	2,468	3,594	178	1,332
1986	7,807	2,619	3,670	176	1,342
1987	10,923	3,154	6,100	217	1,453
1988	9,062	3,280	3,806	213	1,763
1989	10,969	4,213	4,555	275	1,927
1990	12,324	5,225	4,645	218	2,023
1991	14,016	6,024	5,271	498	2,212
1992	14,317	6,848	5,352	525	1,576
1993	14,310	7,074	5,059	526	1,652
1994	14,570	7,534	4,835	493	1,708

Year	TOTAL	Science, Aeronautics, & Technology	Human Space Flight	Other[b]	Mission Support
1995[c]	$13,854	$5,936	$5,515	$(130)	$2,533
1996	13,886	5,929	5,457	17	2,483
1997	13,711	5,590	5,540	19	2,562
1998	13,649	5,690	5,560	19	2,380
1999	13,655	5,654	5,480	21	2,500
2000	13,602	5,582	5,488	21	2,511
2001	14,361	6,235	5,496	28	2,602
2002[d]	14,893	8,095	6,773	25	—
2003	15,391	9,215	6,149	27	—

Year	TOTAL	Exploration, Science, & Aeronautics	Exploration Capabilities	Other[b]	Mission Support
2004[E]	$15,379	$7,830	$7,521	$ 28	$ —
2005[E]	16,245	7,690	8,526	29	—

Source: Office of Management and Budget, "Budget of the United States Government" (Annually).
 a Separate budget category beginning in 1984; funds formerly included under Research and Development.
 b Includes trust funds, Office of the Inspector General, National Space Grant Program, & GSA building delegation.
 c 1995 features major budget account restructuring.
 d Mission Support, as a separate category, discontinued; funds merged into other categories.

NATIONAL AERONAUTICS AND SPACE ADMINISTRATION OUTLAYS
Fiscal Years 1986-2005
(Millions of Dollars)

Year	TOTAL	Research and Development	Space Flight Control and Data Communications[a]	Contruction of Facilities	Research & Program Management[b]
1986	$ 7,404	$2,615	$3,267	$189	$1,332
1987	7,591	2,436	3,597	149	1,409
1988	9,092	2,916	4,362	166	1,648
1989	11,052	3,922	5,030	190	1,909
1990	12,429	5,094	5,117	218	2,000
1991	13,878	5,765	5,590	326	2,196
1992	13,961	6,579	5,118	463	1,802
1993	14,305	7,086	5,025	557	1,638
1994	13,695	6,758	4,899	371	1,666
1995[c]	5,098	3,286	1,409	305	98
1996[c]	1,022	510	241	265	6
1997[c]	317	101	92	122	2
1998[c]	138	40	34	64	—
1999[c]	47	18	2	27	—
2000[c]	31	18	1	12	—

Year	TOTAL	Science, Aeronautics, & Technology	Human Space Flight	Other[b]	Mission Support
1995[c]	$ 8,280	$2,708	$3,528	$ 15	$2,029
1996[c]	12,858	5,017	5,452	16	2,373
1997[c]	14,043	5,891	5,656	19	2,477
1998[c]	14,068	6,015	5,551	19	2,483
1999[c]	13,617	5,785	5,417	20	2,395
2000[c]	13,411	5,477	5,497	21	2,416
2001[d]	14,199	5,752	5,829	32	2,586
2002[f]	14,430	7,532	6,337	27	534
2003[f]	14,552	8,358	6,034	25	135
2004[Efg]	5,388	3,756	1,540	—	92
2005[Eg]	1,246	923	323	—	—

Year	TOTAL	Exploration, Science, & Aeronautics	Exploration Capabilities	Other[b]	Mission Support
2004[Eg]	$ 9,216	$4,071	$5,114	$ 31	$ —
2005[Eg]	15,140	7,132	7,979	29	—

Source: Office of Management and Budget, "Budget of the United States Government" (Annually).
  a Separate budget category beginning in 1984; funds formerly included under Research and Development.
  b Includes trust funds, Office of Inspector General, National Space Grant Program, & GSA building delegation.
  c 1995 featured major budget account restructuring. Note: 1995-2000 outlays split between old and new account structure.
  d Continuing minimal outlays reported under old account structure included under Other beginning in 2001.
  f Mission Support, as a separate category, is being discontinued; funds merged into other categories.
  g 2004 featured another budget account restructuring. 2004-2005 outlays split between old and new account structure.

NATIONAL AERONAUTICS AND SPACE ADMINISTRATION
BUDGET AUTHORITY BY MAJOR BUDGET ACCOUNT
FOR SELECTED PROGRAMS
Fiscal Years 2003-2005
(Millions of Dollars)

	2003	2004ᴱ	2005ᴱ
TOTAL	$15,388	$15,378	$16,244
EXPLORATION CAPABILITIES	$ 8,030	$ 7,521	$ 8,456
International Space Station	$ 1,462	$ 1,498	$ 1,863
Space Shuttle	3,301	3,945	4,319
Space Flight Support	352	432	492
Human & Robotic Technology	NA	679	1,094
Transportation Systems	NA	967	689
Space Launch Initiative	1,815	NA	NA
Mission & Science Measurement Tech.	304	NA	NA
Innovative Tech. Transfer Partnerships	162	NA	NA
Institutional Support	1,633	NA	NA
EXPLORATION, SCIENCE, & AERONAUTICS	$ 7,333	$ 7,830	$ 7,760
Space Science	$ 3,531	$ 3,971	$ 4,138
Biological & Physical Research	883	985	1,049
Earth Science	1,717	1,613	1,485
Aeronautics Technology	1,004	1,034	919
Education	199	226	169
INSPECTOR GENERAL	$ 25	$ 27	$ 28

Source: NASA.

DEPARTMENT OF DEFENSE SPACE PROGRAMS
PROCUREMENT[a] AND RDT&E
Fiscal Years 2003, 2004, and 2005
(Millions of Dollars)

Agency and Program	2003 Procurement	2003 RDT&E	2004[E] Procurement	2004[E] RDT&E	2005[E] Procurement	2005[E] RDT&E
AIR FORCE						
Advanced EHF	$ —	$802.6	$ —	$802.3	$ 98.6	$612.0
Defense Satellite Comm Sys	21.8	2.0	12.0	—	6.6	—
Defense Space Reconn Pgm	279.4	41.6	215.4	96.0	332.4	219.3
Defense Support Program	105.7	1.9	112.1	—	116.5	—
DMSP	69.4	5.0	67.5	0.9	74.2	—
EELV	175.6	55.8	604.8	7.9	611.0	27.0
Maui Space Surveillance Sys	—	47.1	—	51.6	—	6.3
Medium Launch Vehicles	47.8	—	89.4	—	102.9	—
MilSat Com	36.1	22.4	42.0	5.5	19.2	0.9
Milstar	—	148.3	—	1.4	—	1.4
NAVSTAR GPS	249.8	364.5	255.5	244.2	330.5	252.4
NPOESS	—	232.1	—	264.7	—	307.7
NUDET Detection System	7.8	20.8	10.7	35.4	7.6	35.4
Rocket Systems Launch Pgm	—	28.7	—	23.0	—	8.0
Satellite Control Network	43.3	16.7	47.9	20.5	43.9	17.8
SBIRS-High	—	775.3	94.7	610.2	—	508.4
Space-Based Radar	—	45.4	—	172.6	—	327.7
Spacelift Range System	106.4	90.8	80.0	69.9	101.5	47.3
Titan Launch Vehicles	254.4	—	45.1	—	74.3	—
Wideband Gapfiller	186.7	13.8	21.8	36.3	40.3	73.5
ARMY						
DSCS	$ 93.5	$ 11.4	$ 98.2	$ 13.5	$ 99.8	$ 9.3
NAVY						
Meteorological and Ocean Sensors	$ —	$ 21.8	$ —	$ 7.9	$ —	$ 4.2
MUOS/Sat Comm	158.9	110.5	234.8	267.7	103.6	571.1

Source: Department of Defense, "Program Acquisition Costs by Weapon System" (Annually) and "Procurement Programs (P-1)" (Annually).
  a Total Obligational Authority for procurement including initial spares.
  b Air Force and BMDO funding.
  c Army and Air Force funding.
KEY: DMSP   = Defense Meteorological Satellite Program
        DSCS   = Defense Satellite Communications System
        EELV   = Evolved Expendable Launch Vehicle
        EHF   = Extremely High Frequency
        GPS   = Global Positioning System
        MUOS   = Mobile User Objective Satellite system
        NPOESS = National Polar-orbiting Operational Environmental Satellite System
        SBIRS   = Space-Based InfraRed System

ORDERS AND BACKLOG OF COMMERCIAL GEOSYNCHRONOUS SATELLITES BY MANUFACTURER[a]
Calendar Years 1999–2003

	1999	2000	2001	2002	2003
ORDERS					
Value[b] (Millions of Dollars)..........	$1,987 [r]	$3,287	$2,380	$1,010	$2,050
Number of Satellites—TOTAL ...	18 [r]	31	25	10	21
Alcatel	2	6	2	2	2
Alenia Aerospazio	—	1	—	—	—
Astrium	1	6	2	2	4
Boeing Satellite Systems	7	4	5	1	2
Chinese Academy of Space Technology	—	—	—	2	—
Israel Aircraft Industries.............	—	—	1	—	—
Lockheed Martin Commercial Space Systems	3	2	5	2	5
NPO PM	—	3	—	—	2
Orbital Sciences	2	—	4	1	2
RSC Energia	2 [r]	—	—	—	—
Space Systems Loral	1	9	6	—	4
BACKLOG[c]					
Value[b] (Millions of Dollars)..........	$8,024 [r]	$9,451 [r]	$9,375 [r]	$9,179 [r]	$9,678
Number of Satellites—TOTAL ...	69 [r]	82 [r]	86 [r]	84 [r]	89
Alcatel	9	12	13	13	14
Alenia Aerospazio	—	1	1	— [r]	—
Astrium	3	9	8	10	13
Boeing Satellite Systems	24	23	19	16	14
Chinese Academy of Space Technology	—	—	—	2	2
Israel Aircraft Industries.............	—	—	1	1	—
Lockheed Martin Commercial Space Systems	13	10	10	11	15
NPO PM	—	3	3	3	4
Orbital Sciences	2	2	6	5	5
RSC Energia	2 [r]	2 [r]	2 [r]	2 [r]	—
Space Systems Loral	16	20	23	21	22

Source: Futron Corporation.
a Excludes canceled orders and orders on hold, without firm funding or business commitment, or with extended construction delay.
b Estimated using best available public information; where not available, used Futron estimates.
c Includes satellites on order during year and may include satellites that have been launched.

ORDERS AND BACKLOG OF COMMERCIAL LAUNCHES BY PROVIDER-COUNTRY

Calendar Years 1999–2003

	1999	2000	2001	2002	2003
ORDERS—TOTAL	28	38	35	21	22
China	1	—	—	—	—
India	—	—	—	—	1
Japan	—	—	—	—	—
Russia	9	—	5	5	5
United States	6	17	15	5	7
Europe	12	16	13	10	5
Other multinational[a]	—	5	2	1	4
BACKLOG—TOTAL	141	129	163	155	111
China	7	7	7	7	3
India	—	—	—	—	1
Japan	8	—	—	—	—
Russia	13	13	18	15	20
United States	55	47	68	60	46
Europe	40	46	53	55	27
Other multinational[a]	18	16	17	18	14

Source: Futron Corporation.
a   Sea Launch.

The world's airlines suffered another disastrous year in 2003, posting additional losses on slightly increasing passenger traffic. Operating losses, at $2.8 billion, improved by $2.1 billion in 2003. Taking into account non-operating expenses such as interest and taxes, the industry's net loss totaled $6.6 billion, or –2.1% of revenue, up from an $11.7 billion loss. International Civil Aviation Organization statistics show that the world's airlines carried 18 million more passengers in 2003 and flew 17 billion (or less than 1%) more passenger-miles. Load factors remained steady at historic high levels, reflecting airlines' ability to fill planes and still lose money.

The United States and U.S. airlines lie at the epicenter of this downturn. Enplanements rose by 34 million or 5.5%; passenger revenue ton-miles also rose by 2.3%; and operating losses lessened from $8.6 billion to $2.2 billion. Operating expenses also increased 2.3%, or $2.7 billion, as carriers worked to restrain capacity growth and other costs. Fuel prices, which were already high, have risen 19% or 13.4 cents per gallon. Fuel cost as a percentage of cash operating expenses rose from 12% to 13% or $1.6 billion, despite the third straight year of falling consumption, according to data from the Air Transport Association of America. Consequently, U.S. scheduled airline operating losses declined significantly—falling $6.4 billion in 2003. Despite this improvement, the combined losses during 2001-2003 totaled $21 billion—far exceeding the $6 billion operating loss of the 1990-1992 downturn.

The world's turbine-engined airline fleet continued to grow in 2003—reaching 26,367 aircraft in service—according to Air BP's "Turbine-Engined Fleets of the World's Airlines." While the number of jets increased from 17,609 to 17,988, the numbers of turboprops and helicopters declined. Among the jet aircraft fleet, the number of Boeing 727s fell by 134 to 788, DC-9s fell by 55 to 483, and approximately 62% of the British Aerospace 111s left the fleet. Perhaps not too surprisingly, smaller aircraft models lead the unit growth. The Airbus A320 family (A318/A319/A320/A321) grew by 218 to 2,027 and Boeing's 737s grew by 132 to 3,946, but regional jets showed both large unit gains and large percentage increases. In particular, the Canadair RJs grew by 260 or 35% and the Embraer ERJ family grew by 84 or 14%.

The number of installed turbojet engines grew by 978 to 45,353 in 2003. Accounting for the growth: CFM International engines increased 549; General Electric, 522; "Other", 272; and International Aero Engines, 229. The number of Rolls-Royce engines declined by one to 4,453 and Pratt & Whitney engines dropped by 593 to 13,317. Pratt & Whitney retains the dominant share with 29.4% of the installed turbine engines in the world's airline fleet.

Based on the latest available data, the number of hours flown by general aviation aircraft in the United States decreased by 7.2% to 27 million in 2002. Similarly, the number of active general aviation aircraft also decreased. However, since the enactment of the General Aviation Revitalization Act of 1994, the number of active single-engine aircraft has increased 16,900 to approximately 144,700 despite the decline of the last three years.

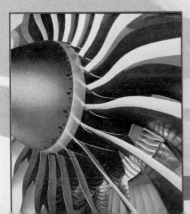

OPERATING REVENUES, EXPENSES, AND RESULTS
OF WORLD SCHEDULED AIRLINES
Calendar Years 2000–2003
(Millions of Dollars)

	2000	2001	2002	2003ᴾ
OPERATING REVENUES:				
Scheduled Services:				
Passenger	$248,940	$232,410	$231,030	
Freight	33,840	32,990	32,740	
Mail..	2,140	2,150	2,140	
				NA
Scheduled Services—Total	$284,920	$267,550	$265,910	
Non-Scheduled Services	11,710	10,470	9,790	
Incidental	31,870	29,480	30,300	
Operating Revenues—Total........	$328,500	$307,500	$306,000	$312,900
OPERATING EXPENSES:				
Flight Operations	$98,790	$ 97,020	$ 95,700	
Maintenance & Overhaul	33,710	36,120	35,130	
Depreciation & Amortization	20,780	22,670	22,190	
User Charges & Station				NA
Expenses	54,720	54,000	52,860	
Passenger Services	31,780	32,670	31,710	
Ticketing, Sales & Promotion	40,450	35,650	33,260	
General, Administrative & Other...	37,570	41,170	40,050	
Operating Expenses—Total........	$317,800	$319,300	$310,900	$315,700
OPERATING RESULT	$ 10,700	($ 11,800)	($ 4,900)	($ 2,800)
Percent of Revenue.....................	3.3%	−3.8%	−1.6%	−0.9%
NET RESULT[a]	$ 3,700	($ 13,000)	($ 11,700)	($ 6,600)
Percent of Revenue.....................	1.1%	−4.2%	−3.8%	−2.1%

Source: International Civil Aviation Organization, "Civil Aviation Statistics of the World" (Annually).
   a   Net Result equals Operating Result minus non-operating items, including interest, income taxes, retirement of property and equipment, affiliated companies, and subsidies.

OPERATING REVENUES AND EXPENSES OF U.S. AIR CARRIERS[a]
DOMESTIC AND INTERNATIONAL OPERATIONS
Calendar Years 1969–2003
(Millions of Dollars)

Year	TOTAL			Domestic Operations			International Operations		
	Operating Revenues	Operating Expenses	Operating Profit (or Loss)	Operating Revenues	Operating Expenses	Operating Profit (or Loss)	Operating Revenues	Operating Expenses	Operating Profit (or Loss)
1969	$ 8,791	$ 8,403	$ 387	$ 6,936	$ 6,613	$ 322	$ 1,855	$ 1,790	$ 65
1970	9,290	9,247	43	7,180	7,181	(1)	2,109	2,066	44
1971	10,046	9,717	328	7,753	7,496	257	2,292	2,221	71
1972	11,163	10,578	584	8,652	8,158	493	2,512	2,420	91
1973	12,419	11,834	585	9,694	9,200	494	2,725	2,633	91
1974	14,703	13,978	725	11,546	10,761	785	3,157	3,218	(60)
1975	15,356	15,229	128	12,020	11,903	117	3,336	3,326	11
1976	17,503	16,781	721	13,899	13,324	575	3,605	3,457	147
1977	19,926	19,018	908	15,822	15,166	657	4,104	3,852	252
1978	22,892	21,527	1,366	18,189	17,172	1,018	4,703	4,355	348
1979	27,227	27,028	199	21,652	21,523	129	5,575	5,505	69
1980	33,728	33,949	(222)	26,404	26,409	(6)	6,543	6,766	(223)
1981	36,211	36,612	(401)	28,788	29,051	(264)	6,390	6,574	(184)
1982	36,066	36,804	(739)	28,728	29,478	(750)	6,435	6,452	(17)
1983	38,593	38,231	362	31,014	31,186	(171)	7,163	6,693	470
1984	44,060	41,946	2,114	35,394	33,812	1,582	7,975	7,485	490
1985	48,580	47,207	1,372	37,629	36,611	1,018	8,302	7,984	319
1986	50,086	48,855	1,231	41,001	39,984	1,060	8,621	8,458	163
1987	56,787	54,339	2,448	45,658	43,925	1,733	10,925	10,226	698
1988	63,679	60,236	3,443	50,187	47,739	2,448	13,402	12,403	998
1989	69,225	67,413	1,812	54,314	52,460	1,855	14,911	14,954	(43)
1990	75,984	77,898	(1,913)	57,994	58,983	(989)	17,990	18,914	(924)
1991	75,158	76,943	(1,785)	56,230	56,758	(528)	18,928	20,185	(1,257)
1992	78,140	80,585	(2,444)	57,654	58,801	(1,147)	20,486	21,784	(1,298)
1993	84,559	83,121	1,438	63,233	61,157	2,076	21,326	21,964	(637)
1994	88,313	85,600	2,713	65,949	63,758	2,191	22,364	21,842	522
1995	94,318	88,455	5,863	70,885	66,120	4,765	23,433	22,335	1,098
1996	101,937	95,728	6,209	76,891	71,573	5,317	25,047	24,155	892
1997	109,568	100,981	8,587	82,250	75,731	6,518	27,318	25,250	2,068
1998	113,465	104,137	9,328	86,494	78,389	8,105	26,971	25,749	1,223
1999	119,038	110,635	8,403	90,931	84,328	6,603	28,107	26,307	1,800
2000	130,299	123,314	6,985	98,896	93,579	5,317	31,403	29,736	1,668
2001	115,227	125,550	(10,323)	86,511	94,892	(8,380)	28,716	30,658	(1,943)
2002	106,702	115,260	(8,557)	79,220	86,697	(7,476)	27,482	28,563	(1,081)
2003[p]	115,738	117,930	(2,192)	88,217	90,872	(2,656)	27,521	27,057	464

Source: Department of Transportation, Office of Airline Information, "Air Carrier Financial Statistics Quarterly" (Quarterly).
a Scheduled and non-scheduled service for all certificated route air carriers. Excludes supplemental air carriers, commuters, and air taxis.

SOURCES OF OPERATING REVENUES OF U.S. AIR CARRIERS[a]
DOMESTIC AND INTERNATIONAL OPERATIONS
Calendar Years 1989–2003
(Millions of Dollars)

Year	TOTAL	Passenger Service[b]	Mail	Freight[b] & Air Express	Excess Baggage	Other[c]
DOMESTIC OPERATIONS						
1989	$54,314	$43,670	$ 767	$5,408	$ 70	$ 4,399
1990	57,994	46,282	747	4,276	76	6,613
1991	56,230	44,594	734	4,487	78	6,337
1992	57,654	45,246	937	4,655	87	6,729
1993	63,233	49,289	974	5,266	91	7,612
1994	65,949	50,504	971	5,844	98	8,531
1995	70,885	53,971	1,050	6,546	92	9,227
1996	76,891	59,381	1,024	7,029	94	9,362
1997	82,250	62,549	1,087	7,497	99	11,017
1998	86,494	64,847	1,423	7,711	105	12,408
1999	90,931	67,777	1,475	8,053	118	13,509
2000	98,896	74,744	1,688	8,804	123	13,537
2001	86,511	64,324	824	8,170	111	13,082
2002	79,220	57,871	431	8,148	132	12,638
2003[p]	88,217	62,043	544	8,798	202	16,631
INTERNATIONAL OPERATIONS						
1989	$14,911	$11,181	$ 188	$2,417	$ 47	$ 1,078
1990	17,990	13,468	223	2,602	43	1,654
1991	18,928	14,103	223	3,134	50	1,419
1992	20,486	15,664	247	2,980	47	1,547
1993	21,326	15,915	237	3,220	49	1,905
1994	22,364	16,300	212	3,606	46	2,201
1995	23,433	16,788	216	3,994	48	2,387
1996	25,047	17,337	255	4,664	47	2,743
1997	27,318	18,320	275	5,156	56	3,511
1998	26,971	17,667	285	5,278	50	3,692
1999	28,107	18,011	264	5,921	46	3,865
2000	31,403	20,419	283	6,566	47	4,089
2001	28,716	18,227	240	6,444	42	3,763
2002	27,482	17,105	228	7,127	48	2,975
2003[p]	27,521	17,201	355	6,921	66	2,979

Source: Department of Transportation, Office of Airline Information, "Air Carrier Financial Statistics Quarterly" (Quarterly).
  a Scheduled and non-scheduled service for all certificated route air carriers. Excludes supplemental air carriers, commuters, and air taxis.
  b Scheduled and charter.
  c Includes subsidy, reservation cancellation fees, miscellaneous operating revenues, and other transport-related revenues.

OPERATING EXPENSES OF U.S. AIR CARRIERS[a]
DOMESTIC AND INTERNATIONAL OPERATIONS
Calendar Years 1989–2003
(Millions of Dollars)

Year	TOTAL	Flying Opera-tions	Mainte-nance	Passen-ger Service	Aircraft & Traffic Ser-vicing	Promo-tion and Sales	Depreci-ation & Amorti zation	Other[b]
DOMESTIC OPERATIONS								
1989	$52,460	$14,749	$ 6,184	$4,775	$ 9,449	$ 8,718	$3,078	$ 5,507
1990	58,983	18,166	6,921	5,220	9,094	9,102	3,273	7,207
1991	56,758	16,831	6,682	5,068	9,140	8,856	3,217	6,964
1992	58,801	17,203	6,884	5,327	9,783	8,936	3,340	7,328
1993	61,157	17,622	7,025	5,241	10,172	9,387	3,621	8,089
1994	63,758	17,912	7,312	5,305	10,543	9,882	3,782	9,023
1995	66,120	18,926	7,656	5,281	11,103	9,974	3,762	9,417
1996	71,573	21,515	8,292	5,577	11,569	10,414	3,878	10,328
1997	75,731	22,156	9,475	5,854	12,058	10,780	3,940	11,469
1998	78,389	21,044	10,311	6,252	12,699	10,743	4,144	13,195
1999	84,328	22,820	11,161	6,763	13,796	10,760	4,657	14,372
2000	93,579	28,565	12,062	7,355	14,827	10,089	5,122	15,558
2001	94,892	27,908	12,113	7,219	15,390	8,949	6,230	17,081
2002	86,697	25,924	11,069	7,049	14,853	6,703	4,989	16,109
2003 [p]	90,872	27,905	10,308	6,471	15,486	6,319	4,988	19,396
INTERNATIONAL OPERATIONS								
1989	$14,954	$ 3,919	$ 1,724	$1,454	$ 2,483	$ 3,108	$ 746	$ 1,520
1990	18,878	5,454	2,051	1,738	2,657	3,833	887	2,295
1991	20,185	5,636	2,152	1,861	2,831	4,602	892	2,210
1992	21,784	5,843	2,148	2,204	3,255	5,229	1,033	2,073
1993	21,964	5,928	1,967	2,175	3,072	5,339	1,077	2,406
1994	21,842	5,842	2,064	2,311	3,336	4,335	1,237	2,716
1995	22,335	6,181	2,273	2,467	3,748	3,527	1,106	3,033
1996	24,155	7,279	2,616	2,596	3,736	3,354	1,483	3,091
1997	25,250	7,462	2,899	2,736	3,823	3,476	1,281	3,571
1998	25,749	7,158	2,955	2,920	3,978	3,374	1,438	3,926
1999	26,307	7,472	2,902	3,067	4,207	3,201	1,614	3,845
2000	29,736	9,504	3,093	3,211	4,565	3,282	1,751	4,329
2001	30,658	9,652	3,196	3,254	4,599	2,828	2,168	4,960
2002	28,563	9,202	3,125	3,090	4,573	2,233	1,923	4,417
2003 [p]	27,057	9,034	3,075	2,742	4,102	1,917	1,688	4,498

Source: Department of Transportation, Office of Airline Information, "Air Carrier Financial Statistics Quarterly" (Quarterly).
a Scheduled and non-scheduled service for all certificated route air carriers. Excludes supplemental air carriers, commuters, and air taxis.
b General and administrative and other transport-related expenses.

JET FUEL COSTS AND CONSUMPTION BY U.S. AIR CARRIERS[a]

Calendar Years 1971–2003

Year	Total Jet Fuel Cost (Millions of Dollars)	Gallons Consumed (Millions)	Cost Per Gallon (Cents)	Cost Index (1982 = 100)	Cost of Fuel as Percent of Cash Operating Expenses
1971	$ 1,121.1	9,836.5	11.4 ¢	11.4	11.8%
1972	1,163.9	9,979.2	11.7	11.7	11.2
1973	1,337.3	10,489.5	12.7	12.8	11.4
1974	2,341.2	9,377.3	25.0	25.1	16.7
1975	2,783.3	9,312.5	29.9	30.0	18.3
1976	3,117.4	9,631.6	32.4	32.5	18.7
1977	3,740.6	10,063.4	37.2	37.3	19.7
1978	4,178.6	10,352.2	40.4	40.5	19.5
1979	6,491.7	11,032.5	58.8	59.1	23.8
1980	9,739.7	10,630.2	91.6	92.0	29.7
1981	10,494.2	9,838.7	106.7	107.1	29.6
1982	9,695.9	9,737.4	99.6	100.0	27.2
1983	9,006.7	10,225.3	88.1	88.5	24.5
1984	9,324.1	11,182.5	83.4	83.7	23.4
1985	9,352.7	10,324.9	90.6	91.0	21.7
1986	7,054.9	10,722.0	65.8	66.1	15.9
1987	7,607.5	11,542.2	65.9	66.2	15.5
1988	7,551.6	12,059.4	62.6	62.9	14.0
1989	8,572.7	14,255.4	60.1	60.4	14.4
1990	11,768.8	15,265.6	77.1	77.4	16.9
1991	9,694.7	14,441.8	67.1	67.4	14.4
1992	9,257.7	14,852.2	62.3	62.6	13.0
1993	8,850.4	14,969.0	59.1	59.4	12.3
1994	8,279.5	15,237.8	54.3	54.6	11.4
1995	8,465.7	15,492.0	54.6	54.9	11.4
1996	10,329.1	15,950.2	64.8	65.0	13.0
1997	10,313.7	16,324.7	63.2	63.4	12.5
1998	8,408.5	16,751.4	50.2	50.4	10.0
1999	9,048.9	17,397.5	52.0	52.2	10.1
2000	14,146.0	18,401.9	76.9	77.2	14.1
2001	13,220.4	17,299.5	76.4	76.7	12.8
2002 [r]	11,036.6	15,491.0	71.2	71.5	11.7
2003	12,648.1	14,951.3	84.6	85.0	13.3

Source: Air Transport Association of America, "Airline Cost Index" (Quarterly).
  a Majors and Nationals.

TOTAL ASSETS AND INVESTMENT IN EQUIPMENT BY U.S. AIR CARRIERS
Calendar Years 1969–2003
(Millions of Dollars)

Year	Total Assets	Value of Flight Equipment	Value of Ground Property & Equipment & Other[a]	Less: Reserves for Depreciation & Overhaul	Equals: Net Value of Owned Operating Property & Equipment	Investment in Operating Property and Equipment as a Percent of Total Assets
1969	$ 12,069	$ 9,943	$ 1,516	$ 3,560	$ 7,899	65.4%
1970	12,913	10,950	1,951	4,120	8,782	68.0
1971	12,998	11,221	2,028	4,649	8,600	66.2
1972	13,635	11,918	2,225	5,115	9,028	66.2
1973	14,464	12,908	2,424	5,693	9,639	66.6
1974	15,200	13,538	2,539	6,252	9,826	64.6
1975	15,064	14,035	2,635	6,823	9,847	65.4
1976	15,454	14,399	2,792	7,585	9,605	62.2
1977	16,869	14,822	2,997	8,141	9,679	57.4
1978	20,745	16,127	3,367	8,799	10,696	51.6
1979	24,907	18,561	3,985	9,746	12,800	51.4
1980	28,900	20,859	4,682	10,309	15,233	52.7
1981	30,513	22,375	5,175	11,028	16,521	54.1
1982	31,525	23,786	5,424	11,405	17,804	56.5
1983	35,213	26,588	6,191	12,910	19,868	56.4
1984	36,769	28,509	6,061	14,043	20,527	55.8
1985	40,978	30,402	6,772	15,467	21,707	53.0
1986	47,105	31,750	8,468	14,764	25,454	54.0
1987	51,436	33,177	9,223	15,580	26,820	52.1
1988	56,047	35,781	10,248	17,450	28,579	51.0
1989	62,454	38,812	11,903	19,018	31,697	50.8
1990	67,769	40,215	13,523	20,593	33,144	48.9
1991	70,332	42,897	14,285	22,009	35,173	50.0
1992	75,426	48,563	15,219	24,445	39,337	52.2
1993	82,399	51,513	15,438	24,949	42,003	51.0
1994	84,442	51,951	15,844	26,476	41,319	48.9
1995	89,782	56,018	16,804	29,056	43,766	48.7
1996	95,184	59,206	16,661	30,029	45,838	48.2
1997	105,226	66,523	17,643	32,789	51,377	48.8
1998	118,308	75,385	19,980	35,992	59,373	50.2
1999	133,711	86,269	21,826	39,060	69,035	51.6
2000	146,300	98,404	22,095	41,880	78,620	53.7
2001	158,516	103,508	23,092	42,666	83,934	52.9
2002	158,186	106,297	24,224	44,366	86,155	54.5
2003[p]	165,160	108,554	23,408	44,495	87,468	53.0

Source: Department of Transportation, Office of Airline Information, "Air Carrier Financial Statistics Quarterly" (Quarterly).
a Includes land and construction in progress

TRAFFIC STATISTICS
WORLD AIRLINE SCHEDULED SERVICE[a]
Calendar Years 1970–2003

Year	Passen-gers Carried	Freight Tons Carried	Passen-ger-Miles Per-formed	Seat-Miles Avail-able	Passen-ger Load Factor	Total (Passen-gers & Baggage, Freight, Mail)	Freight	Mail
						Ton-Miles Performed		
	(Millions)		(Billions)		(Percent)	(Billions)		
1970	383	6.7	286	522	55%	38.82	8.23	2.10
1971	411	7.4	307	568	54	41.42	9.06	1.99
1972	450	8.0	348	609	57	46.69	10.29	1.90
1973	489	9.1	384	667	58	51.91	12.01	1.97
1974	514	9.5	408	688	59	55.27	13.03	1.98
1975	534	9.6	433	733	59	58.08	13.27	1.99
1976	576	10.3	475	789	60	63.88	14.75	2.08
1977	610	11.1	508	837	61	68.79	16.19	2.17
1978	679	11.7	582	902	65	77.77	17.77	2.24
1979	754	12.1	659	999	66	86.89	19.19	2.35
1980	748	12.2	677	1,071	63	89.72	20.12	2.52
1981	752	12.0	695	1,092	64	92.81	21.15	2.60
1982	766	12.8	710	1,115	64	94.84	21.60	2.65
1983	798	13.5	739	1,151	64	100.28	24.05	2.74
1984	848	14.8	794	1,226	65	109.05	27.17	2.95
1985	899	15.1	850	1,293	66	114.86	27.29	3.01
1986	960	16.2	902	1,389	65	122.47	29.58	3.11
1987	1,028	17.7	988	1,471	67	134.57	33.10	3.22
1988	1,082	19.0	1,060	1,568	68	145.29	36.48	3.31
1989	1,109	19.9	1,102	1,621	68	152.73	39.14	3.46
1990	1,165	20.3	1,177	1,740	68	161.12	40.27	3.65
1991	1,135	19.3	1,147	1,727	66	158.04	40.11	3.48
1992	1,146	19.5	1,199	1,821	66	165.86	42.90	3.51
1993	1,142	19.9	1,211	1,873	65	171.67	46.88	3.58
1994	1,233	22.6	1,305	1,969	66	187.29	52.89	3.71
1995	1,304	24.5	1,397	2,087	67	201.34	56.94	3.86
1996	1,391	25.6	1,511	2,215[r]	68	217.24	61.10	3.97
1997	1,457	29.1	1,599	2,317	69	235.76	70.47	4.10
1998	1,471	29.2	1,633	2,385	68	238.78	69.74	3.94
1999	1,562	31.0	1,739	2,517	69	253.73	74.43	3.92
2000[r]	1,672	33.5	1,888	2,663	71	276.70	80.88	4.14
2001[r]	1,640	31.8	1,833	2,655	69	265.87	75.89	3.63
2002	1,639	34.6	1,842	2,589	71	272.02	82.09	3.13
2003[p]	1,657	38.0	1,859	2,603	71	276.94	85.79	3.16

Source: International Civil Aviation Organization (ICAO).
  a Includes international and domestic traffic on scheduled service performed by the airlines of the 188 states which were members of ICAO in 2003.

TRAFFIC STATISTICS
U.S. AIR CARRIER SCHEDULED SERVICE[a]
Calendar Years 1969–2003

Year	Revenue Ton-Miles (Millions) TOTAL	Revenue Ton-Miles (Millions) Passenger	Revenue Ton-Miles (Millions) Cargo[b]	Total Available Ton-Miles (Millions)	Total Revenue Load Factor (Percent)	Aircraft Revenue Miles (Millions)	Average Overall Flight Stage Length (Miles)	Average Available Seats per Aircraft Mile
1969	16,898	12,197	4,701	38,664	43.7%	2,385	443	112
1970	18,166	13,171	4,994	41,693	43.6	2,426	473	117
1971	18,685	13,565	5,120	44,139	42.3	2,378	476	125
1972	20,746	15,241	5,506	45,583	45.5	2,376	471	129
1973	22,242	16,196	6,046	49,019	45.4	2,448	477	135
1974	22,425	16,292	6,133	46,848	47.9	2,258	478	140
1975	22,186	16,281	5,905	47,254	46.9	2,241	476	143
1976	24,121	17,899	6,222	49,325	48.9	2,320	480	146
1977	25,909	19,322	6,587	52,284	49.6	2,419	490	149
1978	29,679	22,678	7,001	54,765	54.2	2,520	502	152
1979	33,390	26,202	7,189	60,844	54.9	2,791	517	154
1980	32,603	25,519	7,084	62,983	51.8	2,816	526	158
1981	31,949	24,889	7,060	61,186	52.2	2,703	519	161
1982	32,850	25,964	6,886	62,401	52.6	2,699	544	167
1983	35,756	28,183	7,573	65,385	54.7	2,809	558	169
1984	38,697	30,512	8,185	72,223	53.6	3,134	575	168
1985	41,329	33,640	7,689	76,059	54.3	3,320	569	168
1986	45,681	36,655	9,026	85,140	53.7	3,725	580	168
1987	50,469	40,453	10,016	92,209	54.7	3,988	606	167
1988	53,800	42,330	11,469	97,899	55.0	4,141	618	169
1989	55,458	43,271	12,187	100,082	55.4	4,193	633	169
1990	58,342	45,793	12,549	107,559	54.2	4,491	649	170
1991	56,925	44,795	12,130	105,599	53.9	4,416	651	169
1992	61,054	47,855	13,199	112,749	54.2	4,661	661	169
1993	63,088	48,968	14,120	115,473	54.6	4,846	669	166
1994	67,989	51,938	16,052	120,798	56.3	5,033	668	163
1995	70,987	54,066	16,921	126,154	56.3	5,293	657	160
1996	75,621	57,866	17,754	131,381	57.6	5,501	668	160
1997	80,852	60,342	20,510	137,544	58.8	5,659	696	160
1998	82,304	61,809	20,496	141,722	58.1	5,838	704	159
1999	86,817	65,205	21,613	149,561	58.0	6,168	715	157
2000	93,163	69,276	23,888	159,441	58.4	6,574	728	154
2001	87,173	65,170	22,003	158,975	54.8	6,514	745	143
2002	88,701	64,110	24,591	158,795	55.9	6,556	755	136
2003[p]	91,565	65,585	25,980	163,530	56.0	7,068	734	127

Source: Department of Transportation, Office of Airline Information, "Air Carrier Traffic Statistics Monthly" (Monthly).
a Includes international and domestic operations.
b Includes freight, air express, U.S. and foreign mail.

PASSENGER STATISTICS
U.S. AIR CARRIER SCHEDULED SERVICE
DOMESTIC AND INTERNATIONAL OPERATIONS
Calendar Years 1989–2003

Year	Revenue Passenger Enplanements (Thousands)	Average Passenger Trip-Length (Miles)	Revenue Passenger Miles (Millions)	Available Seat Miles (Millions)	Revenue Passenger Load Factor[a]
DOMESTIC OPERATIONS					
1989	416,331	793	329,975	530,079	62.3
1990	423,565	803	340,231	563,065	60.4
1991	412,360	806	332,566	543,638	61.2
1992	431,693	806	347,931	557,989	62.4
1993	443,172	799	354,177	571,489	62.0
1994	481,755	787	378,990	585,438	64.7
1995	499,000	791	394,708	603,917	65.4
1996	530,708	802	425,596	626,389	67.9
1997	542,001	817	442,640	640,319	69.1
1998	559,653	812	454,430	649,362	70.0
1999	582,880	824	480,134	687,502	69.8
2000	610,601	833	508,403	714,454	71.2
2001	570,125	843	480,348	695,200	69.1
2002	560,107	850	476,004	676,949	70.3
2003[p]	593,048	842	499,224	689,170	72.4
INTERNATIONAL OPERATIONS					
1989	37,361	2,750	102,739	154,297	66.6
1990	41,995	2,803	117,695	170,310	69.1
1991	39,941	2,889	115,389	171,561	67.3
1992	43,415	3,009	130,622	194,784	67.1
1993	45,348	2,988	135,508	200,151	67.7
1994	47,093	2,981	140,391	198,893	70.6
1995	48,773	2,992	145,948	203,160	71.8
1996	50,526	3,029	153,067	208,682	73.3
1997	52,724	3,049	160,779	216,913	74.1
1998	53,232	3,074	163,656	224,728	72.8
1999	53,079	3,239	171,913	230,917	74.4
2000	55,549	3,319	184,354	242,496	76.0
2001	52,003	3,295	171,352	235,311	72.8
2002	52,769	3,129	165,098	215,606	76.6
2003[p]	53,475	2,929	156,626	204,732	76.5

Source: Department of Transportation, Office of Airline Information, "Air Carrier Traffic Statistics Monthly" (Monthly).
   a Revenue passenger miles as a percent of available seat miles.

AIR CARGO STATISTICS
U.S. COMMERCIAL AIR CARRIERS
Fiscal Years 1970–2003
(Millions of Revenue-Ton-Miles)

Year	TOTAL	Freight/Express/Mail	
		Domestic	International
1970	4,606	2,679	1,927
1971	4,758	2,653	2,105
1972	5,857	3,050	2,808
1973	5,839	3,310	2,530
1974	6,167	3,550	2,617
1975	5,725	3,309	2,416
1976	6,112	3,470	2,643
1977	6,315	3,676	2,639
1978	7,003	4,083	2,920
1979	7,211	4,217	2,994
1980	7,255	4,105	3,150
1981	6,979	4,078	2,901
1982	6,895	3,847	3,048
1983	7,715	4,539	3,177
1984	8,857	5,228	3,629
1985	8,653	4,994	3,659
1986	10,311	5,989	4,322
1987	12,130	7,010	5,119
1988	14,136	8,075	6,061
1989	15,954	8,821	7,133
1990	1ι .9	8,987	7,242
1991	16,327	8,913	7,414
1992	16,793	9,474	7,319
1993	18,420	10,374	8,046
1994	20,790	11,323	9,467
1995	23,228	12,416	10,812
1996	24,217	12,782	11,435
1997	26,954	13,455	13,499
1998	28,347	13,830	14,517
1999	28,102	13,975	14,127
2000 [r]	30,057	14,699	15,358
2001 [r]	28,485	13,938	14,547
2002	27,763	12,967	14,796
2003 [E]	32,887	14,670	18,217

Source: Federal Aviation Administration, Office of Aviation Policy & Plans.
Note: Beginning in 2003, international includes contract service by U.S. carriers for foreign carriers.

WORLD AIRLINE FLEET OF TURBINE-ENGINED AIRCRAFT BY MODEL
Calendar Years 1999–2003

	1999	2000	2001	2002	2003
TOTAL..	24,128	25,173	25,963	26,109ʳ	26,367
Turbojets—TOTAL......................	15,453	16,405	17,291	17,609	17,988
Aerospatiale SE-210 Caravelle	12	9	5	5	5
Aerospatiale Corvette...............	2	2	2	2	2
Airbus A300..............................	389	408	396	388	389
Airbus A310..............................	220	217	216	206	187
Airbus A318..............................	—	—	—	—	9
Airbus A319..............................	206	309	398	475	541
Airbus A320..............................	773	880	994	1,090	1,207
Airbus A321..............................	143	165	215	244	270
Airbus A330..............................	131	170	201	242	273
Airbus A340..............................	161	181	200	208	246
Antonov 72/74	9	15	19	20	20
Antonov 124	17	17	17	17	17
Antonov 225	1	1	1	1	1
Avro RJ-70/85/100	138	158	163	162	172
B.Ae./Aerospatiale Concorde....	13	12	12	12	—
B.Ae. 146.................................	203	206	195	176	168
B.Ae. One-Eleven	101	97	88	86	33
B.Ae. (HS) 125	11	13	15	16	18
Beech 400 Beechjet	3	3	3	2	2
Boeing 707/720	94	86	76	59	54
Boeing 717	11	44	92	108	125
Boeing 727	1,189	1,144	1,077	922	788
Boeing 737	3,176	3,431	3,667	3,814	3,946
Boeing 747	1,041	1,027	1,029	1,018	1,002
Boeing 757	879	924	952	974	999
Boeing 767	752	799	816	845	857
Boeing 777	261	313	373	419	462
Canadair CL-601 Challenger	2	1	1	1	3
Canadair Regional Jet..............	351	451	559	735	995
Cessna Citation I/II/III...............	34	41	39	37	47
Dassault Falcon 10/20/50	71	69	73	69	67
Dornier/Fairchild 328 Jet	11	43	67	79	85
Embraer ERJ-135/140/145	186	345	497	616	700
Fokker F-28 Fellowship	169	172	148	146	134
Fokker 70	42	42	42	44	44
Fokker 100	277	271	257	267	219
Gulfstream II/III/IV G-1159	14	14	12	12	13
Ilyushin IL-62	83	85	105	100	99
Ilyushin IL-76	226	257	285	297	290
Ilyushin IL-86	79	81	87	83	82
Ilyushin IL-96	8	8	9	9	9
Israel Aircraft 1121/1124	10	8	8	9	10
Learjet	85	86	85	85	80
Lockheed L-1011 Tristar	135	117	102	93	78
Lockheed L-1329 Jetstar..........	1	1	1	1	—
MBB Hansa HFB-320...............	9	9	6	6	6
McDonnell Douglas DC-8.........	225	227	200	171	163
McDonnell Douglas DC-9.........	714	676	627	538	483
McDonnell Douglas DC-10	340	319	317	255	212

(Continued on next page)

WORLD AIRLINE FLEET OF TURBINE-ENGINED AIRCRAFT BY MODEL
Calendar Years 1999–2003, continued

	1999	2000	2001	2002	2003
Turbojets (continued)					
McDonnell Douglas MD-11	187	188	191	182	182
McDonnell Douglas MD-80	1,180	1,164	1,141	1,118	1,020
McDonnell Douglas MD-90	109	110	106	105	104
Tupolev Tu-134	188	193	202	188	205
Tupolev Tu-154	446	439	482	453	457
Tupolev Tu-204	9	11	14	14	18
Yakolev Yak-40/42	326	356	406	385	390
Turbine-Powered					
Helicopters—TOTAL	1,449	1,438	1,429	1,378ʳ	1,377
Aerospatiale SA-315 Lama	2	—	—	—	—
Aerospatiale SA-316 Alouette III ..	5	5	2	1	1
Aerospatiale SA-318 Alouette II ...	1	1	1	1	1
Aerospatiale (Nurtanio)					
SA-330 Puma	22	19	3	6	6
Aerospatiale AS-332 Super Puma	72	74	92	93	95
Aerospatiale AS-350 Ecureuil/					
Astar	125	124	124	119	123
Aerospatiale AS-355 Ecureuil 2/					
Twinstar...................................	28	26	23	32	18
Aerospatiale SA-365 Dauphin II	36	43	45	34	54
Agusta A109	—	—	2	3	3
Bell (Agusta/Fuji) 204.................	4	4	4	4	4
Bell 205	15	14	14	14	14
Bell 206 Jetranger/Longranger	363	353	323	308	294
Bell 212	120	115	115	108	110
Bell 214	14	13	11	11	11
Bell 222 UT.................................	2	2	1	1	2
Bell 407	53	54	74	70	71
Bell 412	56	59	71	75	73
Bell 430	—	—	—	—	2
Boeing 107	15	15	15	15	15
Boeing Vertol BV-234	9	9	9	9	9
Eurocopter EC-120	—	2	2	5	5
Hughes (Kawasaki) 500/369D	13	12	9	9	9
Kamov Ka-26	19	16	16	16	16
MBB BK-117	10	8	7	7	8
MBB/Nurtanio Bo.105	101	100	106	85	83
MD Helicopters MD-900	—	—	—	4	4
Mil Mi-2	28	26	26	26	26
Mil Mi-6	6	6	—	6	6
Mil Mi-8	107	102	96	88	78
Mil Mi-14....................................	1	1	1	1	1
Mil Mi-26....................................	5	8	8	8	7
Sikorsky S-55T	—	1	—	—	—
Sikorsky S-58T	1	—	1	1	1
Sikorsky S-61	79	81	85	74	75
Sikorsky S-64	22	24	5	5	5
Sikorsky S-76	115	121	138	139	147

(Continued on next page)

WORLD AIRLINE FLEET OF TURBINE-ENGINED AIRCRAFT BY MODEL
Calendar Years 1999–2003, continued

	1999	2000	2001	2002	2003
Turboprops—TOTAL....................	7,226	7,330	7,243	7,122	7,002
Aerospatiale N.262/Mohawk 298	12	12	14	10	10
Aerospatiale/Aeritalia ATR 42	296	311	306	245	302
Aerospatiale/Aeritalia ATR 72	222	223	255	267	262
Airtech CN-235	33	23	23	17	14
Antonov An-8	6	4	6	6	6
Antonov An-12	81	114	112	114	113
Antonov An-22	1	1	1	1	1
Antonov An-24/26/30/32	475	526	582	566	566
B.Ae. ATP..................................	55	49	28	33	32
B.Ae. Viscount..........................	12	12	—	3	3
B.Ae. (HP-137) Jetstream 31......	258	223	190	186	164
B.Ae. Jetstream 41	92	93	90	91	91
B.Ae. HS-748	118	109	110	93	91
Beech 18 Turbo	9	9	8	8	4
Beech 90 King Air	46	39	39	34	34
Beech 99	110	142	146	142	144
Beech 100 King Air	47	51	48	47	51
Beech 200/300 Super King Air....	112	131	134	136	147
Beech 1300...............................	9	8	7	6	9
Beech 1900C/D	469	490	397	426	405
Canadair CL-44	4	3	3	1	1
CASA/Nurtanio C-212 Aviocar....	110	109	108	95	91
Cessna 208 Caravan I	647	661	705	746	754
Cessna F406 Caravan II............	30	29	33	29	31
Cessna 425/441 Conquest I/II	19	15	15	15	16
Convair 580/600/640..................	106	104	103	104	89
DHC-2/3 Turbo Beaver/Otter	24	28	35	36	36
DHC-5 Buffalo	1	1	1	1	1
DHC-6 Twin Otter	365	349	345	348	343
DHC-7 Dash 7	69	67	68	63	58
DHC-8 Dash 8	489	523	557	556	574
Dornier DO-228.........................	121	103	105	107	110
Dornier DO-328.........................	83	91	89	85	89
Douglas DC-3T Turbo Express...	3	3	3	5	5
Embraer EMB-110 Bandeirante..	199	181	181	176	149
Embraer EMB-120 Brasilia	307	300	290	281	256
Embraer EMB-121 Xingu	3	1	1	1	1
Fokker/Fairchild F-27/FH-227 Friendship..............................	276	257	251	218	209
Fokker 50...................................	188	184	170	167	155
GAF Nomad	16	12	12	11	11
Grumman G-73 Turbo Mallard....	6	6	6	6	6
Grumman G-159 Gulfstream I	27	17	14	4	4

(Continued on next page)

WORLD AIRLINE FLEET OF TURBINE-ENGINED AIRCRAFT BY MODEL
Calendar Years 1999–2003, continued

	1999	2000	2001	2002	2003
Turboprops (continued)					
Handley Page Herald	1	1	1	—	—
Harbin YU-12 II	48	46	47	43	38
IAI Arava	4	3	2	1	1
Ilyushin IL-18	41	38	44	38	39
Ilyushin IL-114	3	3	3	3	3
LET L-410	141	178	186	197	217
Lockheed L-188 Electra...........	43	40	35	34	32
Lockheed L-100/L-382 Hercules	44	43	41	43	45
Mitsubishi MU-2B	21	18	22	19	15
Nihon AMC YS-11	46	37	33	35	29
Piaggio P-180 Avanti	—	—	1	1	2
Pilatus Britten-Norman BN-2T					
Turbo Islander	5	5	4	4	4
Pilatus PC-6 Turbo Porter	23	27	25	25	17
Pilatus PC-XII	21	22	22	29	21
Piper PA-31T/42 Cheyenne	22	19	18	14	22
Piper T-1040	13	9	9	6	6
PZL (Antonov) An-28	27	43	42	51	44
Rockwell Turbo Commander	8	8	9	7	7
Saab SF-340A/B	414	447	380	376	367
Saab 2000	43	48	48	51	47
Shorts SC-5 Belfast	2	2	1	—	—
Shorts SC-7 Skyliner/Skyvan ...	27	26	25	28	25
Shorts 330	37	39	39	33	32
Shorts 360	102	101	106	102	94
Swearingen Merlin	58	50	52	51	23
Swearingen Metro	398	392	385	371	387
Transall C-160	6	6	6	6	6
Xian (Antonov) Y-7/Y-8/MA-60 ...	65	65	66	68	51
TOTAL AIRCRAFT IN SERVICE	<u>24,128</u>	<u>25,173</u>	<u>25,963</u>	<u>26,109^r</u>	<u>26,367</u>
Number Manufactured in U.S. ...	13,537	13,857	13,988	13,842	13,678
Percent Manufactured in U.S. ...	56.1%	55.0%	53.9%	53.0%	51.9%
Turbojet Aircraft in Service	<u>15,453</u>	<u>16,405</u>	<u>17,291</u>	<u>17,609</u>	<u>17,988</u>
Number Manufactured in U.S. ...	10,430	10,714	10,906	10,758	10,617
Percent Manufactured in U.S. ...	67.5%	65.3%	63.1%	61.1%	59.0%
Turboprop Aircraft in Service	<u>7,226</u>	<u>7,330</u>	<u>7,243</u>	<u>7,122</u>	<u>7,002</u>
Number Manufactured in U.S. ...	2,226	2,266	2,207	2,234	2,221
Percent Manufactured in U.S. ...	30.8%	30.9%	30.5%	31.4%	31.7%
Turbine-Powered Helicopters					
in Service	<u>1,449</u>	<u>1,438</u>	<u>1,429</u>	<u>1,378^r</u>	<u>1,377</u>
Number Manufactured in U.S. ...	881	877	875	850	840
Percent Manufactured in U.S. ...	60.8%	61.0%	61.2%	61.5%^r	61.0%

Source: Air BP Lubricants, "Turbine-Engined Fleets of the World's Airlines," compiled by Aviation Data Service, Inc. (Annually).
NOTE: "Turbine-Engined Fleets of the World's Airlines" covers aircraft in airline service as of December 31. Excludes air taxi operators.

NUMBER AND PERCENT OF CIVIL TURBOJET ENGINES
IN WORLD AIRLINE FLEET BY MANUFACTURER AND AIRCRAFT MODEL
As of December 2003

Aircraft Manufacturer and Model	Total Installed Engines	Engine Manufacturers					
		P&W	GE	RR	CFM	IAE	Other
TOTAL ENGINES	45,353	13,317	7,201	4,453	10,160	1,908	8,314
PERCENT OF TOTAL ...	100.0%	29.4%	15.9%	9.8%	22.4%	4.2%	18.3%
Airbus A300[a]	520	26%	74%	–%	–%	–%	–%
Airbus A300B4-600R	316	53	47	–	–	–	–
Airbus A310[a]	162	32	68	–	–	–	–
Airbus A310-300	278	46	54	–	–	–	–
Airbus A318	14	–	–	–	100	–	–
Airbus A319[a]	14	–	–	–	–	100	–
Airbus A319[b]	1,078	–	–	–	70	30	–
Airbus A320[a]	36	–	–	–	100	–	–
Airbus A320-200	2,400	–	–	–	55	45	–
Airbus A321[a]	176	–	–	–	48	52	–
Airbus A321-200	392	–	–	–	56	44	–
Airbus A330-200	298	31	26	43	–	–	–
Airbus A330-300	256	46	13	41	–	–	–
Airbus A340[a]	408	–	–	24	76	–	–
Airbus A340-300X	584	–	–	–	100	–	–
Antonov AN-72	16	–	–	–	–	–	100
Antonov AN-74	28	–	–	–	–	–	100
Antonov AN-124	72	–	–	–	–	–	100
AS Corvette	4	100	–	–	–	–	–
AS Caravelle	10	80	–	20	–	–	–
Avro Int'l RJ	668	–	–	–	–	–	100
BAe 1-11	132	–	–	100	–	–	–
BAe 146	792	–	–	–	–	–	100
BAe/HS 125	42	5	–	–	–	–	95
Beech 400 Beechjet	16	100	–	–	–	–	–
Boeing B-707	332	100	–	–	–	–	–
Boeing B-717	250	–	–	100	–	–	–
Boeing B-727 series[a]	1,050	85	–	15	–	–	–
Boeing B-727-200 Adv F	714	100	–	–	–	–	–
Boeing B-727-200 ADV...	1,140	100	–	–	–	–	–
Boeing B-737[a]	572	51	–	–	49	–	–
Boeing B-737-200 ADV...	1,232	100	–	–	–	–	–
Boeing B-737-300	2,092	–	–	–	100	–	–
Boeing B-737-400	934	–	–	–	100	–	–
Boeing B-737-500	766	–	–	–	100	–	–
Boeing B-737-700	964	–	–	–	100	–	–
Boeing B-737-800	1,466	–	–	–	100	–	–
Boeing B-747[a]	2,116	44	46	10	–	–	–
Boeing B-747-200B	456	71	11	18	–	–	–
Boeing B-747-400	1,684	40	34	25	–	–	–
Boeing B-757[a]	452	24	–	76	–	–	–
Boeing B-757-200	1,564	47	–	53	–	–	–
Boeing B-767[a]	324	15	85	–	–	–	–
Boeing B-767-200ER......	262	46	54	–	–	–	–
Boeing B-767-300	202	25	75	–	–	–	–
Boeing B-767-300ER......	976	36	58	6	–	–	–
Boeing B-777[a]	258	53	7	40	–	–	–

(Continued on next page)

NUMBER AND PERCENT OF CIVIL TURBOJET ENGINES
IN WORLD AIRLINE FLEET BY MANUFACTURER AND AIRCRAFT MODEL
As of December 2003, continued

Aircraft Model	Number						
Boeing B-777-200ER	658	22%	37%	41%	–%	–%	–%
Canadair CL 600/601	6	–	67	–	–	–	33
Canadair RJ series[a]	36	–	100	–	–	–	–
Canadair Regional Jet[b]	454	–	100	–	–	–	–
Canadair Regional Jet 200	1,232	–	100	–	–	–	–
Canadair Regional Jet 700	246	–	100	–	–	–	–
Cessna 500s	82	95	–	5	–	–	–
Cessna 650	6	–	–	–	–	–	100
Cessna 750	2	–	–	–	–	–	100
Dassault Falcon	150	–	87	–	–	–	13
Embraer ERJ-135	210	–	–	–	–	–	100
Embraer ERJ-140	148	–	–	–	–	–	100
Embraer ERJ-145	1,042	–	–	–	–	–	100
Fairchild Dornier 328 Jet	166	100	–	–	–	–	–
Fokker F-28	296	–	–	100	–	–	–
Fokker 70	82	–	–	100	–	–	–
Fokker 100	528	–	–	100	–	–	–
Gulfstream II/III/IV	26	–	–	100	–	–	–
IAI 1124/1125	20	–	–	–	–	–	100
Ilyushin IL-62	416	–	–	–	–	–	100
Ilyushin IL-76[a]	160	–	–	–	–	–	100
Ilyushin IL-76MD	484	–	–	–	–	–	100
Ilyushin IL-76TD	608	–	–	–	–	–	100
Ilyushin IL-86	336	–	–	–	–	–	100
Ilyushin IL-96	36	–	–	–	–	–	100
Learjet 23/24/25	124	–	100	–	–	–	–
Learjet 35/36/45/55/60	88	9	–	–	–	–	91
Lockheed JetStar	4	–	–	–	–	–	100
Lockheed L-1011	312	–	–	100	–	–	–
MBB HFB-320 Hansa Jet	12	–	100	–	–	–	–
Douglas DC-8	772	58	–	–	42	–	–
Douglas DC-9[a]	424	100	–	–	–	–	–
Douglas DC-9-30	688	100	–	–	–	–	–
Douglas DC-10	765	7	93	–	–	–	–
MDC MD-11	582	39	61	–	–	–	–
MDC MD-80s[a]	284	100	–	–	–	–	–
MDC MD-82	1,140	100	–	–	–	–	–
MDC MD-83	530	100	–	–	–	–	–
MDC MD-88	314	100	–	–	–	–	–
MDC MD-90-30	232	–	–	–	–	100	–
Rockwell Sabreliner	2	–	100	–	–	–	–
Tupolev TU-134[a]	168	–	–	–	–	–	100
Tupolev TU-134A3	230	–	–	–	–	–	100
Tupolev TU-154[a]	174	–	–	–	–	–	100
Tupolev TU-154B2	525	–	–	–	–	–	100
Tupolev TU-154M	744	–	–	–	–	–	100
Tupolev TU-204	28	–	–	29	–	–	71
Yakovlev YAK-40	972	–	–	–	–	–	100
Yakovlev YAK-42	291	–	–	–	–	–	100

Source: Aerospace Industries Association, based on data from Aviation Data Service.
  a Data for major (100 or more aircraft) series excluded and reported separately.
  b Series bearing same designation as model number, but qualifies for separate reporting as a major series.
KEY: AS = Aerospatiale; BAe = British Aerospace; CFM = CFM International; GE = General Electric;
      IAE = International Aero Engines; IAI = Israel Aircraft Industries; MBB = Messerschmitt Bolkow Blohm;
      MDC = McDonnell Douglas; P&W = Pratt & Whitney; RR = Rolls-Royce.

ACTIVE[a] U.S. AIR CARRIER FLEET
BY TYPE OF AIRCRAFT, NUMBER OF ENGINES, AND MODEL
As of December 1999–2003

	1999	2000	2001	2002	2003
TOTAL	8,228	8,055	8,497	8,194	8,176
Turbojets—TOTAL	5,630	5,956	6,296	6,383	6,523
Four-Engine—TOTAL	441	432	419	365	337
Boeing 707	1	—	1	—	—
Boeing 747	188	190	209	175	180
B.Ae./AVRO 146	46	54	54	53	53
McDonnell Douglas DC-8	206	188	155	137	104
Three-Engine—TOTAL	1,181	1,061	996	790	602
Boeing 727	811	720	674	514	361
Lockheed L-1011	66	52	24	20	17
McDonnell Douglas DC-10/MD-11	304	289	298	256	224
Twin-Engine—TOTAL	4,008	4,463	4,881	5,228	5,584
Airbus A-300	68	85	113	119	132
Airbus A-310	39	39	46	46	51
Airbus A-318	—	—	—	—	4
Airbus A-319	40	111	170	218	238
Airbus A-320	162	207	231	278	308
Airbus A-321	—	—	23	28	29
Airbus A-330	—	5	9	9	13
BAe HS-125	1	—	—	—	—
Beech 400	1	—	1	—	—
Boeing 717	2	22	57	83	95
Boeing 737	1,179	1,280	1,359	1,396	1,387
Boeing 757	555	585	599	647	652
Boeing 767	278	315	340	366	361
Boeing 777	53	89	96	129	129
Canadair CL-600	187	251	324	459	693
Cessna C500/C501/C525/C650	9	—	—	1	5
Dassau AMD	27	—	26	—	—
Embraer ERJ-135	7	39	69	123	158
Embraer ERJ-145	95	151	217	275	346
Fokker F-28	145	145	133	86	77
Israel Aircraft 1124	1	—	1	—	—
Learjet LR-24/25/31/35	20	17	4	2	1
McDonnell Douglas DC-9/MD-80/ MD-90	1,133	1,122	1,060	963	905
Mitsubishi MU-300	5	—	2	—	—
North American NA-265	1	—	1	—	—
Turboprops—TOTAL	1,788	1,475	1,494	1,250	1,123
Four-Engine—TOTAL	28	29	24	17	16
De Havilland DHC-7	6	7	4	2	2
Lockheed 188 Electra	14	14	12	9	8
Lockheed 382	8	8	8	6	6

(Continued on next page)

ACTIVE[a] U.S. AIR CARRIER FLEET
BY TYPE OF AIRCRAFT, NUMBER OF ENGINES, AND MODEL
As of December 1999–2003, continued

	1999	2000	2001	2002	2003
Twin-Engine—TOTAL	1,759	1,440	1,470	1,233	1,107
Airtech CN-235	1	1	1	1	—
Beech BE90	6	1	3	1	1
Beech BE99	38	9	14	9	9
Beech BE100	4	3	3	3	4
Beech BE200	19	7	8	6	3
Beech BE300	—	—	2	—	—
Beech BE1900	239	224	185	163	172
B.Ae. ATP	9	—	—	—	—
B.Ae. Jetstream	184	145	100	89	83
CASA C212 Aviocar	4	4	4	9	8
Cessna CE208B	167	44	159	38	50
Cessna C441	2	1	—	4[r]	3
Convair 580/600/640	12	10	5	5	1
Curtis C-46	—	1	2	2	2
DeHavilland DHC-6	54	38	51	27	25
DeHavilland DHC-8	180	183	190	183	170
Dornier DO328	39	65	85	87	79
Embraer EMB110	1	1	1	1	1
Embraer EMB120	225	197	176	160	136
Fairchild/Fokker F-27/FH-227	38	38	38	38	34
Grumman G-73	3	5	5	5	5
Gulfstream 695	—	—	—	1	—
Gulfstream GA1159	—	—	3	—	—
Mitsubishi MU-2	14	13	—	—	—
Piper PA31T	6	4	4	4	5
Piper 42	2	—	—	—	—
Saab-Fairchild SF340	275	272	255	232	210
Shorts SC-7	3	3	3	3	3
Shorts SD-3	20	10	13	6	4
SNAIS ATR-42	79	69	66	64	16
SNAIS ATR-72	60	70	65	63	62
Swearingen SA-226	3	1	2	2	—
Swearingen SA-227	72	27	27	27	21
Single-Engine—TOTAL	1	—	—	—	—
Piston-Engine—TOTAL	688	585	580	528	498
Four-Engine—TOTAL	19	17	16	12	13
Douglas DC-6	19	17	16	12	13
Three-Engine—TOTAL	3	3	3	3	3
Pilatus Britten-Norman BN2A-MK-3 Turbo Islander	3	3	3	3	3
Twin-Engine—TOTAL	292	255	173	154	143
Single-Engine—TOTAL	374	310	388	359	339
Helicopters—TOTAL	122	39	127	33	32

Source: Federal Aviation Administration.
NOTE: Includes certificated route air carriers, supplemental air carriers (charters), multi-engine aircraft in passenger service of commuters, and all aircraft over 12,500 pounds operated by Part 121 and Part 135 commuter operators.
a "Active aircraft" equals the average number of aircraft reported in operation during the last quarter of the year.

ACTIVE U.S. MILITARY AIRCRAFT[a]
Fiscal Years 1980–2003

Year	TOTAL[a]	Fixed-Wing Aircraft				Helicopters
		TOTAL	Jet	Turboprop	Piston	
1980	18,969	11,362	8,794	1,869	699	7,607
1981	19,363	11,645	9,111	1,943	591	7,718
1982	21,728	12,063	9,647	1,900	516	9,665
1983	18,652	11,603	9,495	1,745	363	7,049
1984	18,833	11,661	9,551	1,777	333	7,172
1985	19,333	11,929	9,640	1,881	408	7,404
1986	20,157	11,919	9,730	1,803	386	8,238
1987	20,514	12,054	9,819	1,865	370	8,460
1988	21,010	12,481	9,954	2,222	305	8,529
1989	19,223	11,893	9,501	2,131	261	7,330
1990	20,017	12,817	10,360	2,199	258	7,200
1991	19,966	12,587	10,221	2,119	247	7,379
1992	19,210	11,936	9,672	2,035	229	7,274
1993	17,231	9,681	7,651	1,852	178	7,550
1994[E]	17,018	9,803	7,786	1,835	182	7,215
1995[E]	16,207	9,277	7,294	1,754	229	6,930
1996[b]	20,554	10,154	7,798	2,199	157	10,400
1997	20,245	9,677	7,364	2,151	162	10,568
1998	15,585	9,187[c]	7,082	1,951	120	6,398
1999	16,062	9,015[d]	6,981	1,908	115	7,047
2000	15,902	8,777[d]	6,738	2,023	5	7,125
2001	16,155	9,024[f]	6,790	2,084	118	7,131
2002	16,037	8,993[f]	6,748	2,092	121	7,044
2003	16,233	9,005[g]	6,748	2,103	121	7,228

Source: Aerospace Industries Association.
a Includes Army, Air Force, Navy, and Marine regular service aircraft, as well as Reserve and National Guard Aircraft.
b Prior years data provided by Office of the Secretary of Defense and limited to aircraft in the continental United States.
c Includes 34 gliders.
d Includes 11 gliders.
f Includes 32 gliders.
g Includes 33 gliders.

ACTIVE U.S. CIVIL AIRCRAFT[a]
As of December 31, 1968–2002
(Thousands)

Year	TOTAL	Air Carrier[b]	General Aviation Aircraft					
				Fixed-Wing Aircraft				
			TOTAL	Multi-Engine	Single-Engine		Rotor-craft[c]	Other[d]
					4-place & over	3-place & less		
1968	126.8	2.586	124.2	16.8	61.0	42.8	2.4	1.3
1969	133.5	2.690	130.8	18.1	63.7	45.0	2.6	1.4
1970	134.4	2.679	131.7	18.3	64.8	44.9	2.3	1.6
1971	133.8	2.642	131.1	17.9	64.5	44.8	2.4	1.7
1972	147.6	2.583	145.0	19.8	71.0	49.4	2.8	1.9
1973	156.1	2.599	153.5	21.9	74.8	51.4	3.1	2.3
1974	164.0	2.472	161.5	23.4	78.9	53.0	3.6	2.5
1975	171.0	2.495	168.5	24.6	82.6	54.4	4.1	2.8
1976	180.8	2.492	178.3	25.7	88.2	56.7	4.5	3.2
1977	186.8	2.473	184.3	26.7	92.0	57.3	4.7	3.6
1978	201.3	2.545	198.8	28.8	101.5	59.2	5.3	4.0
1979	213.9	3.609	210.3	31.3	106.0	62.4	5.9	4.8
1980	214.9	3.808	211.0	31.7	107.9	60.5	6.0	4.9
1981	217.2	3.973	213.2	33.3	108.0	59.9	7.0	5.0
1982	213.9	4.027	209.8	34.2	106.5	57.7	6.2	6.2
1983	217.5	4.203	213.3	34.6	107.1	59.1	6.5	5.9
1984	225.3	4.370	220.9	35.6	109.9	62.0	7.1	6.3
1985	201.2	4.678	196.5	31.3	98.5	54.9	6.0	5.8
1986	210.2	4.909	205.3	32.0	102.0	58.3	6.5	6.5
1987	208.0	5.253	202.7	30.8	100.4	59.3	5.9	6.3
1988	201.9	5.660	196.2	30.1	98.1	55.6	6.0	6.4
1989	210.8	5.778	205.0	31.9	100.5	58.4	7.0	7.2
1990	204.1	6.083	198.0	30.6	97.6	56.4	6.9	6.6
1991	202.9	6.054	196.9	29.7	97.8	55.1	6.2	8.1
1992	193.0	7.320	185.7	26.8	91.6	53.2	6.0	8.0
1993	184.4	7.297	177.1	22.8	91.6	42.5	4.7	15.5
1994	180.3	7.370	172.9	22.3	87.3	40.5	4.7	18.1
1995	190.0	7.411	188.1	24.6	93.6	44.1	5.8	19.9
1996	194.8	7.478	191.1	25.6	93.8	44.3	6.6	20.9
1997	200.0	7.616	192.4	26.2	95.0	45.7	6.8	18.8
1998	212.8	8.111	204.7	29.9	103.6	41.8	7.4	22.1
1999	227.7	8.228	219.5	32.8	109.3	42.6	7.4	27.3
2000	225.6	8.055	217.5	33.2	108.0	42.1	7.2	27.1
2001	219.9	8.497	211.4	31.7	106.3	39.7	6.8	27.0
2002	219.4	8.194	211.2	31.7	105.5	39.2	6.6	28.3

Source: Federal Aviation Administration.
  a "Active aircraft" must have a current U.S. registration and have flown during the calendar year. Prior to 1971, only a current U.S. registration was necessary.
  b Includes certificated route air carriers, supplemental air carriers (charters), multi-engine aircraft in commuter passenger service, and all aircraft over 12,500 pounds operated by air taxis, commercial operators, and travel clubs.
  c Includes autogiros; excludes air carrier helicopters.
  d Includes gliders, dirigibles, balloons, and experimental aircraft.

U.S. GENERAL AVIATION[a]
TYPE OF AIRCRAFT AND HOURS FLOWN
Calendar Years 1998–2002

	1998	1999	2000	2001	2002
NUMBER OF ACTIVE AIRCRAFT BY TYPE (Thousands)					
All Aircraft—TOTAL	204.7	219.5	217.5	211.4	211.2
Fixed-Wing:	175.2	184.7	183.3	177.7	176.3
Piston:	163.0	171.9	170.5	163.3	161.1
Single-Engine	144.2	150.9	149.4	145.0	143.5
Twin-Engine	18.7	20.9	21.0	18.2	17.5
Other	0.1	0.1	0.1	0.1	0.1
Turboprop:	6.2	5.7	5.8	6.6	6.8
Twin-Engine	5.1	4.6	5.0	5.6	5.7
Other	1.1	1.0	0.7	1.0	1.1
Turbojet:	6.1	7.1	7.0	7.8	8.4
Twin-Engine	5.5	6.4	6.2	5.6	7.7
Other	0.6	0.7	0.8	0.8	0.7
Rotorcraft:	7.4	7.4	7.2	6.8	6.6
Piston	2.5	2.6	2.7	2.3	2.4
Turbine	4.9	4.9	4.5	4.5	4.3
Balloons, Dirigibles, and Gliders...	5.6	6.8	6.7	6.5	6.4
Experimental	16.5	20.5	20.4	20.4	21.9
HOURS FLOWN BY TYPE OF AIRCRAFT (Thousands)					
All Aircraft—TOTAL	28,100	31,756	30,975[r]	29,133[r]	27,040
Fixed-Wing: Piston	20,402	22,895	22,199	20,883	18,891
Turboprop	1,765	1,811	2,031	1,913	1,850
Turbojet	2,226	2,738	2,755	2,658	2,745
Rotorcraft: Piston	430	556	531	583	454
Turbine	1,912	2,188	1,777	1,559	1,422
Balloons, Dirigibles, and Gliders...	295	318	374	324	333
Experimental	1,071	1,247	1,307	1,214	1,345
AVERAGE HOURS FLOWN ANNUALLY BY TYPE					
All Aircraft—TOTAL	137.3	144.7	142.4	137.8	128.0
Fixed-Wing: Piston	125.2	133.2	130.2	127.9	117.3
Turboprop	285.8	319.0	352.5	290.0	270.4
Turbojet	367.0	384.6	393.5	341.3	328.6
Rotorcraft: Piston	169.0	217.0	198.1	254.2	192.9
Turbine	391.8	448.0	397.6	347.0	331.0
Balloons, Dirigibles, and Gliders...	52.8	47.1	55.8	49.6	52.2
Experimental	64.9	60.8	64.0	59.4	61.3

Source: Federal Aviation Administration.
a Excludes commuters.

U.S. GENERAL AVIATION
ACTIVE AIRCRAFT AND HOURS FLOWN BY PRIMARY USE
Calendar Years 1998–2002

Primary Use	1998	1999	2000	2001	2002
ACTIVE AIRCRAFT AS OF DECEMBER 31 (Thousands)					
TOTAL	204.7	219.5	217.5	211.4	211.2
Executive	11.3	10.8	11.0	10.5	10.8
Business	32.6	24.5	25.2	25.5	24.2
Air Taxi[a]	4.9	4.3	3.7	3.6	3.9
Instructional	11.4	16.1	14.9	14.3	13.2
Personal	124.3	147.1	148.2	144.0	146.0
Aerial Application	4.6	4.3	4.3	3.8	4.0
Aerial Observation	3.2	3.2	5.1	5.0	4.5
Aerial Other	NA	0.4	1.0	0.6	0.9
Sight Seeing	0.7	0.8	0.9	0.9	0.6
Public Use	4.0	4.1	NA	NA	NA
Air Tours............................	0.3	0.3	0.3	0.4	0.3
External Load	0.3	0.2	0.2	0.2	0.2
Medical	NA	0.8	0.9	0.9	1.0
Other Work	1.1	2.4	1.8	1.5	1.7
Other	6.0	NA	NA	NA	NA
HOURS FLOWN (Thousands)					
TOTAL	28,100	31,756	30,972	29,134	27,040
Executive	3,213	3,616	3,765	3,411	3,275
Business	3,523	3,598	3,604	3,583	3,287
Air Taxi[a]	2,400	1,897	1,694	1,491	1,346
Instructional	3,961	5,893	5,375	5,075	4,182
Personal	9,781	11,294	11,711	11,314	11,025
Aerial Application	1,306	1,415	1,401	1,093	1,182
Aerial Observation	812	1,243	1,621	1,596	1,366
Aerial Other	NA	120	244	189	187
Sight Seeing	169	220	198	201	134
Air Tours............................	183	146	224	190	149
Public Use	1,373	1,111	NA	NA	NA
Medical	NA	461	442	456	441
External Load	153	128	171	177	97
Other Work	286	613	522	359	369
Other	940	NA	NA	NA	NA

Source: Federal Aviation Administration, "General Aviation and Air Taxi Activity Survey" (Annually).
   a   Air taxis under 12,500 pounds.

ACTIVE U.S. CIVIL AIRCRAFT
BY PRIMARY USE AND TYPE OF AIRCRAFT
As of December 31, 2002

Primary Use	TOTAL	Fixed-Wing			Rotor-craft[a]	Other[b]
		Turbojet	Turboprop	Piston		
TOTAL......................	219,438	14,738	8,091	161,615	6,681	28,313
Air Carrier—TOTAL	8,194	6,383	1,250	528	33	—
Large	7,576	6,379	1,159	38	—	—
Small	618	4	91	490	33	—
General Aviation—TOTAL	211,244	8,355	6,841	161,087	6,648	28,313
Executive..........................	10,810	5,691	2,417	1,947	551	203
Business	24,153	1,119	1,386	20,619	463	566
Air Taxi[c]	3,898	685	779	2,212	216	6
Instructional	13,203	95	42	11,775	536	755
Personal	145,996	618	1,086	117,365	1,373	25,555
Aerial Application	3,971	5	510	2,759	581	116
Aerial Observation..............	4,535	—	113	2,632	1,748	43
Aerial Other	899	—	174	431	260	35
Sight Seeing	641	—	—	130	65	446
Air Tours	259	—	—	110	99	50
External Load	151	—	—	—	145	7
Medical	996	26	224	190	532	23
Other Work	1,733	117	110	918	80	508

Source: Federal Aviation Administration.
NOTE: Detail may not add to totals because of estimating procedures.
  a Includes helicopters and autogiros.
  b Includes gliders, dirigibles, balloons, and experimental aircraft.
  c Limited to Air taxis under 12,500 pounds. Otherwise, aircraft included in "Air Carrier."

U.S. CIVIL AND JOINT-USE AIRCRAFT FACILITIES[a]
BY STATE AND BY TYPE
As of December 31, 2003

State	Total[a]	Public[b]	Paved	Lighted	State	Total[a]	Public[b]	Paved	Lighted
Alabama	268	97	176	106	Nevada	128	53	67	40
Alaska	649	408	74	179	New Hampshire	121	26	56	23
Arizona	307	80	174	89	New Jersey	381	53	160	60
Arkansas	308	99	182	114	New Mexico	175	62	80	55
California	942	263	670	284	New York	582	163	225	153
Colorado	426	79	184	85	North Carolina	371	114	162	122
Connecticut	153	25	93	32	North Dakota	308	90	87	90
Delaware	48	11	17	15	Ohio	718	175	288	178
Dist. of Col.	16	3	15	4	Oklahoma	439	149	217	132
Florida	811	133	355	187	Oregon	451	98	173	85
Georgia	442	109	198	122	Pennsylvania	799	138	330	151
Hawaii	48	13	40	16	Rhode Island	27	8	17	7
Idaho	251	121	88	57	South Carolina	190	67	88	75
Illinois	872	118	306	191	South Dakota	185	76	80	79
Indiana	631	111	175	117	Tennessee	296	81	163	98
Iowa	324	124	179	138	Texas	1,858	387	873	459
Kansas	413	144	143	131	Utah	142	47	90	49
Kentucky	204	63	116	65	Vermont	85	18	20	11
Louisiana	485	81	262	91	Virginia	419	67	171	95
Maine	146	66	49	34	Washington	491	138	232	140
Maryland	231	38	87	51	West Virginia	119	37	72	38
Massachusetts	235	44	125	46	Wisconsin	555	131	194	151
Michigan	476	232	201	176	Wyoming	119	42	59	43
Minnesota	514	158	164	147	**50 States—TOTAL**	19,513	5,267	8,568	5,227
Mississippi	239	83	122	87	Puerto Rico	45	11	37	13
Missouri	542	131	239	148	Virgin Islands	8	2	3	2
Montana	269	122	111	92	S. Pacific[c]	19	10	12	7
Nebraska	304	91	119	90	**TOTAL**	19,585	5,290	8,620	5,249

FACILITIES BY CLASS

Class	TOTAL[a]	Public[b]	Private
Airports	13,734	5,003	8,731
Heliports	5,286	80	5,206
Seaplane Bases	478	204	274
Stolports	87	3	84
TOTAL	19,585	5,290	14,295

Source: Federal Aviation Administration.
  a Included in these data are facilities having joint civil-military use.
  b "Public" refers to use, whether publicly or privately owned.
  c American Samoa, Guam, and Trust Territories.

HELIPORTS/HELIPADS[a] IN THE UNITED STATES BY STATE
As of 2003

State	TOTAL Helipads in State	Private Use		Public Use	
		Heliports & Helistops	Helipads at Airports	Heliports & Helistops	Helipads at Airports
Alabama	95	94	—	—	1
Alaska	39	29	2	7	1
Arizona	119	110	2	1	6
Arkansas	84	81	—	—	3
California	418	395	2	—	21
Colorado	174	170	—	—	4
Connecticut	95	89	—	3	3
Delaware	15	14	—	1	—
District of Columbia	18	17	—	1	—
Florida	282	274	2	4	2
Georgia	111	109	—	—	2
Hawaii	20	18	—	—	2
Idaho	42	40	1	—	1
Illinois	264	255	4	4	1
Indiana	126	120	4	2	—
Iowa	89	88	—	—	1
Kansas	43	38	1	—	4
Kentucky	58	58	—	—	—
Louisiana	250	242	2	4	2
Maine	14	12	—	—	2
Maryland	73	70	1	—	2
Massachusetts	141	140	—	—	1
Michigan	89	86	1	2	—
Minnesota	55	54	—	—	1
Mississippi	50	49	—	1	—
Missouri	135	131	1	1	2
Montana	33	30	—	2	1
Nebraska	39	37	1	—	1
Nevada	34	31	—	—	3
New Hampshire	64	63	—	—	1

(Continued on next page)

HELIPORTS/HELIPADS[a] IN THE UNITED STATES BY STATE

As of 2003, continued

State	TOTAL Helipads in State	Private Use		Public Use	
		Heliports & Helistops	Helipads at Airports	Heliports & Helistops	Helipads at Airports
New Jersey	257	250	—	4	3
New Mexico	27	25	2	—	—
New York	173	158	3	7	5
North Carolina	74	70	—	4	—
North Dakota	16	15	—	—	1
Ohio	204	192	1	10	1
Oklahoma	93	88	—	5	—
Oregon	105	101	3	1	—
Pennsylvania	326	315	1	8	2
Rhode Island	17	16	—	1	—
South Carolina	33	30	—	—	3
South Dakota	30	30	—	—	—
Tennessee	100	98	1	—	1
Texas	463	449	4	5	5
Utah	46	44	—	—	2
Vermont	19	19	—	—	—
Virginia	137	133	—	—	4
Washington	144	136	3	1	4
West Virginia	37	35	—	—	2
Wisconsin	91	89	—	—	2
Wyoming	27	25	—	—	2
TOTAL	**5,480**	**5,255**	**42**	**78**	**105**

Source: Helicopter Association International, "2004 Helicopter Annual" (Annually).
NOTE: 96.7 percent of all U.S. helicopter landing areas are private, while 3.3 percent are public.
a Excludes temporary heliports, offshore heliports, and infrequently used helicopter landing sites.

The National Science Foundation (NSF) estimates that the United States funded a total of $284 billion of R&D in 2003—the latest figures available. Industry shouldered the largest, but declining, share of R&D spending. In 2000, industry's share of total R&D spending was 69%. That figure has fallen a percentage point or so each year; and by 2003, the $180 billion spent by industry on R&D accounted for some 63% of the total. At the same time, the federal government's spending has risen in absolute terms and as a percentage of the total. In 2000, the federal government supplied a little more than 25% of the R&D dollars in the United States. By 2003, the federal government's $85 billion accounted for 30%. At $196 billion, industry also performed the majority of R&D, according to the NSF's Annual Survey of Industrial R&D. Colleges and universities combined were the next-largest R&D performer in 2003, accounting for $40 billion of the year's R&D dollars. The federal government accounted for $25 billion.

Funding for aerospace industry-performed R&D rebounded $1.8 billion, or 23%, in 2002—again using the latest figures available from the NSF. Federal funding of aerospace industry R&D totaled $4.3 billion—up from $3.8 billion—and company funding grew $1.3 billion to $5.3 billion. The prior year marked the lowest level in two decades before adjustment for inflation

and even longer after. Coincident with this increase in funding, the number of R&D-performing scientists and engineers (R&D S&Es) employed by the aerospace industry jumped from 19,100 in 2002 to 32,500 in 2003.

Similarly, the percentage of R&D S&Es employed in the aerospace industry, which had fallen to a record-low 1.8%, increased to 3.0% in 2003.

In FY 2003, federal outlays for R&D (total, not just aerospace) increased $14 billion—the third year of real growth—after languishing for six years at the same real spending level. DoD outlays rose $8.9 billion to $54 billion, while NASA R&D spending increased 13% to $7.7 billion and Energy R&D rose 7.6%. The DoD continued to be the government's largest single spender on R&D, accounting for half of all federal funding. Other agencies, such as the NSF, the National Institutes of Health, and the Transportation and Agriculture Departments saw their collective R&D outlays increase 11% to $33 billion. Further, in FY 2004, federally-funded R&D is scheduled to rise $14 billion to $115 billion. DoD R&D is due to increase $7.6 billion and Energy R&D will grow 18% or $1.3 billion. Likewise, NASA's R&D funding will grow 6.6% or $0.5 billion.

Ballistic Missile Defense (BMD) continues to dominate DoD's RDT&E account. BMD funding totaled $6.7 billion in FY 2003 and is scheduled to increase to $9.1 billion in FY 2005. Other DoD aerospace programs receiving the greatest levels of RDT&E funding in FY 2003 included: Joint Strike Fighter, $3.3 billion; F-22 Raptor, $909 million; RAH-66 Comanche, $866 million; Advanced EHF, $803 million; SBIRS-High, $775 million; and V-22 Osprey, $444 million.

TOTAL U.S. FUNDS FOR RESEARCH AND DEVELOPMENT BY SOURCE AND PERFORMER[a]
Calendar Years 2000–2003
(Millions of Dollars)

Source of Funds	TOTAL, All Performers	Performer				
		Federal Government	Industry	Colleges & Universities	Federally-Funded Research & Development Centers	Non-Profit Institutions
2000[r]						
All Sources—TOTAL......	$264,634	$17,917	$199,539	$30,566	$5,742	$10,869
Federal Government	66,326	17,917	19,118	17,637	5,742	5,912
Gov't, Non-Federal	2,238	—	—	2,238	—	—
Industry	183,689	—	180,421	2,165	—	1,103
Colleges & Universities	6,211	—	—	6,211	—	—
Nonprofit Institutions........	6,170	—	—	2,316	—	3,854
2001						
All Sources—TOTAL......	$274,211	$21,048	$200,525	$33,518	$6,225	$12,894
Federal Government	73,340	21,048	18,919	19,654	6,225	7,494
Gov't, Non-Federal	2,382	—	—	2,382	—	—
Industry	184,893	—	181,606	2,177	—	1,110
Colleges & Universities	6,778	—	—	6,778	—	—
Nonprofit Institutions........	6,818	—	—	2,528	—	4,290
2002[p]						
All Sources—TOTAL......	$276,434	$23,788	$194,614	$36,846	$7,132	$14,054
Federal Government	80,490	23,788	19,320	22,052	7,132	8,198
Gov't, Non-Federal	2,548	—	—	2,548	—	—
Industry	178,514	—	175,294	2,150	—	1,070
Colleges & Universities	7,332	—	—	7,332	—	—
Nonprofit Institutions........	7,550	—	—	2,764	—	4,786
2003[E]						
All Sources—TOTAL......	$283,795	$24,959	$196,112	$40,262	$7,421	$15,042
Federal Government	85,280	24,959	19,697	24,499	7,421	8,704
Gov't, Non-Federal	2,710	—	—	2,710	—	—
Industry	179,615	—	176,415	2,123	—	1,077
Colleges & Universities	7,944	—	—	7,944	—	—
Nonprofit Institutions........	8,247	—	—	2,986	—	5,261

Source: National Science Foundation, "Annual Survey of Industrial Research and Development" (Annually).

a Source/performer detail not available by industry.

FEDERAL OUTLAYS FOR CONDUCT OF RESEARCH AND DEVELOPMENT
Fiscal Years 1991–2005
(Millions of Dollars)

Year	TOTAL	DoD	NASA	Energy[a]	Other[b]
CURRENT DOLLARS					
1991	$ 62,183	$35,330	$ 7,072	$5,892	$13,890[r]
1992	64,728	35,504	7,617	6,043	15,566[r]
1993	68,378	37,666	8,088	6,036	16,588
1994	66,453[r]	35,474	7,878	5,904	17,196[r]
1995	68,432	35,356	8,992	6,195	17,889
1996	68,439	36,936	8,083	6,135	17,285
1997	71,073	37,702	9,374	5,819	18,178
1998	72,803	37,558	9,881	5,971	19,393
1999	74,136	37,571	9,433	6,077	21,055
2000	73,947	38,279	6,369	6,282	23,017
2001	80,089	41,157	6,473	6,613	25,846
2002	87,911	44,903	6,772	6,830[r]	29,406[r]
2003	101,440	53,778	7,665	7,350[r]	32,642
2004[E]	115,006	61,347	8,174	8,671	36,814
2005[E]	123,991	67,041	8,921	8,608	39,421
CONSTANT DOLLARS[c][r]					
1991	$ 73,764	$41,910	$ 8,389	$6,989	$16,477
1992	74,899	41,083	8,814	6,993	18,012
1993	77,368	42,618	9,151	6,830	18,769
1994	73,608	39,293	8,726	6,540	19,047
1995	74,237	38,355	9,755	6,721	19,407
1996	72,846	39,315	8,604	6,530	18,398
1997	74,352	39,441	9,806	6,087	19,017
1998	75,249	38,820	10,213	6,172	20,044
1999	75,634	38,330	9,624	6,200	21,480
2000	73,947	38,279	6,369	6,282	23,017
2001	78,258	40,216	6,325	6,462	25,255
2002	84,408	43,114	6,502	6,558	28,234
2003	95,834	50,806	7,241	6,949	30,838
2004[E]	107,242	57,205	7,622	8,086	34,329
2005[E]	114,193	61,743	8,216	7,928	36,306

Source: Office of Management and Budget, "The Budget of the United States Government" (Annually).
   a   Includes defense and nondefense-related atomic energy R&D with nondefense energy R&D.
   b   Includes but not limited to NSF, National Institutes of Health, DoT, & Agriculture.
   c   Based on Fiscal Year GDP deflator, 2000=100.

FUNDS FOR INDUSTRIAL RESEARCH AND DEVELOPMENT
IN ALL INDUSTRIES AND THE AEROSPACE INDUSTRY
BY FUNDING SOURCE
Calendar Years 1988–2002
(Millions of Dollars)

Year	All Industries[a]			Aerospace Industry[b]		
	TOTAL	Federal Funds	Company Funds[c]	TOTAL	Federal Funds	Company Funds[c]
CURRENT DOLLARS						
1988	$ 97,015	$30,343	$ 66,672	$24,168	$18,402	$5,766
1989	102,055	28,554	73,501	22,331	16,828	5,503
1990	109,727	28,125	81,602	20,635	15,248	5,387
1991	116,952	26,372	90,580	16,629	11,096	5,533
1992	119,110	24,722	94,388	17,158	10,287	6,871
1993	117,400	22,809	94,591	15,056	9,372	5,684
1994	119,595	22,463	97,131	14,260	8,794	5,466
1995	132,103	23,451	108,652	16,951	11,462	5,489
1996	144,667	23,653	121,015	16,224	10,515	5,710
1997	157,539	23,928	133,611	17,865	10,904	6,961
1998	169,180	24,164	145,016	16,359	9,838	6,521
1999	182,711ʳ	22,535	160,176ʳ	14,425	9,117	5,309
2000	199,539	19,118	180,421	10,319	6,424	3,895
2001	198,505	16,899	181,606	7,868	3,785	4,083
2002	190,809	16,401	174,408	9,654	4,306	5,349
CONSTANT DOLLARS[d]						
1988	$128,157	$40,083	$ 88,074	$31,926	$24,309	$7,617
1989	129,676	36,282	93,394	28,375	21,382	6,992
1990	134,469	34,467	100,002	25,288	18,686	6,602
1991	138,569	31,246	107,322	19,703	13,147	6,556
1992	137,859	28,613	109,245	19,859	11,906	7,953
1993	132,805	25,802	107,003	17,032	10,602	6,430
1994	132,442	24,876	107,565	15,792	9,739	6,053
1995	143,434	25,463	117,972	18,405	12,445	5,960
1996	154,065	25,190	128,876	17,278	11,198	6,081
1997	165,135	25,082	140,053	18,726	11,430	7,297
1998	175,316	25,040	150,276	16,952	10,195	6,758
1999	186,630	23,018	163,612	14,734	9,313	5,423
2000	199,539	19,118	180,421	10,319	6,424	3,895
2001	193,853	16,503	177,350	7,684	3,696	3,987
2002	183,647	15,785	167,861	9,292	4,144	5,148

Source: National Science Foundation, "Annual Survey of Industrial Research and Development" (Annually).
   a Includes all manufacturing industries, plus those non-manufacturing industries known to conduct or finance research and development.
   b Companies classified in NAICS code 3364, having as their principal activity the manufacture of aerospace products and parts. Prior to 1999, data categorized using SIC system and reported combining codes 372 and 376.
   c Company funds include all funds for industrial R&D work performed within company facilities except funds provided by the Federal Government. Excluded are company-financed research and development contracted to outside organizations such as research institutions, universities and colleges, or other non-profit organizations.
   d Based on GDP deflator, 2000=100.

FUNDS FOR INDUSTRIAL RESEARCH AND DEVELOPMENT IN THE AEROSPACE INDUSTRY BY TYPE OF RESEARCH AND FUNDING SOURCE
Calendar Years 1965–2002
(Millions of Dollars)

Year	TOTAL	Basic Research			Applied Research			Development		
		TOTAL	Federal Funds	Com-pany Funds	TOTAL	Federal Funds	Com-pany Funds	TOTAL	Federal Funds	Com-pany Funds
1965	$ 5,148	$ 71	$ 41	$ 30	$ 735	$ 563	$ 172	$ 4,342	$ 3,921	$ 421
1966	5,526	69	36	33	773	563	210	4,685	4,162	523
1967	5,669	71	33	38	726	490	236	4,871	4,071	800
1968	5,765	68	26	42	677	426	251	5,021	4,145	876
1969	5,882	65	24	41	597	347	250	5,220	4,216	1,004
1970	5,219	63	20	43	565	352	213	4,591	3,718	873
1971	4,881	54	37	17	461	279	182	4,365	3,583	782
1972	4,950	60	44	16	451	267	184	4,438	3,722	716
1973	5,052	50	21	29	512	308	204	4,491	3,633	858
1974	5,278	51	19	32	609	360	249	4,617	3,735	882
1975	5,713	54	17	37	614	381	233	5,044	4,119	925
1976	6,339	54	21	33	666	365	301	5,619	4,521	1,098
1977	7,033	56	25	31	753	419	334	6,223	5,017	1,206
1979 [a]	8,041	86	44	42	880	499	381	7,076	5,314	1,762
1981 [a]	11,968	131	60	71	1,484	897	587	10,353	7,738	2,615
1983	13,853	146	NA	NA	3,466	NA	NA	10,241	7,668	2,573
1984	16,033	247	NA	NA	3,067	NA	NA	12,718	9,870	2,848
1985	17,619	304	162	142	3,785	2,776	1,009	13,530	10,483	3,047
1986	21,050	311	208	103	3,198	1,571	1,627	17,541	13,205	4,336
1987	24,488	425	335	90	2,949	1,709	1,239	21,115	16,475	4,640
1988	25,900	366	263	104	2,997	1,915	1,082	22,537	17,700	4,838
1989	25,638	668	553	116	3,081	2,113	968	21,889	16,967	4,921
1990	25,356	658	519	139	3,340	1,931	1,409	21,358	16,766	4,592
1991	16,983	364	302	62	2,091	1,105	986	14,528	10,043 [b]	4,485
1992	17,158	270	235	35	1,739	976	763	15,148	9,076	6,072
1993	15,056	NA	NA	NA	1,453	825	628	NA	NA	NA
1994	14,260	NA	NA	NA	<1,473	<816	<657	12,787	7,978	4,809
1995	16,951	252	250	2	1,987	564	1,423	14,712	10,648	4,064
1996	16,224	NA	NA	108	<2,858	<1,251	<1,607	13,259	9,264	3,995
1997	17,865 [c]	NA	NA	10	NA	NA	1,508	13,275	9,115	4,159
1998	16,359 [c]	NA	NA	172	NA	NA	272	12,800	8,136	4,664
1999	14,425	NA	NA	173	<2,712	<2,057	655	11,541	7,060	4,480
2000	10,319	NA	NA	NA	<3,553	<2,493	<1,060	6,766	3,931	2,835
2001	7,868	<530	<229	301	1,639	735	904	>5,693	>2,821	2,877
2002	9,654	NA	NA	347	<2,039	<947	1,092	7,268	3,358	3,910

Source: National Science Foundation, "Annual Survey of Industrial Research and Development" (Annually).
  a Break-outs by Research Type and Funding Source available only for odd-numbered years between 1977 and 1983.
  b Computed by AIA as difference between total and company funds. Figure withheld by NSF because of imputation of more than 50 percent.
  c Funding by type of research not revised nor published despite revised totals.

RESEARCH AND DEVELOPMENT FUNDS AS PERCENT OF NET SALES
ALL MANUFACTURING INDUSTRIES AND THE AEROSPACE INDUSTRY
Calendar Years 1978–2002

Year	All Manufacturing Industries[a]		Aerospace Industry[b]	
	Total Funds	Company Funds	Total Funds	Company Funds
1978	2.9%	2.0%	13.3%	3.2%
1979	2.6	1.9	12.9	3.5
1980	3.0	2.1	13.7	3.8
1981	3.1	2.2	16.0	4.6
1982	3.8	2.6	17.1	5.1
1983	3.9	2.6	15.2	4.1
1984	3.9	2.6	15.4	4.0
1985	4.4	3.0	14.9	3.9
1986	4.7	3.2	13.4	4.0
1987	4.6	3.1	14.7	3.6
1988	4.5	3.1	16.3	3.9
1989	4.3	3.1	13.5	3.3
1990	4.2	3.1	11.8	3.1
1991	4.2	3.2	12.1	4.0
1992	4.2	3.3	11.8	4.7
1993	3.8	3.1	12.5	4.7
1994	3.6	2.9	13.8	5.3
1995	3.6	2.9	12.9	4.2
1996	4.0	3.3	12.9	4.5
1997	3.9	3.3	8.4	3.3
1998	3.7	3.2	7.2	2.9
1999	3.7	3.2	8.8	3.2
2000	3.6	3.3	7.3	2.8
2001	4.0	3.6	5.7	3.0
2002	3.6	3.2	4.1	2.3

Source: National Science Foundation, "Annual Survey of Industrial Research and Development" (Annually).
 a Includes all manufacturing industries known to conduct or finance research and development.
 b Companies classified in NAICS code 3364, having as their principal activity the manufacture of aerospace products and parts. Prior to 1999, data categorized using SIC system and reported combining codes 372 and 376.

FEDERAL AERONAUTICS RESEARCH AND DEVELOPMENT
Fiscal Years 1987–2003
(Millions of Dollars)

Year	TOTAL	NASA[a]	DoD[b]	DoT[c]
BUDGET AUTHORITY				
1987	$ 5,824	$ 698	$4,179	$ 946
1988	6,974	723	4,989	1,262
1989	10,656	872	8,240	1,544
1990	10,690	932	7,867	1,891
1991	9,417	968	6,149	2,300
1992	11,110	1,117	7,366	2,627
1993	11,359	1,245	7,582	2,532
1994	10,703	1,546	6,848	2,309
1995	10,718	1,310	7,196	2,212
1996	10,159	1,315	6,792	2,052
1997	9,721	1,252	6,323	2,146
1998	9,682	1,327	6,256	2,099
1999	8,997	1,194	5,532	2,271
2000	9,848	1,060	6,587	2,201
2001	9,867	926	6,149	2,792
2002	10,932[r]	997	6,995	2,940[r]
2003	13,360	1,004	9,432	2,924
OUTLAYS				
1987	$ 5,867	$ 622	$4,182	$1,063
1988	6,340	679	4,448	1,213
1989	8,491	855	6,420	1,216
1990	10,009	889	7,649	1,471
1991	9,501	1,017	6,793	1,691
1992	10,011	1,122	6,790	2,099
1993	11,162	1,212	7,572	2,378
1994	11,137	1,330	7,203	2,604
1995	11,155	1,153	7,132	2,870
1996	10,837	1,187	6,974	2,676
1997	10,430	1,302	6,600	2,528
1998	10,122	1,339	6,354	2,429
1999	9,499	1,217	5,913	2,369
2000	9,577	1,014	6,320	2,243
2001	9,735	867	6,297	2,571
2002	10,410	956	6,655	2,799
2003	12,127	974	8,314	2,839

Source: NASA, "Aeronautics and Space Report of the President" (Annually).
  a Research and Development, Construction of Facilities, Research and Program Management.
  b Research, Development, Test, and Evaluation of aircraft and related equipment.
  c Federal Aviation Administration: Research, Engineering, and Development; and Facilities, Engineering, and Development.

DEPARTMENT OF DEFENSE OUTLAYS
FOR RESEARCH, DEVELOPMENT, TEST, AND EVALUATION
Fiscal Years 1972–2005
(Millions of Dollars)

Year	TOTAL	Air Force	Army	Navy	Other
1972	$ 7,881	$ 3,205	$1,779	$ 2,427	$ 470
1973	8,157	3,362	1,912	2,404	479
1974	8,582	3,240	2,190	2,623	529
1975	8,866	3,308	1,964	3,021	573
1976	8,923	3,338	1,842	3,215	528
Tr.Qtr.	2,203	830	437	778	161
1977	9,795	3,618	2,069	3,481	627
1978	10,508	3,626	2,342	3,825	715
1979	11,152	4,080	2,409	3,826	837
1980	13,127	5,017	2,707	4,381	1,021
1981	15,278	6,341	2,958	4,783	1,196
1982	17,729	7,794	3,230	5,240	1,465
1983	20,554	9,182	3,658	5,854	1,861
1984	23,117	10,353	3,812	6,662	2,289
1985	27,103	11,573	3,950	8,054	3,527
1986	32,283	13,417	3,984	9,667	5,215
1987	33,596	13,347	4,721	9,176	6,352
1988	34,792	14,302	4,624	8,828	7,038
1989	37,002	14,912	4,966	9,291	7,833
1990	37,458	14,443	5,513	9,160	8,342
1991	34,589	13,050	5,559	7,586	8,371
1992	34,632	11,998	5,978	7,826	8,830
1993	36,968	12,338	6,218	8,944	9,467
1994	34,786	12,513	5,746	7,990	8,537
1995	34,710	12,052	5,081	9,230	8,347
1996	36,561	13,056	4,925	9,404	9,175
1997	37,027	14,040	4,859	8,220	9,908
1998	37,420	14,499	4,881	7,836	10,204
1999	37,363	14,172	5,027	8,052	10,112
2000	37,606	13,839	4,777	8,857	10,133
2001	40,599	14,310	5,837	9,465	10,987
2002	44,389	14,228	6,569	10,360	13,232
2003	53,098	17,271	7,041	12,192	16,594
2004 [E]	60,593	19,592	8,730	14,033	18,238
2005 [E]	66,207	20,601	9,974	15,607	20,025

Source: Office of Management and Budget, "The Budget of the United States Government" (Annually).

DEPARTMENT OF DEFENSE APPROPRIATIONS FOR RESEARCH, DEVELOPMENT, TEST, AND EVALUATION
Fiscal Years 2003–2005
(Millions of Dollars)

	2003	2004^E	2005^E
TOTAL...	$58,307	$64,693	$68,942

BY APPROPRIATION

Army	$ 7,595	$10,201	$10,436
Navy	13,700	14,969	16,346
Air Force...	18,935	20,294	21,115
Defense Agencies	17,839	18,927	20,740
Operational Test & Evaluation	240	302	305

RECAP OF BUDGET ACTIVITIES

Basic Research	$ 1,369	$ 1,404	$ 1,330
Applied Research	4,269	4,423	3,878
Advanced Technology Development	5,091	6,254	5,343
Advanced Component Development & Prototypes	10,637	13,306	15,352
System Development & Demonstration	13,393	15,902	19,271
RDT&E Management Support	4,046	3,278	3,261
Operational Systems Development........................	19,503	20,126	20,508

RECAP OF FYDP PROGRAMS

Strategic Forces	$ 228	$ 302	$ 375
General Purpose Forces	3,925	4,272	4,919
Intelligence and Communications	13,519	13,865	13,808
Mobility Forces	643	770	836
Guard and Reserve Forces	9	5	—
Research and Development (FYDP Program 6)....	39,053	44,278	47,948
Central Supply and Maintenance	342	396	249
Training Medical and Other...................................	0	3	3
Administration and Associated Activities	124	203	310
Support of Other Nations	4	29	35
Special Operations Forces	462	571	459

Source: Department of Defense Budget, "RDT&E Programs (R-1)" (Annually).

DEPARTMENT OF DEFENSE PRIME CONTRACT AWARDS
FOR RESEARCH, DEVELOPMENT, TEST, AND EVALUATION
Fiscal Years 1999–2003
(Millions of Dollars)

Program Categories	1999	2000	2001	2002	2003
TOTAL..	$19,437	$19,246	$21,444	$26,908	$33,069
Research..	1,785	1,756	2,213	3,164	3,841
Exploratory Development....................	2,255	2,509	2,835	3,111	3,664
Other Development / Support	15,397	14,981	16,396	20,633	25,564
Aircraft—TOTAL	$ 4,108	$ 4,037	$ 4,361	$ 5,526	$ 8,104
Research..	156	261	276	393	534
Exploratory Development....................	110	305	319	250	343
Other Development / Support	3,842	3,471	3,766	4,883	7,219
Missile and Space Systems—TOTAL ..	4,793	4,556	5,361	6,268	6,923
Research..	188	55	81	324	347
Exploratory Development....................	536	580	881	1,052	1,355
Other Development / Support	4,069	3,921	4,399	4,891	5,220
Electronics & Communications Equipment—TOTAL	3,173	2,645	3,192	3,688	3,780
Research..	212	162	252	376	430
Exploratory Development....................	320	352	424	422	505
Other Development / Support	2,640	2,132	2,516	2,890	2,844
All Other—TOTAL[a]	7,364	8,008	8,530	11,426	14,262
Research..	1,230	1,278	1,604	2,071	2,520
Exploratory Development....................	1,289	1,272	1,211	1,387	1,461
Other Development / Support	4,846	5,457	5,715	7,969	10,280

Source: Department of Defense, "Prime Contract Awards by Service Category and Federal Supply Classification" (Annually).
a "All Other" includes ships, tank-automotive, weapons, ammunition, services, and other.

DEPARTMENT OF DEFENSE PRIME CONTRACT AWARDS OVER $25,000 FOR RESEARCH, DEVELOPMENT, TEST, AND EVALUATION BY REGION AND TYPE OF CONTRACTOR

Fiscal Year 2003

Region	TOTAL	Type of Contractor		
		Educational Institutions	Other Non-Profit Institutions[a]	Business Firms
TOTAL (Millions of Dollars)	$31,520	$1,124	$1,633	$28,757
New England	$ 2,721	$ 533	$ 249	$ 1,939
Middle Atlantic	3,449	133	179	3,136
East North Central	1,346	57	43	1,246
West North Central	1,092	25	2	1,065
South Atlantic	4,764	115	474	4,173
East South Central	4,027	34	3	3,990
West South Central	5,124	41	85	4,998
Mountain	1,452	65	7	1,379
Pacific[b]	7,545	120	590	6,832
PERCENT OF TOTAL	100.0%	100.0%	100.0%	100.0%
New England	8.6%	47.5%	15.2%	6.7%
Middle Atlantic	10.9	11.8	11.0	10.9
East North Central	4.3	5.1	2.6	4.3
West North Central	3.5	2.2	0.1	3.7
South Atlantic	15.1	10.2	29.0	14.5
East South Central	12.8	3.1	0.2	13.9
West South Central	16.3	3.7	5.2	17.4
Mountain	4.6	5.8	0.5	4.8
Pacific[b]	23.9	10.7	36.1	23.8

Source: Department of Defense, Washington Headquarters Services, Information Technology Management Directorate.
a Includes contracts with other government agencies.
b Includes Alaska and Hawaii.

MILITARY AIRCRAFT PROGRAMS
RESEARCH, DEVELOPMENT, TEST, AND EVALUATION[a]
BY AGENCY AND MODEL
Fiscal Years 2003, 2004, and 2005
(Millions of Dollars)

Agency and Model	2003	2004[E]	2005[E]
AIR FORCE			
B-1B Lancer	$ 150.4	$ 87.9	$ 59.5
B-2 Spirit	232.1	165.9	245.0
B-52 Stratofortress	52.0	28.4	25.8
C-5 Galaxy	273.8	346.5	333.0
C-17 Globemaster III	155.8	183.9	199.7
C-130J Hercules	132.2	117.9	186.5
E-3 AWACS	163.7	267.8	288.8
E-4B Sentry	47.4	44.0	11.2
E-8C JSTARS	62.1	57.8	89.2
F-15E Eagle	70.7	122.4	115.2
F-16 Falcon	77.6	96.1	99.6
F-22 Raptor	909.3	928.6	564.5
F-117A Nighthawk	3.7	14.6	29.7
KC-10 Extender	20.1	2.3	18.5
Multi-Sensor C2 Aircraft	—	—	538.9
U-2 Dragon Lady	24.1	46.6	87.7
ARMY			
AH-64D Longbow Apache	$ 44.4	$ 1.7	$ —
CH-47 Chinook	3.3	14.1	12.9
*RAH-66 Comanche	865.6	1,068.0	—
UH-60 Black Hawk	112.0	156.6	67.6
DEFENSE AIRBORNE RECONNAISSANCE OFFICE			
UAVs[b]	$ 748.1	$ 805.4	$1,364.1
NAVY			
AV-8B Harrier	$ 17.7	$ 8.6	$ 12.3
E-2C Hawkeye	107.0	343.3	597.0
EA-6B Prowler	53.9	35.4	34.0
EA-18 Growler	—	—	357.5
F/A-18 Hornet	204.1	173.7	134.6
H-1 Super Cobra	232.2	91.0	90.4
*JSF[c]	3,274.3	4,251.7	4,571.9
MH-60R Strikehawk	89.9	76.1	78.8
MH-60S KnightHawk	23.2	58.5	81.2
P-3 Modernization/MMA	66.5	86.0	505.6
V-22 Osprey	444.1	505.4	395.4
VH-XX Executive Helo	—	195.2	777.4

Source: Department of Defense Budget, "Program Acquisition Costs by Weapon System" (Annually) and "RDT&E Programs (R-1)" (Annually).

NOTE: See Aircraft Production Chapter for aircraft program procurement authorization data.
  a Total Obligational Authority.
  b Air Force, Navy, and Army funding.
  c Air Force and Navy funding.
  * Programs in R&D only.

EMPLOYMENT AND COST OF R&D SCIENTISTS AND ENGINEERS
ALL INDUSTRIES AND AEROSPACE INDUSTRY
Calendar Years 1979–2003

Year	Employment[a]			Cost Per R&D Scientist and Engineer[d]	
	All Industries[b] (Thousands)	Aerospace[c] (Thousands)	Aerospace as a Percent of All Industries	All Industries[b]	Aerospace[c]
1979	423.9	86.5	20.4%	$ 87,400	$ 93,300
1980	450.6	85.9	19.1	94,900	101,600
1981	487.8	95.2	19.5	103,900	128,400
1982	509.8	91.1	17.9	111,600	148,800
1983	540.9	103.1	19.1	116,000	143,600
1984	584.1	111.5	19.1	124,000	156,000
1985	622.5	130.2	20.9	130,200	161,700
1986	671.0	144.8	21.6	128,500	149,800
1987	695.8	136.3	19.6	128,800	180,400
1988	708.6	136.4	19.2	132,300	193,300
1989	722.5	134.8	18.7	134,500	207,300
1990	743.6	115.3	15.5	141,300	213,700
1991	773.4	100.2	13.0	148,600	177,000
1992	779.3	92.9	11.9	157,912	180,552
1993	764.7	97.9	12.8	153,336	176,450
1994	768.5	72.8	9.5	157,459	186,898
1995	746.1	63.5	8.5	167,339	213,328
1996	832.8	95.5	11.5	168,362	170,733
1997	885.7	94.6	10.7	171,499	208,217
1998	951.5	77.0	8.1	173,589	228,159
1999	997.7	66.4	6.7	179,997	237,058
2000	1,033.7	55.3	5.3	192,327	256,692
2001	1,041.3	25.1	2.4	188,917	356,018
2002	1,060.2	19.1	1.8	179,475	374,186
2003	1,066.1	32.5	3.0	NA	NA

Source: National Science Foundation.

a Employment as of January. Scientists and engineers working less than full time have been included in terms of their full time equivalent number.

b All manufacturing industries and those non-manufacturing industries known to conduct or finance research and development.

c Companies classified in NAICS code 3364, having as their principal activity the manufacture of aerospace products and parts. Prior to 1999, data categorized using SIC system and reported combining codes 372 and 376.

d The arithmetic mean of the numbers of R&D scientists and engineers reported for January in two consecutive years, divided into the total R&D expenditures of each industry during the earlier year.

Even as the manufacturing sector as a whole saw total trade increase, aerospace trade declined in 2003. Trade balances for both groups worsened, with the aerospace trade surplus down by $2.4 billion despite a decline in imports.

Aerospace exports, at $53 billion, constituted 7.3% of the total value of U.S.-exported merchandise. Three years ago, when aerospace exports recently bottomed at $55 billion, aerospace accounted for 7.0%; and five years ago that percentage recently peaked at 9.4% of merchandise exports.

Civil products comprised 84% of the total value of aerospace exports in 2003. Reduced by declining commercial transport production, civil exports decreased $3.3 billion to $44 billion. Declines in general aviation aircraft exports and aircraft engine parts exports compounded the effect of the $2.2 billion fewer jetliner exports.

Military products, which constituted 16% of aerospace exports, decreased to $8.4 billion. While military parts exports increased $0.3 billion, complete aircraft declined by roughly half. In particular, fighter/bomber exports dropped to nothing and helicopter exports fell 81% after rebounding 67% in 2002.

Aerospace imports fell $1.8 billion to $25 billion. Accounting for much of the decline, aircraft engine imports fell 33%, or $1.3 billion, to $2.5 billion. Imports of commercial transport aircraft also declined in 2003 from 136 to 124. In 2003, the value of imported jetliners fell to $4.1 billion. Similarly, general aviation aircraft imports, in dollars, decreased 5.4% last year.

The Japan was the largest importer of U.S. aerospace exports—$6.0 billion in 2003. The next five largest in order were: United Kingdom, $4.8 billion; France, $3.8 billion; Singapore, $3.4 billion; Canada, $3.1 billion; and Germany, $2.7 billion. Five of these six countries, which imported a total of $20 billion of U.S. aerospace exports, are also leading aerospace producers. The U.S. imported from Canada, $7.7 billion; France, $6.3 billion; United Kingdom, $3.1 billion; Germany, $1.9 billion; and Japan, $1.4 billion. Their combined aerospace exports to the United States totaled $21 billion, indicating a somewhat balanced trade between aerospace-producing countries in aggregate.

The Export-Import Bank of the United States (Eximbank) promotes U.S. exports by offering foreign customers loans and loan guarantees competitive with the official export credit organizations of our foreign competitors. In FY 2003, Eximbank loans and guarantees enabled the purchase of 74 jet aircraft worth $5.1 billion—up from the 60 jet aircraft worth $3.1 billion in FY 2001, but down from the 123 jet aircraft worth $7.6 billion in FY 1999.

U.S. TOTAL AND AEROSPACE FOREIGN TRADE[a]
Calendar Years 1969–2003
(Millions of Dollars)

Year	Total U.S. Merchandise Trade			Aerospace		
	Trade Balance	Exports	Imports	Trade Balance	Exports	Imports
1969	$ 1,289	$ 37,332	$ 36,043	$ 2,831	$ 3,138	$ 307
1970	3,225	43,176	39,952	3,097	3,405	308
1971	(1,476)[b]	44,087	45,563	3,830	4,203	373
1972	(5,729)	49,854	55,583	3,230	3,795	565
1973	2,390	71,865	69,476	4,360	5,142	782
1974	(3,884)	99,437	103,321	6,350	7,095	745
1975	9,551	108,856	99,305	7,045	7,792	747
1976	(7,820)	116,794	124,614	7,267	7,843	576
1977	(28,353)	123,182	151,534	6,850	7,581	731
1978	(30,205)	145,847	176,052	9,058	10,001	943
1979	(23,922)	186,363	210,285	10,123	11,747	1,624
1980	(19,696)	225,566	245,262	11,952	15,506	3,554
1981	(22,267)	238,715	260,982	13,134	17,634	4,500
1982	(27,510)	216,442	243,952	11,035	15,603	4,568
1983	(52,409)	205,639	258,048	12,619	16,065	3,446
1984	(106,703)	223,976	330,678	10,082	15,008	4,926
1985	(117,712)	218,815	336,526	12,593	18,725	6,132
1986	(138,279)	227,159	365,438	11,826	19,728	7,902
1987	(152,119)	254,122	406,241	14,575	22,480	7,905
1988	(118,526)	322,426	440,952	17,860	26,947	9,087
1989	(109,399)	363,812	473,211	22,083	32,111	10,028
1990	(101,718)	393,592	495,311	27,282	39,083	11,801
1991	(66,723)	421,730	488,453	30,785	43,788	13,003
1992	(84,501)	448,164	532,665	31,356	45,018	13,662
1993	(115,568)	465,091	580,659	27,235	39,418	12,183
1994	(150,630)	512,626	663,256	25,010	37,373	12,363
1995	(158,801)	584,742	743,543	21,561	33,071	11,509
1996	(170,214)	625,075	795,289	26,602	40,270	13,668
1997	(180,522)	689,182	869,704	32,239	50,374	18,134
1998	(229,758)	682,138	911,896	40,960	64,071	23,110
1999	(328,821)	695,797	1,024,618	37,381	62,444	25,063
2000	(436,104)	781,918	1,218,022	26,734	54,679	27,944
2001	(411,899)	729,100	1,140,999	26,035	58,508	32,473
2002	(468,263)	693,103	1,161,366	29,533	56,775	27,242
2003	(535,455)	724,030	1,259,485	27,111	52,504	25,393

Source: Bureau of the Census, Foreign Trade Division and Aerospace Industries Association, based on data from International Trade Administration.

NOTE: The Commerce Department began reporting international trade using the Harmonized Tariff Schedules of the United States in 1989. Previous years based on the Tariff Schedules of the United States Annotated.

a Total U.S. and aerospace foreign trade are reported as (1) exports of domestic merchandise, including Department of Defense shipments and undocumented exports to Canada, free alongside-ship basis, (2) imports for consumpti□□□ customs value basis.

b First U.S. trade deficit since 1888.

TOTAL U.S. EXPORTS AND EXPORTS OF AEROSPACE PRODUCTS
Calendar Years 1969–2003
(Millions of Dollars)

Year	Total Exports of U.S. Merchandise[a]	TOTAL	Percent of Total U.S. Exports	Civil Total	Trans-ports	Military
1969	$ 37,332	$ 3,138	8.4%	$ 2,027	$ 947	$ 1,111
1970	43,176	3,405	7.9	2,516	1,283	889
1971	44,087	4,203	9.5	3,080	1,567	1,123
1972	49,854	3,795	7.6	2,954	1,119	841
1973	71,865	5,142	7.2	3,788	1,664	1,354
1974	99,437	7,095	7.1	5,273	2,655	1,822
1975	108,856	7,792	7.2	5,324	2,397	2,468
1976	116,794	7,843	6.7	5,677	2,468	2,166
1977	123,182	7,581	6.2	5,049	1,936	2,532
1978	145,847	10,001	6.9	6,018	2,558	3,983
1979	186,363	11,747	6.3	9,772	4,998	1,975
1980	225,566	15,506	6.9	13,248	6,727	2,258
1981	238,715	17,634	7.4	13,312	7,180	4,322
1982	216,442	15,603	7.2	9,608	3,834	5,995
1983	205,639	16,065	7.8	10,595	4,683	5,470
1984	223,976	15,008	6.7	9,659	3,195	5,350
1985	218,815	18,725	8.6	12,942	5,518	5,783
1986	227,159	19,728	8.7	14,851	6,276	4,875
1987	254,122	22,480	8.8	15,768	6,377	6,714
1988	322,426	26,947	8.4	20,298	8,766	6,651
1989	363,812	32,111	8.8	25,619	12,313	6,492
1990	393,592	39,083	9.9	31,517	16,691	7,566
1991	421,730	43,788	10.4	35,548	20,881	8,239
1992	448,164	45,018	10.0	36,906	22,379	8,111
1993	465,091	39,418	8.5	31,823	18,146	7,596
1994	512,626	37,373	7.3	30,050	15,931	7,322
1995	584,742	33,071	5.7	25,079	10,606	7,991
1996	625,075	40,270	6.4	29,477	13,624	10,792
1997	689,182	50,374	7.3	40,075	21,028	10,299
1998	682,138	64,071	9.4	51,999	29,168	12,072
1999	695,797	62,444	9.0	50,624	25,694	11,820
2000	781,918	54,679	7.0	45,566	19,615	9,113
2001	729,100	58,508	8.0	49,371	22,151	9,137
2002	693,103[r]	56,775	8.2	47,348	21,661	9,427
2003	724,030	52,504	7.3	44,060	19,434	8,445

Source: Bureau of the Census, Foreign Trade Division and Aerospace Industries Association, based on data from International Trade Administration.
NOTE: International trade reported using Harmonized Tariff Schedules after 1988.
a Includes DoD shipments and undocumented exports to Canada, free alongside-ship basis.

U.S. EXPORTS OF AEROSPACE PRODUCTS[a]
BY MAJOR COUNTRIES OF DESTINATION
Calendar Years 1999–2003
(Millions of Dollars)

Country of Destination	1999	2000	2001	2002	2003
Australia	$1,426	$1,284	$1,112	$3,182	$2,356
Brazil	1,575	1,636	2,473	1,867	1,373
Canada	3,438	3,747	4,071	3,321	3,133
China	2,491	1,794	2,591	3,526	2,684
France	5,322	4,691	5,248	5,566	3,798
Germany	4,325	4,581	4,417	2,991	2,733
Ireland	650	731	778	844	1,004
Israel	1,789	877	1,275	954	925
Italy	1,426	873	823	1,854	1,820
Japan	5,401	4,257	3,795	5,071	5,966
Korea, South	1,899	2,157	2,844	2,742	2,062
Mexico	571	518	778	609	881
Netherlands	1,566	1,796	1,285	1,438	2,544
Saudi Arabia	3,299	1,960	1,432	315	438
Singapore	2,069	1,387	4,160	3,500	3,352
Spain	1,305	1,381	720	663	569
Sweden	1,295	1,347	608	494	453
Taiwan	2,237	1,622	1,609	1,114	1,283
Turkey	957	1,307	842	1,033	408
United Kingdom	7,845	6,478	6,536	4,319	4,772

Source: Aerospace Industries Association, based on data from the International Trade Administration.
a Includes all civil products, free alongside-ship basis; excludes military products whose country of destination are not reported.

U.S. IMPORTS OF AEROSPACE PRODUCTS[a]
BY MAJOR COUNTRIES OF ORIGIN
Calendar Years 1999–2003
(Millions of Dollars)

Country of Origin	1999	2000	2001	2002	2003
Australia	$ 144	$ 109	$ 137	$ 125	$ 123
Brazil	1,285	1,494	1,973	1,868	1,861
Canada	5,087	6,253	7,985	7,003	7,709
France	6,313	8,071	8,721	7,591	6,306
Germany	2,707	3,364	3,775	2,488	1,869
Israel	428	515	576	589	561
Italy	736	506	527	711	418
Japan	1,710	1,614	1,986	1,507	1,410
Korea, South	186	195	302	214	203
Mexico	158	149	162	399	354
Netherlands	161	173	173	167	168
Singapore	87	96	122	126	124
Sweden	147	132	159	127	108
Switzerland	164	164	174	170	154
United Kingdom	4,968	4,197	4,818	3,600	3,084

Source: Aerospace Industries Association, based on data from the International Trade Administration.
a Includes civil and military products, c.i.f. (Cost, Insurance, and Freight) basis.

U.S. EXPORTS OF AEROSPACE PRODUCTS
Calendar Years 2000–2003
(Millions of Dollars)

Use and Type	2000	2001	2002	2003
TOTAL...................................	$54,679	$58,508	$56,775	$52,504
CIVIL—TOTAL............................	$45,566	$49,371	$47,348	$44,060
Complete Aircraft—TOTAL.........	$22,156	$24,787	$25,617	$22,682
Transports..................................	19,615	22,151	21,661	19,434
General Aviation[a].......................	1,136	1,357	1,180	909
Helicopters.................................	170	170	116	203
Used Aircraft..............................	1,208	1,078	2,640	2,111
Other, incl. Spacecraft[b].............	167	188	351	218
Aircraft Engines—TOTAL...........	4,610	5,258	4,347	4,367
Turbine Engines..........................	4,510	5,142	4,226	4,244
Piston Engines...........................	101	116	121	123
Aircraft and Engine Parts incl. Spares—TOTAL..................	18,660	19,169	17,054	16,818
Aircraft Parts & Accessories.......	12,289	12,606	10,815	10,907
Aircraft Engine Parts..................	6,371	6,563	6,239	5,911
MILITARY—TOTAL......................	$ 9,113	$ 9,137	$ 9,427	$ 8,445
Complete Aircraft—TOTAL[c]........	$ 2,556	$ 2,096	$ 1,574	$ 746
Fighters & Fighter Bombers.......	1,287	339	366	—
Transports..................................	408	645	—	—
Helicopters.................................	594	572	957	178
Used Aircraft..............................	85	247	205	456
Other, incl. Spacecraft[b].............	303	432	348	252
Aircraft Engines—TOTAL...........	333	281	310	333
Turbine Engines..........................	248	147	230	229
Piston Engines...........................	85	134	80	104
Aircraft and Engine Parts incl. Spares—TOTAL..................	5,049	5,503	6,063	6,341
Aircraft Parts & Accessories.......	4,151	4,602	4,657	4,838
Aircraft Engine Parts..................	898	901	1,405	1,502
Guided Missiles, Rockets, & Parts—TOTAL............................	1,053	1,119	1,178	884
Guided Missiles & Rockets.........	402	223	244	290
Missile & Rocket Parts...............	643	893	919	579
Missile & Rocket Engines...........	9	3	15	15
Missile & Rocket Engine Parts...	—	—	—	—

Source: Aerospace Industries Association, based on data from International Trade Administration.
    a All fixed-wing aircraft under 33,000 pounds.
    b Products within this category are not designated civil or military by the Harmonized Tariff Schedules. Historically, aircraft herein have been predominantly civil. Also, spacecraft not included in "Complete Aircraft—Total."
    c Includes aircraft exported under Military Assistance Programs and Foreign Military Sales.

U.S. IMPORTS OF AEROSPACE PRODUCTS
Calendar Years 2000–2003
(Millions of Dollars)

Use and Type	2000	2001	2002	2003
TOTAL.....................................	$27,944	$32,473	$27,242	$25,393
CIVIL—TOTAL...............................	$21,994	$25,670	$21,334	$20,393
Complete Aircraft—TOTAL	$12,388	$14,709	$12,647	$12,329
Transports	5,560	6,686	4,576	4,059
General Aviation.............................	5,005	6,283	6,384	6,040
Helicopters	489	419	332	367
Other, including Used Aircraft, & Gliders, Balloons, & Airships[a]........	1,334	1,321	1,355	1,862
Aircraft Engines—TOTAL	1,864	2,418	1,887	1,259
Turbine Engines[b]...........................	1,846	2,394	1,845	1,232
Piston Engines	17	23	42	27
Aircraft & Engine Parts—TOTAL ...	7,742	8,543	6,800	6,805
Aircraft Parts and Accessories[b].....	4,679	5,250	3,948	4,011
Turbine Engine Parts[b]	2,554	2,880	2,440	2,389
Piston Engine Parts........................	121	147	136	135
Spacecraft, Other Parts & Accessories[bc]..............................	389	266	276	270
MILITARY—TOTAL	$ 5,951	$ 6,804	$ 5,908	$ 5,000
Complete Aircraft—TOTAL.............	$ 11	$ 2	$ 33	$ 5
Aircraft Engines—TOTAL	1,884	2,432	1,915	1,288
Turbine Engines[b]...........................	1,846	2,394	1,845	1,232
Piston Engines including Parts.......	38	37	70	57
Aircraft & Engine Parts—TOTAL....	4,056	4,370	3,960	3,707
Aircraft Parts[b]...............................	1,129	1,216	1,202	1,057
Turbine Engine Parts[b]	2,543	2,856	2,430	2,403
Spacecraft, Missiles, Rockets, Other Parts, & Accessories[bc]	384	298	329	247

Source: Aerospace Industries Association, based on data from International Trade Administration.
 a Products within this category are not designated civil or military by the Harmonized Tariff Schedules. Historically, these products have been predominantly civil.
 b Category contains products whose use (civil or military) is unspecified by the Harmonized Tariff Schedules. Figures for those products distributed equally between civil and military.
 c Includes satellites, propulsion engines, and parts.

U.S. EXPORTS OF MILITARY AIRCRAFT[a]
Calendar Years 1999–2003

Type of Aircraft	1999	2000	2001	2002	2003
NUMBER OF AIRCRAFT	309	344	260	264	203
Fighters and Fighter Bombers	68	36	13	14	—
Transports	17	8	3	—	—
Helicopters	75	63	37	64	48
New Aircraft, NEC	66	88	96	52	61
Used or Rebuilt Aircraft	83	149	111	134	94
VALUE (Millions of Dollars)	$4,221	$2,556	$2,096	$1,574	$ 746
Fighters and Fighter Bombers	$2,543	$1,287	$ 339	$ 366	$ —
Transports	878	408	645	—	—
Helicopters	358	594	572	957	178
New Aircraft, NEC	140	181	293	47	111
Used or Rebuilt Aircraft	303	85	247	205	456

Source: Aerospace Industries Association, based on data from the International Trade Administration.
  a Includes aircraft exported under Military Assistance Programs and Foreign Military Sales.
NEC Not elsewhere classified.

U.S. EXPORTS OF CIVIL AIRCRAFT
Calendar Years 1999–2003

Type and Size	1999	2000	2001	2002	2003
NUMBER OF AIRCRAFT[a]	1,451	1,472	1,480	1,341	1,715
Helicopters—TOTAL	181	304	309	294	399
Under 2,200 lbs	147	259	277	259	356
Over 2,200 lbs	34	45	32	35	43
General Aviation—TOTAL	503	411	446	321	349
Single-Engine	253	186	194	110	182
Multi-Engine, under 4,400 lbs	66	61	70	55	49
Multi-Engine, 4,400-10,000 lbs	113	60	52	41	42
Multi-Engine, 10,000-33,000 lbs	71	104	130	115	76
Transports—TOTAL	341	268	253	262	214
Passenger Aircraft, over 33,000 lbs	326	255	238	247	204
Cargo Aircraft, over 33,000 lbs	13	12	15	15	10
Other, over 33,000 lbs, incl. Pass./Cargo Combi	2	1	—	—	—
Other Aircraft—TOTAL[a]	426	489	472	464	753
Used or Rebuilt Aircraft	426	489	472	464	753
Other Aircraft, including Balloons, Gliders, & Kites	563	535	567	562	517
VALUE (Millions of Dollars)	$28,450	$22,156	$24,787	$25,617	$22,682
Helicopters—TOTAL	$ 137	$ 170	$ 170	$ 116	$ 203
Under 2,200 lbs	24	70	54	38	74
Over 2,200 lbs	113	120	116	78	129
General Aviation—TOTAL	1,309	1,136	1,357	1,180	909
Single-Engine	140	80	102	75	99
Multi-Engine, under 4,400 lbs	24	21	39	21	23
Multi-Engine, 4,400-10,000 lbs	519	227	199	139	172
Multi-Engine, 10,000-33,000 lbs	627	809	1,016	945	616
Transports—TOTAL	25,694	19,615	22,151	21,661	19,434
Passenger Aircraft, over 33,000 lbs	23,733	17,472	19,487	18,785	17,340
Cargo Aircraft, over 33,000 lbs	1,621	1,963	2,664	2,876	2,094
Other, over 33,000 lbs, incl. Pass./Cargo Combi	340	180	—	—	—
Other Aircraft—TOTAL[a]	1,311	1,235	1,109	2,660	2,136
Used or Rebuilt Aircraft	1,286	1,208	1,078	2,640	2,111
Other Aircraft, including Balloons, Gliders, & Kites	25	27	31	21	26

Source: Aerospace Industries Association, based on data from International Trade Administration.
a Numbers of gliders, balloons, & kites excluded from civil aircraft totals.

U.S. IMPORTS OF COMPLETE AIRCRAFT
Calendar Years 2000–2003

Use and Type	2000	2001	2002	2003
NUMBER OF AIRCRAFT	2,159	2,140	2,441	2,389
Civil Aircraft—TOTAL.........................	2,143	2,129	2,413	2,379
New Complete Aircraft:				
Helicopters	238	229	169	174
General Aviation:				
Single-Engine...............................	142	144	223	334
Multi-Engine, under 4,400 lbs	4	—	4	1
Multi-Engine, 4,400-10,000 lbs	7	14	25	10
Multi-Engine, Turbojet/Turbofan,				
10,000-33,000 lbs	286	345	343	320
Multi-Engine, Other, including				
Turboshaft, 10,000-33,000 lbs	21	16	2	—
Transports, Multi-Engine, over				
33,000 lbs.......................................	147	167	136	124
Other Civil Aircraft:				
Gliders[a]	133	122	158	154
Balloons & Airships[a]	75	80	44	132
Others including Kites[a]..................	849	739	1,041	879
Used or Rebuilt	241	273	268	251
Military Aircraft—TOTAL.....................	16	11	28	10
New Complete Aircraft	2	—	4	6
Used or Rebuilt	14	11	24	4
TOTAL VALUE (Millions of Dollars)	$12,399.1	$14,711.1	$12,680.2	$12,334.0
Civil Aircraft—TOTAL.........................	$12,388.3	$14,709.0	$12,647.2	$12,329.0
New Complete Aircraft:				
Helicopters	489.3	419.1	331.9	367.4
General Aviation:				
Single-Engine...............................	134.8	161.2	136.5	205.7
Multi-Engine, under 4,400 lbs	2.5	—	1.7	0.3
Multi-Engine, 4,400-10,000 lbs	15.0	35.8	70.0	29.4
Multi-Engine, Turbojet/Turbofan,				
10,000-33,000 lbs	4,647.8	5,879.4	6,141.3	5,805.0
Multi-Engine, Other, including				
Turboshaft, 10,000-33,000 lbs	205.0	206.4	34.1	—
Transports, Multi-Engine, over				
33,000 lbs.......................................	5,559.6	6,685.8	4,576.4	4,059.2
Other Civil Aircraft:				
Gliders[a]	2.3	2.0	3.1	1.8
Balloons & Airships[a]......................	8.2	9.9	6.7	6.5
Others including Kites[a]..................	9.5	9.0	7.2	3.8
Used or Rebuilt	1,314.4	1,300.4	1,338.2	1,849.9
Military Aircraft—TOTAL.....................	$ 10.9	$ 2.1	$ 33.0	$ 5.0
New Complete Aircraft	0.2	—	5.6	4.3
Used or Rebuilt	10.7	2.1	27.4	0.6

Source: Aerospace Industries Association, based on data from International Trade Administration.
   a Products within this category are not designated civil or military by the Harmonized Tariff Schedules. Historically, these
   products have been predominantly civil.

U.S. EXPORTS OF COMMERCIAL TRANSPORT AIRCRAFT[a]
Calendar Years 1999–2003

Region of Destination	1999	2000	2001	2002	2003
NUMBER OF AIRCRAFT	341	268	253	262	214
Canada & Greenland	4	—	9	12	11
Latin America & Caribbean	19	12	17	14	14
Europe	169	142	85	74	70
Middle East	55	38	28	26	14
Asia	81	57	81	87	79
Oceania	9	11	12	35	19
Africa	4	8	21	14	7
VALUE (Millions of Dollars)	$25,694	$19,615	$22,151	$21,661	$19,434
Canada & Greenland	$ 237	$ —	$ 510	$ 382	$ 373
Latin America & Caribbean	807	607	1,184	660	672
Europe	11,852	10,015	6,892	5,981	5,670
Middle East	3,797	2,231	2,570	2,130	1,277
Asia	7,872	5,618	8,818	9,384	9,363
Oceania	725	710	816	2,329	1,614
Africa	404	433	1,360	796	465

Source: Aerospace Industries Association, based on data from the International Trade Administration.
a Airframe weight exceeding 33,000 pounds.

U.S. EXPORTS OF CIVIL HELICOPTERS[a]
Calendar Years 1999–2003

Region of Destination	1999	2000	2001	2002	2003
NUMBER OF AIRCRAFT	181	304	309	294	399
Canada & Greenland	9	14	6	11	16
Latin America & Caribbean	25	55	59	13	22
Europe...	100	126	123	124	182
Middle East	1	4	16	53	20
Asia	25	60	46	35	32
Oceania...	17	23	49	46	71
Africa	4	22	10	12	56
VALUE (Millions of Dollars)...........	$136.6	$169.9	$169.7	$116.0	$202.9
Canada & Greenland	$ 4.8	$ 6.1	$ 2.0	$ 6.3	$ 18.8
Latin America & Caribbean	15.2	24.7	12.2	6.3	23.8
Europe...	56.4	60.8	53.7	35.2	64.3
Middle East	1.6	13.9	13.9	9.4	0.5
Asia	55.1	56.9	72.5	49.5	21.6
Oceania...	1.4	3.1	6.6	7.2	18.3
Africa	0.2	4.4	8.8	2.2	55.7

Source: Aerospace Industries Association, based on data from the International Trade Administration.
a Excludes used helicopters.

U.S. IMPORTS OF CIVIL HELICOPTERS[a]
Calendar Years 1999–2003

Country of Origin	1999	2000	2001	2002	2003
NUMBER OF AIRCRAFT	217	238	229	169	174
Canada	146	144	113	73	82
France	47	64	80	71	62
Germany	8	14	11	9	13
Italy	13	12	23	14	15
Others[b]	3	4	2	2	2
VALUE (Millions of Dollars)	$431.7	$489.3	$419.1	$331.9	$367.4
Canada	$330.0	$355.0	$267.4	$191.5	$194.8
France	50.0	60.1	70.4	88.5	100.6
Germany	20.3	38.0	29.2	22.0	35.9
Italy	31.4	35.3	50.8	26.2	35.8
Others[b]	0.1	0.9	1.4	3.6	0.3

Source: Aerospace Industries Association, based on data from the International Trade Administration.
a Excludes used helicopters.
b Includes 2 from Japan and 1 from New Zealand in 1999; 3 from Japan and 1 from Switzerland in 2000; 2 from Sweden in 2001; 1 from Japan and 1 from Sweden in 2002; and 2 from Japan in 2003.

U.S. EXPORTS OF GENERAL AVIATION AIRCRAFT[a]
Calendar Years 1999–2003

Region of Destination	1999	2000	2001	2002	2003
NUMBER OF AIRCRAFT	503	411	446	321	349
Canada & Greenland	22	39	33	32	30
Latin America & Caribbean	181	89	100	58	54
Europe...................................	189	180	191	134	160
Middle East	19	18	30	18	4
Asia......................................	26	23	41	22	25
Oceania.................................	32	26	18	33	48
Africa....................................	34	36	33	24	28
VALUE (Millions of Dollars).......	$1,309.0	$1,136.4	$1,357.0	$1,179.6	$908.9
Canada & Greenland .... $	54.6	$ 195.1	$ 141.4	$ 126.7	$ 71.8
Latin America & Caribbean	324.4	234.6	252.9	236.9	162.1
Europe...................................	571.3	449.4	612.9	436.5	437.0
Middle East	96.6	67.8	78.0	65.8	2.3
Asia......................................	97.8	103.2	170.2	113.5	71.1
Oceania.................................	55.7	15.6	30.5	127.3	77.9
Africa....................................	108.5	70.7	71.3	73.0	86.8

Source: Aerospace Industries Association, based on data from the International Trade Administration.
a All fixed-wing aircraft under 33,000 pounds.

U.S. IMPORTS OF GENERAL AVIATION AIRCRAFT[a]
Calendar Years 1999–2003

Country of Origin	1999	2000	2001	2002	2003
NUMBER OF AIRCRAFT	432	460	519	597	665
Brazil	84	92	117	115	100
Canada..	139	134	153	247	322
France	78	84	106	106	100
Germany	26	39	39	41	30
Israel	19	32	33	25	20
Poland	9	2	—	1	—
Russia	3	1	1	—	5
Sweden	1	—	—	—	—
Switzerland....................................	50	56	56	33	44
United Kingdom.............................	—	—	1	3	2
Other	23	20	13	26	42
VALUE (Millions of Dollars).......	$4,279.1	$5,005.0	$6,282.7	$6,383.7	$6,040.4
Brazil	$1,162.8	$1,411.5	$1,877.4	$1,828.3	$1,633.3
Canada..	1,737.5	1,839.8	2,603.3	2,800.2	3,097.9
France	1,015.8	1,201.4	1,160.3	1,256.2	986.0
Germany	97.6	191.3	209.0	74.0	2.8
Israel	135.1	234.6	283.8	264.6	189.6
Poland	1.3	0.2	—	0.1	—
Russia	0.4	0.1	0.1	—	2.0
Sweden	9.0	—	—	—	—
Switzerland....................................	112.7	119.6	128.3	89.7	96.2
United Kingdom.............................	—	—	0.0	4.1	3.8
Other	6.9	6.4	20.4	66.5	28.9

Source: Aerospace Industries Association, based on data from the International Trade Administration.
  a All fixed-wing aircraft under 33,000 pounds.

U.S. EXPORTS OF AIRCRAFT ENGINES
Calendar Years 2001–2003
(Values in Millions of Dollars)

Type of Engine	2001		2002		2003	
	Number	Value	Number	Value	Number	Value
TOTAL..................................	31,495	$5,539	22,140	$4,657	21,287	$4,701
Turbine Engines—TOTAL....	9,962	$5,289	8,711	$4,456	8,641	$4,473
Civil	8,717	5,142	7,627	4,226	6,898	4,244
Military.................................	1,245	147	1,084	230	1,743	229
Piston Engines—TOTAL......	21,533	250	13,429	202	12,646	227
Civil, New, under 500 HP ...	1,894	20	1,283	20	931	21
Civil, New, over 500 HP	830	18	1,339	22	613	8
Civil, Used...........................	8,568	78	3,451	79	4,619	94
Military.................................	10,241	34	7,356	80	6,483	104

Source: Aerospace Industries Association, based on data from the International Trade Administration.

U.S. IMPORTS OF AIRCRAFT ENGINES[a]
Calendar Years 2001–2003
(Values in Millions of Dollars)

Type of Engine	2001		2002		2003	
	Number	Value	Number	Value	Number	Value
TOTAL..................................	7,999	$4,826	7,928	$3,770	6,133	$2,513
Turbine Engines	3,375	$4,789	3,218	$3,690	2,805	$2,463
Piston Engines—TOTAL	4,624	38	4,710	80	3,328	50
Military................................	1,756	14	2,404	38	1,688	23
Civil, New, Small	1,342	4	812	5	203	1
Civil, New, Large	948	4	475	9	111	5
Civil, Used	578	15	1,019	29	1,326	21

Source: Aerospace Industries Association, based on data from the International Trade Administration.
   a New and used.

EXPORT-IMPORT BANK
TOTAL AUTHORIZATIONS OF LOANS AND GUARANTEES
AND AUTHORIZATIONS IN SUPPORT OF AIRCRAFT EXPORTS
Fiscal Years 1989–2003
(Millions of Dollars)

Year	Total Authorizations	Authorizations in Support of Aircraft Exports			
		TOTAL	Percent of Total Authorizations	Commercial Jet Aircraft[a]	Other Aircraft[b]
LOANS[c]					
1989	$ 695	$ 166.4	23.9%	$ 158.0	$ 8.4
1990	614	5.0	0.8	—	5.0
1991	777	—	—	—	—
1992	817	—	—	—	—
1993	1,748	—	—	—	—
1994	3,016	—	—	—	—
1995	1,598	—	—	—	—
1996	1,236	—	—	—	—
1997	1,549	—	—	—	—
1998	103	—	—	—	—
1999	903	590.8	65.4	590.8	—
2000	933	75.7	8.1	75.7	—
2001	871	—	—	—	—
2002	296	—	—	—	—
2003	58	5.6	9.6	—	5.6
GUARANTEES[d]					
1989	$1,292	$ 496.4	38.4%	$ 390.4	$ 106.0
1990	3,333	1,666.3	50.0	224.7	1,441.6
1991	6,034	606.0	10.1	566.9	40.0
1992	7,301	1,667.0	22.8	1,597.1	69.9
1993	9,095	3,488.6	38.4	3,488.6	—
1994	7,609	2,959.0	38.9	2,959.0	—
1995	5,712	977.0	17.1	977.0	—
1996	6,412	1,155.0	18.0	1,155.0	—
1997	7,761	1,959.0	25.2	1,959.0	—
1998	6,151	2,542.5	41.3	2,542.5	—
1999	8,299	5,543.8	66.8	5,543.8	—
2000	8,413	3,647.4	43.4	3,437.8	209.6
2001	6,101	2,736.5	44.8	2,540.5	196.0
2002	7,408	3,823.1	51.6	3,800.9	22.2
2003	7,745	4,647.7	60.0	4,419.9	227.8

Source: Export-Import Bank of the United States.
  a Includes complete aircraft, engines, parts, and retrofits.
  b Includes business aircraft, general aviation aircraft, helicopters, and related goods and services.
  c Loans are commitments for direct financing by the Export-Import Bank to foreign buyers of U.S. equipment and services, which are made to commercial banks and may subsequently be guaranteed by the Export-Import Bank, in which case the value of the loans is also included with Guarantees.
  d Guarantees by the Export-Import Bank provide assurances of repayment of principal and interest on loans made by private lending institutions, such as commercial banks, for major export transactions. Excludes insurance.

EXPORT-IMPORT BANK
SUMMARY OF COMMERCIAL JET AIRCRAFT AUTHORIZATIONS
FOR LOANS[a] AND GUARANTEES[b]
Fiscal Years 1976–2003
(Values in Millions of Dollars)

Year	No. of Jet Aircraft[c] Loans	No. of Jet Aircraft[c] Guarantees	Export Value[c] Loans	Export Value[c] Guarantees	No. of New Commitments Loans	No. of New Commitments Guarantees	Gross Authorizations Loans	Gross Authorizations Guarantees
New Authorizations:								
1976	77	6	$1,017	$ 139	34	11	$ 398	$ 87
Tr.Qtr.	15	5	219	182	6	3	94	59
1977	31	25	330	902	16	14	138	294
1978	29	5	479	253	18	5	189	77
1979	118	7	2,938	317	35	10	1,399	239
1980	136	21	3,975	901	36	24	1,693	1,088
1981	121	18	4,568	637	26	17	2,550	533
1982	11	6	441	113	5	2	199	78
1983	21	9	779	619	3	4	384	601
1984	37	8	1,023	327	7	4	532	294
1985	—	14	19	481	1	5	13	289
1986	3	13	74	451	1	9	46	277
1987	—	27	22	1,449	1	14	13	808
1988	—	2	—	94	—	2	—	73
1989	3	5	253	459	1	2	158	390
1990	—	6	—	264	—	2	—	225
1991	—	12	—	665	—	3	—	567
1992	—	37	—	1,889	—	12	—	1,597
1993	—	70	—	4,122	—	27	—	3,489
1994	—	59	—	3,507	—	19	—	2,959
1995	—	27	—	1,205	—	12	—	974
1996	—	18	—	1,089	—	8	—	923
1997	—	34	—	2,357	—	14	—	1,959
1998	—	65	—	3,059	—	24	—	2,543
1999	17	106	1,170	6,464	2	32	591	5,544
2000	5	53	150	4,047	2	17	76	3,438
2001	—	60	—	3,052	—	12	—	2,540
2002	—	72	—	4,370	—	17	—	3,801
2003	—	74	—	5,083	—	22	—	4,420

Source: Export-Import Bank of the United States.
a Loans are commitments for direct financing by the Export-Import Bank to foreign buyers of U.S. equipment and services, which are made by the Export-Import Bank to commercial banks and which subsequently may be guaranteed by the Export-Import Bank in which case the value of the loans is included with Guarantees.
b Guarantees by the Export-Import Bank provide assurances of repayment of principal and interest on loans made by private lending institutions, such as commercial banks, for major export transactions. Excludes insurance.
c For Export-Import Bank commitments including both loan and guarantee authorization, number of aircraft and export value reported under "Loans."

EXPORT-IMPORT BANK
AUTHORIZATIONS OF LOANS AND GUARANTEES
IN SUPPORT OF EXPORTS OF COMMERCIAL JET AIRCRAFT
Fiscal Years 2002–2003
(Values in Millions of Dollars)

Customer (Country/Airline)	Number and Aircraft Model or Related Product	Export Value	Authorizations				Guar-antees
			Loans (Direct Credits)				
			Amount	Percent Cover-age[a]	Interest Rate	Repay-ment Terms[b]	Amount
FY 2003							
TOTAL	74 aircraft	$5,083	$—	—%	—%	—	$4,420
Australia/Virgin Blue Airlines	~6 x 737	NA	—	—	—	—	$ 230
Bahrain/Bahrain Royal Flight	1 x 747	NA	—	—	—	—	108
Ethiopia/Ethiopian Airlines	2 x 737, 2 x 767	NA	—	—	—	—	226
Hong Kong/Cathay Pacific Airways	2 x 777	NA	—	—	—	—	305
India/Jet Airways	1 x 737	NA	—	—	—	—	39
Ireland/Ryanair...................	~13 x 737	NA	—	—	—	—	461
Italy/Alitalia.........................	6 x 777	NA	—	—	—	—	544
Kenya/Kenya Airways	2 x 737	NA	—	—	—	—	67
Korea/Korean Air Lines	NA	NA	—	—	—	—	404
Morocco/Royal Air Maroc ...	2 x 737	NA	—	—	—	—	66
Netherlands/KLM Royal Dutch Airlines	2 x 777	NA	—	—	—	—	216
Oman/Oman Air	1 x 737	NA	—	—	—	—	35
Pakistan/Pakistan International Airlines.......	3 x 777	NA	—	—	—	—	351
Panama/Compania Panamena de Aviation ...	6 x 737	NA	—	—	—	—	183
Romania/Tarom Romanian Air Transport	2 x 737	NA	—	—	—	—	78
Singapore/Singapore Airlines Cargo	2 x 747	NA	—	—	—	—	259
South Africa/SAFAIR..........	5 x 737	NA	—	—	—	—	173
Taiwan/China Airlines.........	3 x 747	NA	—	—	—	—	386
Uzbekistan/Uzbekistan Airways	1 x 767	NA	—	—	—	—	77
Vietnam/Vietnam Airlines ...	2 x 777	NA	—	—	—	—	210

(Continued on next page)

EXPORT-IMPORT BANK
AUTHORIZATIONS OF LOANS AND GUARANTEES
IN SUPPORT OF EXPORTS OF COMMERCIAL JET AIRCRAFT
Fiscal Years 2002–2003, continued
(Values in Millions of Dollars)

Customer (Country/Airline)	Number and Aircraft Model or Related Product	Export Value	Authorizations				Guar-antees
			Loans (Direct Credits)				
			Amount	Percent Cover-age[a]	Interest Rate	Repay-ment Terms[b]	Amount
FY 2002							
TOTAL	72 aircraft	$4,370	$—	—%	—%	—	$3,801
Algeria/Air Algerie	1 x 737	NA	—	—	—	—	$ 10
Australia/Quantas Airways	~12 x 737	NA	—	—	—	—	567
Austria/Austrian Airlines	NA	NA	—	—	—	—	203
Canada/WestJet Airlines	? x 737	NA	—	—	—	—	478
Ireland/Ryanair	~7 x 737	NA	—	—	—	—	221
Israel/El Al Isreal Airlines	1 x 777	NA	—	—	—	—	102
Korea/Asiana Airlines	1 x 747, 1 x 777	NA	—	—	—	—	93
Korea/Korean Airlines	NA	NA	—	—	—	—	411
Luxembourg/Cargolux Airlines International	1 x 747	NA	—	—	—	—	113
Malaysia/Ministry of Finance	NA	NA	—	—	—	—	617
Morocco/Royal Air Maroc	1 x 737	NA	—	—	—	—	36
Panama/Copa Airlines	3 x 737	NA	—	—	—	—	114
Taiwan/EVA Airways	1 x 747	NA	—	—	—	—	131
Thailand/Thai Airways International	2 x 747	NA	—	—	—	—	241
Turkey/Turkish Airlines	2 x 737	NA	—	—	—	—	68
Unallocable/GATX Financial Corporation	NA	NA	—	—	—	—	397

Source: Aerospace Industries Association, based on data from the Export-Import Bank of the United States.
NOTE: For definitions of Loans and Guarantees, see Export-Import Bank tables on previous pages.
a   Amount of loan as percent of export value.
b   Number of payments and frequency (S=semi-annual).

The aerospace industry, which employed 4.0% of all manufacturing and 6.5% of durable goods manufacturing workers, reduced its workforce in 2003 by 35,000. On an annual average basis, the aerospace industry employed 583,000 workers with an annual payroll of $29 billion. The aircraft sector employed 369,000, while the missiles and space sector employed 70,000, and the instruments manufacturing industry provided another 144,000 jobs.

Of the jobs lost in 2003, the aircraft and parts manufacturing sector accounted for 27,600 of them. Engine sector employment eased 5,300, while the complete aircraft manufacturing sector dropped 14,500, and the aircraft parts manufacturing cut 7,800. Also declining, the missiles and space sector's employment dropped by 4,000 and the instruments manufacturing industry employment fell by 4,000.

Earnings of production workers increased on average to $22.26 per hour, up from $21.46 in 2002. Production workers doing aircraft final assembly earned the highest hourly wage— $25.40. Production workers in the aircraft engine sector were

next with $23.51 per hour; followed by missiles and space workers, $21.41, instruments workers, $19.28, and aircraft parts workers, $18.36.

Workers in the engine sector logged the highest average overtime—6.1 hours per week, up from 6.0 in 2002. Similarly, these workers logged the longest average workweek—43.6 hours. This compares with 42.5 for other aircraft parts, 42.0 in the missiles and space sector, 40.7 for aircraft final assembly, and 40.0 for instruments.

The Bureau of Labor Statistics (BLS) reported that the hourly labor cost, including benefits, averaged $50.70 for all workers in the aircraft manufacturing industry. This was composed of $29.65 in wages and salaries and $21.05 in benefits.

The aerospace industry suffered one work stoppage in 2003. A total of 4,000 employees and 40,000 work-days went idle, according to statistics published by the BLS. The year before, three work-stoppages idled 7,500 workers and 118,100 work-days were lost.

National employment of R&D-performing scientists and engineers across all industries has steadily grown since 1995, while aerospace employment of R&D-performing scientists has steadily declined (until this year). In 1996, 95,500 R&D scientists and engineers found employment in the aerospace industry. By 2002, that number had dropped to 19,100. The aerospace share of national employment had fallen to the lowest level on record—just 1.8%. However, employment rebounded some in 2003, up to 32,500, or 3.0%, of national employment.

ANNUAL AVERAGE EMPLOYMENT IN ALL MANUFACTURING, DURABLE GOODS, AND AEROSPACE INDUSTRIES
Calendar Years 1979–2003
(Thousands)

Year	All Manu-facturing Industries	Durable Goods Industries	Aerospace Industry[a]		
				As Percent of	
			Total	All Manufac-turing	Durable Goods
1979	19,426	12,220	1,007	5.2%	8.2%
1980	18,733	11,679	1,080	5.8	9.2
1981	18,634	11,611	1,087	5.8	9.4
1982	17,363	10,610	1,038	6.0	9.8
1983	17,048	10,326	1,019	6.0	9.9
1984	17,920	11,050	1,058	5.9	9.6
1985	17,819	11,034	1,151	6.5	10.4
1986	17,552	10,795	1,241	7.1	11.5
1987	17,609	10,767	1,282	7.3	11.9
1988	17,906	10,969	1,294	7.2	11.8
1989	17,985	11,004	1,314	7.3	11.9
1990	17,695	10,736	1,121[b]	6.3	10.4
1991	17,068	10,219	1,040	6.1	10.2
1992	16,799	9,945	936	5.6	9.4
1993	16,774	9,900	825	4.9	8.3
1994	17,021	10,131	728	4.3	7.2
1995	17,241	10,372	673	3.9	6.5
1996	17,237	10,485	672	3.9	6.4
1997	17,419	10,704	714	4.1	6.7
1998	17,560	10,910	741	4.2	6.8
1999	17,322	10,830	709	4.1	6.5
2000	17,263	10,876	666	3.9	6.1
2001	16,441	10,335	661	4.0	6.4
2002[r]	15,259	9,483	618	4.1	6.5
2003	14,525	8,970	583	4.0	6.5

Source: Bureau of Labor Statistics and Aerospace Industries Association estimates.
    a See Glossary for detailed explanation of "Aerospace Employment."
    b BLS discontinued reporting employment-related statistics using the SIC in 2003; and now uses the NAICS. Prior years--back to 1990--revised for consistency.

ANNUAL PAYROLL[r]
OF ALL MANUFACTURING AND AEROSPACE INDUSTRIES
Calendar Years 1979–2003
(Millions of Dollars)

Year	All Manufacturing Industries[a]	Aerospace Industry[b]			Aerospace As Percent of All Manufacturing
		TOTAL	Production Workers	Other Workers	
1979	$335,200	$16,409	$ 6,926	$ 9,483	4.9%
1980	356,200	19,523	8,204	11,319	5.5
1981	387,600	21,558	8,733	12,825	5.6
1982	385,700	22,470	8,616	13,854	5.8
1983	400,700	23,437	8,646	14,790	5.8
1984	445,400	25,741	9,369	16,372	5.8
1985	468,500	28,964	10,538	18,426	6.2
1986	480,700	31,994	11,825	20,170	6.7
1987	496,900	33,677	12,534	21,143	6.8
1988	529,900	35,262	12,581	22,681	6.7
1989	547,900	36,982	13,327	23,655	6.7
1990	561,300	35,635	14,360	21,276	6.3
1991	562,300	34,643	13,839	20,804	6.2
1992	583,400	33,262	13,053	20,209	5.7
1993	592,300	30,521	11,821	18,700	5.2
1994	620,400	28,471	10,964	17,506	4.6
1995	647,400	26,696	10,267	16,430	4.1
1996	673,600	28,075	11,179	16,896	4.2
1997	717,600	31,687	13,374	18,313	4.4
1998[c]	675,200	33,083	14,084	18,999	4.9
1999	697,100	31,276	12,880	18,396	4.5
2000	749,300	31,490	12,347	19,143	4.2
2001	708,800	31,127	12,560	19,567	4.5
2002	675,200	29,772	11,306	18,466	4.4
2003	668,800	28,925	10,872	18,053	4.3

Source: Bureau of Economic Analysis, "Survey of Current Business" (Monthly) and Aerospace Industries Association estimates based on data from the Bureau of Labor Statistics.
a See Glossary for explanation of "Payroll, All Manufacturing."
b Based on combined annual average employment and average weekly earnings for SICs 372 and 376.
c Manufacturing as defined by NAICS. Prior years categorized by SIC.

EMPLOYMENT IN THE AEROSPACE INDUSTRY[ar]
Calendar Years 1990–2003
(Thousands)

Year (NAICS)	TOTAL, Aircraft, Missiles, Space Vehicles, & Parts, and Instruments	Aircraft, Engines, & Parts (3364AC)	Missiles, Space Vehicles, & Parts (3364MS)	Search, Detection, & Navigation Instruments (334511)
TOTAL EMPLOYMENT				
1990	1,121	672	169	280
1991	1,040	631	153	256
1992	936	577	133	226
1993	825	512	113	201
1994	728	454	98	175
1995	673	425	89	158
1996	672	432	82	158
1997	714	472	83	159
1998	741	495	84	163
1999	709	468	79	161
2000	666	438	78	149
2001	661	435	76	150
2002	618	397	74	148
2003	583	369	70	144
PRODUCTION WORKERS				
1990	547	360	53	135
1991	501	338	45	119
1992	446	304	37	105
1993	389	264	32	93
1994	340	232	29	80
1995	313	216	26	70
1996	317	226	24	67
1997	346	261	23	62
1998	361	275	23	63
1999	337	252	22	63
2000	304	227	21	56
2001	297	226	19	53
2002	263	204	16	44
2003	248	118	15	45

Source: Bureau of Labor Statistics and Aerospace Industries Association estimates.
Note: BLS discontinued reporting employment-related statistics using the SIC in 2003; and now uses the NAICS. Prior years--back to 1990--revised for consistency.
a Annual average. See Glossary for detailed explanation of "Aerospace Employment."

EMPLOYMENT IN THE AIRCRAFT, ENGINES, AND PARTS INDUSTRY[ar]

Calendar Years 1990–2003
(Thousands)

Year (NAICS)	TOTAL (3364AC)	Aircraft (336411)	Engines and Parts (336412)	Other Parts & Equipment (336413)
TOTAL EMPLOYMENT				
1990	672.2	389.7	147.6	134.9
1991	631.4	364.1	139.3	128.0
1992	577.3	339.1	123.2	115.0
1993	511.5	306.5	106.2	98.8
1994	454.3	275.3	92.5	86.5
1995	425.1	249.0	90.5	85.6
1996	432.0	249.4	92.1	90.6
1997	471.9	270.8	97.1	104.0
1998	495.0	281.5	100.5	113.0
1999	468.0	263.3	98.5	106.2
2000	438.4	242.7	98.1	97.6
2001	434.5	241.3	95.6	97.6
2002	396.7	220.2	87.9	88.6
2003	369.1	205.7	82.6	80.8
PRODUCTION WORKERS				
1990	359.6	192.7	86.6	80.3
1991	337.5	178.7	81.9	76.9
1992	304.1	162.6	72.1	69.4
1993	263.8	144.4	60.1	59.3
1994	232.0	127.3	52.6	52.1
1995	216.4	112.2	51.8	52.4
1996	226.4	114.7	54.7	57.0
1997	260.5	132.4	60.1	68.0
1998	274.6	138.9	60.6	75.1
1999	252.1	127.3	55.3	69.5
2000	227.2	110.3	54.1	62.8
2001	225.7	108.5	53.6	63.6
2002	203.7	97.2	49.9	56.6
2003	188.0	91.3	46.1	50.6

Source: Bureau of Labor Statistics.
Note: BLS discontinued reporting employment-related statistics using the SIC in 2003; and now uses the NAICS. Prior years--back to 1990--revised for consistency.
a Annual average. See Glossary for detailed explanation of "Aerospace Employment."

AVERAGE WEEKLY EARNINGS IN THE AEROSPACE INDUSTRY [r]
Production Workers Only
Calendar Years 1979–2003

| Year (NAICS) | TOTAL,[a] Aircraft, Missiles, Space Vehicles, & Parts, and Instruments | Aircraft and Parts (3364AC) | | | | Guided Missiles, Space Vehicles, & Parts (3364MS) | Search, Detection, & Navigation Instruments (334511) |
		TOTAL[a]	Aircraft (336411)	Engines & Parts (336412)	Other Parts & Equipment (336413)		
AVERAGE WEEKLY EARNINGS[b]							
1979	$351	$351	$360	$ 361	$322	$347	NA
1980	389	390	404	394	358	378	NA
1981	424	426	444	422	396	410	NA
1982	460	462	485	454	426	447	NA
1983	486	487	513	476	453	480	NA
1984	513	516	532	523	486	496	NA
1985	531	534	547	542	506	515	NA
1986	545	550	568	561	520	517	NA
1987	556	558	578	567	523	541	NA
1988	573	575	596	582	529	567	NA
1989	593	594	616	616	542	589	NA
1990[c]	608	631	660	655	533	582	$559
1991	632	656	695	673	546	601	574
1992	665	694	738	709	576	622	594
1993	691	722	761	735	615	659	614
1994	728	761	803	775	645	697	641
1995	732	764	812	792	634	716	637
1996	774	808	861	837	675	745	668
1997	818	851	919	863	708	792	687
1998	822	855	932	865	704	794	692
1999	816	849	923	883	686	803	687
2000	855	902	992	924	726	803	681
2001	882	929	1,025	955	744	848	694
2002	901	936	1,025	968	757	906	732
2003	927	963	1,033	1,025	780	942	771

Source: Bureau of Labor Statistics and Aerospace Industries Association estimates.
  a TOTAL columns are employment-based weighted averages.
  b Includes overtime premiums.
  c BLS discontinued reporting employment-related statistics using the SIC in 2003; and now uses the NAICS. Prior years--back to 1990--revised for consistency.

AVERAGE HOURLY EARNINGS IN THE AEROSPACE INDUSTRY[r]
Production Workers Only
Calendar Years 1979–2003

Year (NAICS)	TOTAL,[a] Aircraft, Missiles, Space Vehicles, & Parts, and Instruments	Aircraft and Parts (3364AC)				Guided Missiles, Space Vehicles, & Parts (3364MS)	Search, Detection, & Navigation Instruments (334511)
		TOTAL[a]	Aircraft (336411)	Engines & Parts (336412)	Other Parts & Equipment (336413)		

AVERAGE HOURLY EARNINGS[b]

Year (NAICS)	TOTAL,[a]	TOTAL[a]	Aircraft (336411)	Engines & Parts (336412)	Other Parts & Equipment (336413)	Guided Missiles (3364MS)	Search (334511)
1979	$ 8.26	$ 8.26	$ 8.50	$ 8.53	$ 7.48	$ 8.25	NA
1980	9.27	9.28	9.66	9.42	8.40	9.22	NA
1981	10.29	10.31	10.74	10.41	9.35	10.06	NA
1982	11.20	11.23	11.85	11.16	10.17	10.95	NA
1983	11.79	11.82	12.58	11.61	10.73	11.59	NA
1984	12.24	12.32	12.91	12.40	11.37	11.82	NA
1985	12.54	12.62	13.18	12.85	11.66	12.14	NA
1986	12.75	12.86	13.48	13.08	11.90	12.20	NA
1987	13.10	13.17	13.74	13.33	12.23	12.73	NA
1988	13.48	13.55	14.18	13.80	12.28	13.13	NA
1989	14.10	14.17	14.89	14.42	12.81	13.70	NA
1990[c]	14.34	14.84	15.73	15.28	12.22	13.69	$13.27
1991	15.06	15.64	16.77	15.83	12.83	14.24	13.72
1992	15.89	16.58	17.76	16.76	13.61	15.32	14.10
1993	16.53	17.28	18.51	17.19	14.36	15.93	14.63
1994	17.20	18.04	19.52	17.82	14.63	16.34	15.06
1995	17.27	18.14	19.96	17.85	14.55	16.43	14.87
1996	17.82	18.68	20.48	18.76	15.00	17.15	15.13
1997	18.25	18.96	20.76	19.12	15.31	18.23	15.31
1998	18.60	19.22	21.09	19.48	15.55	18.71	15.87
1999	19.02	19.70	21.79	20.04	15.61	18.91	16.31
2000	19.81	20.63	23.07	20.76	16.23	19.31	16.69
2001	20.57	21.36	24.06	21.27	16.83	19.92	17.46
2002	21.46	22.19	24.94	21.95	17.68	20.65	18.37
2003	22.26	23.04	25.40	23.51	18.36	21.41	19.28

Source: Bureau of Labor Statistics and Aerospace Industries Association estimates.
a TOTAL columns are employment-based weighted averages.
b Includes overtime premiums.
c BLS discontinued reporting employment-related statistics using the SIC in 2003; and now uses the NAICS. Prior years--back to 1990--revised for consistency.

AVERAGE HOURS IN THE AEROSPACE INDUSTRY [r]
Production Workers Only
Calendar Years 1990–2003

| Year (NAICS) | TOTAL,[a] Aircraft, Missiles, Space Vehicles, & Parts, and Instruments | Aircraft and Parts (3364AC) | | | | Guided Missiles, Space Vehicles, & Parts (3364MS) | Search, Detection, & Navigation Instruments (334511) |
		TOTAL[a]	Aircraft (336411)	Engines & Parts (336412)	Other Parts & Equipment (336413)		
AVERAGE WEEKLY HOURS							
1990	42.4	42.6	42.0	42.9	43.7	41.8	42.1
1991	42.0	42.0	41.5	42.5	42.6	42.1	41.8
1992	41.9	41.9	41.6	42.3	42.3	40.8	42.1
1993	41.8	41.9	41.1	42.8	42.8	41.2	42.0
1994	42.4	42.3	41.1	43.5	44.1	42.2	42.6
1995	42.4	42.3	40.7	44.4	43.6	42.4	42.8
1996	43.5	43.4	42.0	44.6	45.0	42.5	44.2
1997	44.8	45.0	44.3	45.1	46.3	42.5	44.9
1998	44.2	44.5	44.2	44.4	45.3	41.4	43.6
1999	42.8	43.2	42.4	44.1	43.9	40.8	42.1
2000	43.1	43.8	43.0	44.5	44.7	41.1	40.8
2001	42.7	43.6	42.6	44.9	44.2	41.0	39.7
2002	41.9	42.3	41.1	44.1	42.9	41.8	39.8
2003	41.6	41.9	40.7	43.6	42.5	42.0	40.0
AVERAGE WEEKLY OVERTIME HOURS							
1990	4.7	5.5	4.7	5.8	7.0	4.9	2.4
1991	4.2	4.8	4.4	5.0	5.4	4.1	2.4
1992	3.8	4.4	4.0	4.8	5.1	3.1	2.1
1993	3.9	4.7	4.0	5.0	5.9	3.2	2.0
1994	4.7	5.5	4.6	5.8	7.6	4.2	2.4
1995	5.2	6.0	4.7	6.5	8.2	4.3	3.0
1996	6.3	7.2	6.0	7.1	9.9	4.6	3.6
1997	7.7	8.7	8.0	7.4	11.4	5.7	4.0
1998	6.6	7.5	6.6	6.6	9.8	5.2	3.5
1999	5.1	5.5	4.7	5.9	6.8	6.3	3.0
2000	5.4	6.0	5.1	6.6	6.9	4.1	3.7
2001	5.2	5.7	4.6	6.7	6.9	3.8	3.2
2002	4.7	5.1	4.4	6.0	5.6	3.4	3.2
2003	4.7	5.3	4.8	6.1	5.5	3.9	2.7

Source: Bureau of Labor Statistics and Aerospace Industries Association estimates.
  a TOTAL columns are employment-based weighted averages.
Note: BLS discontinued reporting employment-related statistics using the SIC in 2003; and now uses the NAICS. Prior years--back to 1990--revised for consistency.

EMPLOYER COSTS FOR EMPLOYEE COMPENSATION IN THE AIRCRAFT MANUFACTURING INDUSTRY

March[a] 1999–2004

	1999	2000	2001	2002	2003	2004[b]
ALL OCCUPATIONS						
TOTAL	$35.33	$37.87	$40.09	$41.75	$45.85	$50.70
Wages and Salaries	24.28	25.47	26.79	27.80	28.71	29.65
Benefits—TOTAL	11.05	12.39	13.30	13.95	17.14	21.05
Paid Leave	3.34	3.51	3.69	3.82	4.02	4.28
Supplemental Pay	1.19	1.67	1.79	1.78	2.81	1.89
Insurance	2.60	2.67	3.13	3.51	4.18	4.50
Retirement & Savings	0.97	1.20	1.36	1.41	2.40	6.43
Legally Required	2.77	2.92	3.12	3.20	3.50	3.66
Other	0.18	0.42	0.21	0.22	0.23	0.29
WHITE-COLLAR OCCUPATIONS						
TOTAL	$38.12	$40.76	$43.63	$44.98	$49.04	
Wages and Salaries	26.88	28.31	29.68	30.64	31.59	
Benefits—TOTAL	11.24	12.44	13.95	14.34	17.45	
Paid Leave	3.71	4.04	4.22	4.36	4.60	NA
Supplemental Pay	0.71	0.81	1.56	1.28	2.24	
Insurance	2.60	2.69	3.19	3.60	4.19	
Retirement & Savings	1.12	1.32	1.50	1.56	2.55	
Legally Required	2.87	2.99	3.23	3.30	3.63	
Other	0.24	0.59	0.26	0.23	0.24	
BLUE-COLLAR OCCUPATIONS						
TOTAL	$30.56	$33.33	$34.18	$36.56	$40.77	
Wages and Salaries	19.84	20.94	22.00	23.26	24.11	
Benefits—TOTAL	10.72	12.39	12.18	13.30	16.67	
Paid Leave	2.70	2.66	2.81	2.95	3.08	NA
Supplemental Pay	2.02	3.13	2.18	2.59	3.77	
Insurance	2.60	2.61	3.02	3.35	4.14	
Retirement & Savings	0.73	1.02	1.10	1.15	2.13	
Legally Required	2.58	2.83	2.94	3.06	3.32	
Other	0.09	0.13	0.13	0.21	0.22	

Source: Bureau of Labor Statistics, "Employer Costs for Employee Compensation" (Annually).
a Based on the pay period including March 12th.
b Unpublished estimates from the BLS. White-collar vs. Blue-collar detail is no longer available since the conversion from SIC to NAICS in 2004.

WORK STOPPAGES IN THE AEROSPACE INDUSTRY
Calendar Years 1979–2003

Year	Number of Strikes[a]	Number of Workers Involved	Work-Days Idle in Year
1979	12	6,600	103,400
1980	17	4,400	92,900
1981	12	6,100	188,900
1982[b]	4	11,900	45,200
1983	2	8,700	404,100
1984	4	14,600	188,200
1985	4	19,700	289,800
1986	—	—	—
1987	—	—	—
1988	3	10,600	415,800
1989	2	58,500	1,848,000
1990	1	2,300	56,700
1991	1	1,500	—
1992	1	3,800	11,400
1993	2	27,800	34,600
1994	—	—	—
1995	1	33,000	1,551,000
1996	2	7,800	90,100
1997	—	—	—
1998	—	—	—
1999	—	—	—
2000	3	22,400	566,400
2001	1	5,000	45,000
2002	3	7,500	118,100
2003	1	4,000	40,000

Source: Bureau of Labor Statistics, "Compensation and Working Conditions" (Quarterly).
a Strikes beginning during calendar year.
b Effective 1982, data not available for work stoppages involving fewer than 1,000 employees.

OCCUPATIONAL INJURY AND ILLNESS INCIDENCE RATES[a]
ALL MANUFACTURING AND AEROSPACE INDUSTRIES
Calendar Years 1998–2002

Manufacturing Sector	1998	1999	2000	2001	2002
All Manufacturing:					
Total Cases	9.7	9.2	9.0	8.1	7.2
Lost Workday Cases	4.7	4.6	4.5	4.1	4.1
Nonfatal Cases Without Lost Workdays....	5.0	4.6	4.5	4.0	3.1
Aircraft and Parts (SIC 372):					
Total Cases	8.7	8.2	7.1	7.7	5.7
Lost Workday Cases	4.2	4.1	3.4	3.7	3.1
Nonfatal Cases Without Lost Workdays....	4.5	4.1	3.7	4.0	2.6
Aircraft (SIC 3721):					
Total Cases	8.9	8.9	7.5	7.4	5.7
Lost Workday Cases	4.3	4.4	3.7	3.8	3.3
Nonfatal Cases Without Lost Workdays....	4.6	4.5	3.7	3.7	2.4
Aircraft Engines and Parts (SIC 3724):					
Total Cases	6.2	5.8	5.5	6.4	3.7
Lost Workday Cases	2.8	2.9	2.2	2.8	1.8
Nonfatal Cases Without Lost Workdays....	3.4	2.9	3.3	3.6	1.9
Aircraft Parts (SIC 3728):					
Total Cases	10.0	8.7	7.6	9.1	7.4
Lost Workday Cases	5.0	4.4	3.7	4.2	3.8
Nonfatal Cases Without Lost Workdays....	5.0	4.3	3.9	4.9	3.6
Guided Missiles, Space Vehicles & Parts (SIC 376):					
Total Cases	3.3	2.8	2.2	2.9	1.6
Lost Workday Cases	1.5	1.3	1.1	1.6	0.9
Nonfatal Cases Without Lost Workdays....	1.8	1.5	1.1	1.3	0.7
Guided Missiles & Space Vehicles (SIC 3761):					
Total Cases	3.0	2.7	2.0	2.4	1.3
Lost Workday Cases	1.3	1.3	1.0	1.3	0.8
Nonfatal Cases Without Lost Workdays....	1.8	1.4	1.0	1.1	0.6
Space Propulsion Units & Parts (SIC 3764):					
Total Cases	3.2	NA	3.0	4.2	NA
Lost Workday Cases	1.6	NA	1.5	2.5	NA
Nonfatal Cases Without Lost Workdays....	1.7	NA	1.6	1.7	NA
Other Space Vehicle Equipment (SIC 3769):					
Total Cases	4.3	3.5	2.2	NA	1.8
Lost Workday Cases	2.6	1.6	1.1	NA	1.1
Nonfatal Cases Without Lost Workdays....	1.8	2.0	1.1	NA	0.7

Source: Bureau of Labor Statistics, "Survey of Occupational Injuries and Illnesses" (Annually).

a Defined as the number of injuries and illnesses per 100 full-time workers. Separate incidence rates also available for occupational injuries only.

EMPLOYMENT IN NATIONAL AERONAUTICS
AND SPACE ADMINISTRATION PROGRAMS
End of Fiscal Years 1966–2005

Year	TOTAL	NASA Employees	Contractor Employees[a]
1966	393,924	33,924	360,000
1967	306,926	33,726	273,200
1968	267,871	32,471	235,400
1969	218,345	31,745	186,600
1970	160,850	31,350	129,500
1971	143,578	29,478	114,100
1972	138,800	27,500	111,300
1973	134,850	26,850	108,000
1974	125,220	25,020	100,200
1975	127,733	24,333	103,400
1976	130,739	24,039	108,000
1977	124,136	23,636	100,500
1978	124,637	23,237	101,400
1979	131,931	22,831	109,100
1980	135,613	22,613	113,000
1981	133,473	21,873	111,600
1982	128,730	22,430	106,300
1983	129,246	22,246	107,000
1984	162,080	22,080	140,000
1985	131,991	21,991	110,000
1986	154,660	21,660	133,000
1987	165,001	22,001	143,000
1988	172,326	22,326	150,000
1989	213,054	23,054	190,000
1990	221,829	23,829	198,000
1991	223,149	24,149	199,000
1992	230,513	24,513	206,000
1993	228,674	24,174	204,500
1994	217,910	23,873	194,037
1995	209,355	22,355	187,000
1996	198,113	21,113	177,000
1997	189,070	20,070	169,000
1998	183,109	19,109	164,000
1999	181,469	18,469	163,000
2000	173,375	18,375	155,000
2001	172,678[r]	18,678	154,000[r]
2002	179,596	18,596	161,000
2003	174,709	18,709	156,000
2004[E]	174,906	18,906	156,000
2005[E]	178,417	19,417	159,000

Source: Office of Management and Budget, "Budget of the United States Government" (Annually) and NASA Headquarters.
a Includes estimates of manpower for hardware and related contracts, as well as actual work-years for support service contracts. Increase in FY 1984 caused by change in estimating methodology to reflect more accurately the mix of support and development contractors.

FEDERAL CIVILIAN EMPLOYMENT[a] IN THE DEPARTMENT OF DEFENSE
Fiscal Years 1969–2005

Year	TOTAL	Civil Functions[b]	Military Functions[c]
1969	1,257,091	31,214	1,225,877
1970	1,159,935	30,293	1,129,642
1971	1,092,804	30,063	1,062,741
1972	1,040,147	30,585	1,009,562
1973	987,281	29,971	957,310
1974	1,002,850	29,072	973,778
1975	983,790	29,069	954,721
1976	951,034	28,648	922,386
1977	940,549	28,912	911,637
1978	933,071	28,962	904,109
1979	914,582	28,592	885,990
1980	907,700	27,700	880,000
1981	981,400	34,400	947,000
1982	1,009,192	31,111	978,081
1983	1,015,622	30,816	984,806
1984	1,040,213	28,681	1,011,532
1985	1,065,624	28,754	1,036,870
1986	1,069,863	28,511	1,041,352
1987	1,059,669	28,352	1,031,317
1988	1,053,000	28,419	1,024,581
1989	1,051,166	28,081	1,023,085
1990	1,048,814	27,651	1,021,163
1991	1,001,183	27,385	973,798
1992	1,000,453	27,584	972,869
1993	958,855	27,055	931,800
1994	896,293	28,001	868,292
1995	849,529	27,790	821,739
1996	806,122	27,180	778,942
1997	771,914	26,164	745,750
1998	732,097	24,855	707,242
1999	705,826	24,830	680,996
2000	685,085	24,800	660,285
2001[r]	685,856	24,920	660,936
2002[r]	677,747	27,872	649,875
2003	668,591	25,780	642,811
2004[E]	673,436	26,088	647,348
2005[E]	675,218	25,986	649,232

Source: Office of Management and Budget, "The Budget of the United States Government" (Annually).
   a Full-time equivalent civilian employment.
   b Data are estimated for portions of Civil Functions.
   c The Department of Defense is exempt from full-time equivalent controls. Data shown are estimated civilian employment for military functions and military assistance.

The aerospace industry generated $7.2 billion in net income after taxes (net profit) on $172 billion of corporate sales last year. Net profit as a percentage of sales rose to 4.2%—the third lowest level since 1995. The corresponding profit margin for all manufacturing corporations was 5.4%—up sharply from 2002's 3.3% and 2001's 0.8%, but the third worst showing since 1993. Similarly, the aerospace industry's net profit as a percentage of shareholders' equity rose to 12.3%. Profits as a percentage of assets, however, declined to 3.3%. For comparison, prior year aerospace returns for equity and assets were 11.7% and 3.7%; and the averages for all manufacturing corporations in 2003 were 12.2% and 4.7%, respectively. Industry-wide working capital improved significantly in 2003.

The aerospace industry's capital equipment expenditures increased 13% to $2.8 billion in 2002, the latest data available. Missile/space sector investment recovered somewhat, rising to $496 million after sharply declining the prior two years. Meanwhile, the aircraft sector's capital equipment investment increased—up $201 million to $2.3 billion.

DoD awarded $43 billion in aircraft procurement contracts in FY 2003. The West South Central and New England regions received $5.8 billion and $2.6 billion more aircraft procurement contracts than they had in the previous year, respectively. South Atlantic, however, did much worse, booking $2.4 billion fewer orders than last year. Awards for missile and space systems increased $1.9 billion to $15 billion and electronics and communications equipment procurement increased $2.4 billion to $18 billion. Companies in the Pacific region received the most missile and space systems contracts, $6.6 billion, while companies in the South Atlantic region garnered the most electronics and communications equipment contracts, $5.9 billion.

Lockheed Martin retained its position as the DoD's largest contractor in FY 2003, winning $22 billion in prime contract awards or about 10% of all the available DoD prime contract dollars that year. The company's contract wins were 29% higher than in 2002 and it was the seventh year in a row that Lockheed Martin topped the DoD list. Boeing made the second spot for the seventh straight year, winning $17.3 billion worth of prime contracts. Rounding out the top ten DoD contractors were: Northrop Grumman, $11.1 billion; General Dynamics, $8.2 billion; Raytheon, $7.9 billion; United Technologies, $4.5 billion; Halliburton, $3.9 billion; General Electric, $2.8 billion; Science Applications International, $2.6 billion; and Computer Sciences, $2.5 billion. Together the top ten contractors accounted for 40% of the 2003 total prime contract dollars awarded, or more than $83 billion.

United Space Alliance topped NASA's contractor list in FY 2003 with awards totaling $1.8 billion. The Boeing Company ranked second with $898 million. At $624 million, Lockheed Martin Space Operations captured third. Other subsidiaries and affiliates of Lockheed Martin and The Boeing Company won additional contracts.

INCOME STATEMENT AND OPERATING RATIOS
FOR AEROSPACE COMPANIES[a]
Calendar Years 2000–2003
(Millions of Dollars)

INCOME STATEMENT	2000	2001	2002	2003
Net Sales, Receipts, Operating Revenues......	$154,877	$168,756	$159,581	$171,753
Less: Depreciation, Depletion, & Amortization of Property, Plant, and Equipment	4,330	3,895	3,581	3,850
Less: All Other Operating Costs & Expenses, including Selling Costs & General & Administrative Expenses...........................	137,714	152,182	143,066	157,499
Income (or Loss) from Operations	$ 12,833	$ 12,679	$ 12,934	$ 10,403
Net Non-Operating Income (Expense)...........	(1,886)	(4,059)	(153)	(1,896)
Income (or Loss) before Income Taxes (= Total Income)	$ 10,947	$ 8,618	$ 7,874	$ 8,504
Less: Provision for Current & Deferred Domestic Income Taxes	3,686	2,054	1,326	1,263
Income (or Loss) after Income Taxes (= Net Profit)..............................	$ 7,260	$ 6,565	$ 6,547	$ 7,243
Cash Dividends Charged to Retained Earnings	2,684	2,561	2,861	2,907
Net Income Retained in Business	$ 4,576	$ 4,003	$ 3,686	$ 4,336
Retained Earnings at Beginning of Year[b]	44,949	52,966	49,771	49,464
Adjustments to Retained Earnings[c]	(633)	(1,597)	(3,304)	(205)
Retained Earnings at End of Year[d]	$ 48,892	$ 55,373	$ 50,153	$ 53,595

OPERATING RATIOS

Income before Taxes as Percent of Net Sales	7.1%	5.1%	4.9%	5.0%
Provision for Current & Deferred Domestic Income Taxes as Percent of Income before Taxes (Total Income)........................	33.7	23.8	16.8	14.9
Income after Taxes (Net Profit) as Percent of Net Sales...	4.7	3.9	4.1	4.2
Income after Taxes (Net Profit) as Percent of Stockholders' Equity[f].............................	14.2	11.6	11.7	12.3
Income after Taxes (Net Profit) as Percent of Total Assets[f]	4.3	3.6	3.7	3.3

Source: Bureau of the Census, "Quarterly Financial Report for Manufacturing, Mining, and Trade Corporations" (Quarterly).
   a Based on sample of corporate entities classified in NAICS code 3364, having as their principal activity the manufacture of aerospace products and parts. Prior to 2001, data categorized using SIC system and reported combining codes 372 and 376.
   b Beginning-of-year retained earnings for any particular year do not equal end-of-year retained earnings for the previous year because of rotation of small companies in survey sample.
   c Other direct credits (or charges) to retained earnings (net), including stock and other non-cash dividends, etc.
   d Retained Earnings at End of Year CALCULATED AS Retained Earnings at Beginning of Year PLUS Income (Loss) after Income Taxes MINUS Cash Dividends Charged to Retained Earnings PLUS Adjustments to Retained Earnings.
   f Average of four quarters.

BALANCE SHEET FOR AEROSPACE COMPANIES[a]
As of December 31, 2000–2003
(Millions of Dollars)

	2000	2001	2002	2003
Assets:				
Current Assets:				
Cash	$ 2,969	$ 3,004	$ 8,083	$ 8,466
Securities, Commercial Paper, & Other				
Short-term Financial Investments	1,353	638	1,112	885
Total Cash and U.S. Government				
and Other Securities	$ 4,322	$ 3,642	$ 9,195	$ 9,351
Receivables (Total)	20,283	19,438	17,644	40,626
Inventories (Gross)	41,683	42,343	40,288	37,081
Other Current Assets	8,987	10,450	9,353	15,967
Current Assets—TOTAL	$ 75,275	$ 75,872	$ 76,481	$103,024
Net Plant, Property, & Equipment	28,274	28,722	27,567	27,808
Other Non-Current Assets	70,908	79,410	79,684	93,538
Assets—TOTAL	$174,457	$184,004	$183,732	$224,370
Liabilities:				
Current Liabilities:				
Short Term Loans	$ 3,901	$ 2,084	$ 1,637	$ 1,200
Trade Accounts & Notes Payable	11,758	10,458	9,184	11,421
Income Taxes Accrued	3,609	1,778	2,726	1,384
Installments Due on Long Term Debts	2,772	2,534	2,722	1,768
Other Current Liabilities	43,668	49,708	45,802	67,982
Current Liabilities—TOTAL	$ 65,709	$ 66,562	$ 62,071	$ 83,755
Long Term Debt	32,418	33,882	32,554	35,782
Other Non-Current Liabilities	23,840	27,054	40,330	42,126
Liabilities—TOTAL	$121,967	$127,497	$134,954	$161,662
Stockholders' Equity:				
Capital Stock	$ 3,276	$ 4,190	($ 1,838)	$ 9,206
Retained Earnings	49,214	52,318	50,615	53,502
Stockholders' Equity—TOTAL	$ 52,490	$ 56,508	$ 48,777	$ 62,708
Liabilities & Stockholders' Equity—TOTAL	$174,457	$184,004	$183,732	$224,370
Net Working Capital	$ 9,566	$ 9,311	$ 14,410	$ 19,269

Source: Bureau of the Census, "Quarterly Financial Report for Manufacturing, Mining, and Trade Corporations" (Quarterly).
a Based on sample of corporate entities classified in NAICS code 3364, having as their principal activity the manufacture of aerospace products and parts. Prior to 2001, data categorized using SIC system and reported combining codes 372 and 376.

NET PROFIT AFTER TAXES
AS A PERCENT OF SALES, ASSETS, AND EQUITY
FOR ALL MANUFACTURING CORPORATIONS
AND THE AEROSPACE INDUSTRY
Calendar Years 1989–2003

PERCENT OF SALES

Year	All Manufacturing Corporations	Non-Durable Goods	Durable Goods	Aerospace[a] Industry
1989	5.0%	5.8%	4.1%	3.3%
1990	4.0	4.9	3.0	3.4
1991	2.5	4.2	0.6	1.8[b]
1992	1.0	3.2	(1.4)	(1.4)[b]
1993	2.8	3.7	1.9	3.6
1994	5.4	5.5	5.2	4.7
1995	5.7	6.1	5.3	3.8
1996	6.0	6.6	5.5	5.6
1997	6.2	6.6	5.8	5.2
1998	6.0	6.1	5.9	5.0
1999	6.2	6.2	6.2	6.5
2000	6.1	6.9	5.4	4.7
2001	0.8	5.7	(3.3)	3.9
2002	3.3	6.0	1.1	4.1
2003	5.4	7.1	3.9	4.2

Year	Percent of Assets[c]		Percent of Equity[c]	
	All Manufacturing	Aerospace[a] Industry	All Manufacturing	Aerospace[a] Industry
1989	5.6%	3.3%	13.7%	10.7%
1990	4.3	3.4	10.7	11.5
1991	2.6	1.9[b]	6.4	6.1[b]
1992	1.0	(1.2)[b]	2.6	(5.2)[b]
1993	2.9	3.5	8.1	13.2
1994	5.8	4.3	15.6	14.8
1995	6.2	3.5	16.2	11.1
1996	6.5	5.1	16.8	17.1
1997	6.6	4.8	16.6	17.3
1998	6.1	4.8	15.7	18.0
1999	6.1	6.2	16.5	21.8
2000	5.9	4.3	15.2	14.2
2001	0.8	3.6	1.9	11.6
2002	2.9	3.7	7.7	11.7
2003	4.7	3.3	12.2	12.3

Source: Bureau of the Census, "Quarterly Financial Report for Manufacturing, Mining, and Trade Corporations" (Quarterly).
   a Based on a sample of corporate entities classified in NAICS code 3364, having as their principal activity the manufacture of aerospace products and parts. Prior to 2001, data categorized using SIC system and reported combining codes 372 and 376.
   b Reflects unusually large non-operating expenses totalling $3.4 and $8.7 billion in 1991 and 1992, respectively, due to restructuring changes and the implementation of a change in accounting for future retirement benefit costs.
   c Average of four quarters
   ( ) Net loss after taxes.

CAPITAL EXPENDITURES
Calendar Years 1968–2002
(Millions of Dollars)

Year	All Manufacturing Industries	Aerospace Industry[a]	Aircraft, Engines, & Parts	Missiles, Space Vehicles, & Parts
1968	$ 20,613	$ 399	$ 282	$ 117
1969	22,291	429	340	89
1970	22,164	244	181	62
1971	20,941	115	59	56
1972	24,073	261	169	92
1973	26,979	362	258	104
1974	35,696	407	283	124
1975	37,262	478	369	109
1976	40,545	557	431	126
1977	47,459	673	508	164
1978	55,209	948	775	174
1979	61,533	1,551	1,301	250
1980	70,113	1,923	1,618	306
1981	78,632	2,006	1,637	369
1982	74,562	2,142	1,680	462
1983	61,931	2,159	1,530	629
1984	75,186	3,050	2,091	960
1985	83,058	3,784	2,429	1,356
1986	76,355	4,145	2,818	1,327
1987	78,650	3,612	2,536	1,075
1988	81,593	3,388	2,362	1,026
1989	98,738	3,921	2,800	1,121
1990	105,018	3,490	2,621	869
1991	103,003	3,407	2,823	584
1992	103,188	3,860	3,384	476
1993	103,133	2,725	2,307	418
1994	112,784	2,363	1,969	395
1995	128,473	2,114	1,734	380
1996	139,323	2,513	2,023	490
1997[b]	151,511	3,132	2,380	752
1998	152,708	3,477	2,613	864
1999	150,325	3,422	2,338	1,084
2000[r]	154,479	2,326	1,894	432
2001	143,651	2,449	2,059	390
2002	144,617	2,756	2,260	496

Source: Bureau of the Census, "Annual Survey of Manufactures" (Annually).
  a Combined total for establishments in Aircraft, Missiles, Space Vehicles, and Parts Manufacturing.
  b Prior to 1997, figures included only new capital expenditures.

KEY OPERATING COSTS FOR SELECTED AEROSPACE
MANUFACTURING CENTERS
As of 2004

State	Location	Total Annual Operating Cost[a] (in Millions)	Hourly Labor Cost		
			Manufacturing	Technical	Clerical
AZ	Phoenix/Tempe	$35.11	$20.75	$34.10	$14.33
AZ	Tucson	33.37	19.79	32.50	13.79
CA	Chula Vista	38.39	21.92	36.04	16.61
CA	El Segundo/Long Beach/ Redondo Beach/Seal Beach/ Torrance	38.58	23.37	38.41	16.30
CA	Sunnyvale	41.96	24.23	39.81	16.89
CO	Denver	36.63	21.89	35.98	15.26
CT	Hartford/Stratford/Windsor Locks	38.57	23.02	37.82	16.05
FL	Melbourne	32.81	19.71	32.36	13.72
GA	Marietta	35.33	21.01	34.51	16.62
GA	Savannah	33.16	20.10	33.03	14.01
IA	Cedar Rapids	34.30	20.73	34.07	14.45
IL	Rockford	36.04	21.53	35.38	15.02
IN	Indianapolis	35.88	20.86	34.72	17.73
KS	Wichita	34.49	20.90	34.34	14.58
MA	Lexington/Marlborough	36.22	21.87	35.95	15.25
MN	Hopkins/Minneapolis	37.11	22.23	37.57	15.49
MO	St. Louis	35.93	21.77	35.77	15.18
NC	Charlotte	34.66	20.75	34.10	14.47
NH	Nashua	37.14	21.87	35.95	15.25
OH	Cleveland	35.94	21.56	35.42	15.02
OH	Cincinnatti/Evandale	35.25	21.29	34.97	14.84
PA	King of Prussia	36.82	22.50	36.96	15.68
SC	Greenville	32.66	19.76	32.48	13.84
TX	Dallas/Ft. Worth/Grand Prairie/ Irving	34.06	20.81	34.21	14.51
UT	Magna	34.02	20.58	33.82	14.35
WA	Auburn/Everett/Renton	37.23	22.21	36.50	15.48

(Continued on next page)

KEY OPERATING COSTS FOR SELECTED AEROSPACE
MANUFACTURING CENTERS
As of 2004, continued

Power (¢/kwh)	Lease Rates ($/sq ft) Industrial	Office	Construction ($/sq ft)	State	Location
5.41¢	$ 6.60	$24.00	$51.93	AZ	Phoenix/Tempe
7.44	4.56	22.00	50.98	AZ	Tucson
10.70	8.88	30.60	62.14	CA	Chula Vista
12.89	4.33	26.55	63.28	CA	El Segundo/Long Beach/ Redondo Beach/Seal Beach/ Torrance
12.48	7.68	44.10	69.70	CA	Sunnyvale
4.87	6.00	17.00	52.00	CO	Denver
7.21	4.40	25.50	62.87	CT	Hartford/Stratford/Windsor Locks
5.65	3.70	16.25	53.62	FL	Melbourne
4.73	3.70	16.00	48.63	GA	Marietta
4.73	3.15	13.05	44.94	GA	Savannah
3.54	3.80	16.75	52.19	IA	Cedar Rapids
5.80	3.60	13.60	63.35	IL	Rockford
3.78	5.00	19.30	55.46	IN	Indianapolis
4.04	2.75	20.00	48.63	KS	Wichita
8.15	4.00	18.00	62.54	MA	Lexington/Marlborough
4.40	3.50	14.00	67.27	MN	Hopkins/Minneapolis
4.13	2.50	22.00	62.33	MO	St. Louis
4.93	5.00	18.50	45.02	NC	Charlotte
8.41	7.50	16.25	55.92	NH	Nashua
6.34	3.50	20.50	69.77	OH	Cleveland
4.50	3.00	20.00	64.43	OH	Cincinnatti/Evandale
6.72	2.88	25.25	67.54	PA	King of Prussia
4.68	2.90	15.25	45.62	SC	Greenville
4.44	3.15	18.00	48.23	TX	Dallas/Ft. Worth/Grand Prairie/ Irving
4.08	3.12	18.28	51.52	UT	Magna
5.69	5.65	19.00	62.04	WA	Auburn/Everett/Renton

Source: The Boyd Company (Princeton, NJ), BizCosts ® data bank.
  a Includes all major geographically-variable operating costs for a representative 200,000 sq. ft. aerospace manufacturing facility. Costs reflect a 500-worker plant site having 250 production employees, 150 engineers, and 100 administrative support workers. Annual costs for electric power, real estate, and construction are scaled accordingly.

DEPARTMENT OF DEFENSE MAJOR CONTRACTORS
Fiscal Years 1999–2003
Listed by rank according to net value of
prime contracts awarded during last fiscal year
(Millions of Dollars)

Company	1999	2000	2001	2002	2003
TOTAL CONTRACT AWARDS.........	$125,037	$133,232	$144,635	$170,783	$208,964
Lockheed Martin Corp.	$ 12,675	$ 15,126	$ 14,687	$ 16,997	$ 21,927
The Boeing Co.	11,568[b]	12,041	13,341	16,552	17,340
Northrop Grumman Corp.[c]	6,721	7,822	7,056	10,760	11,126
General Dynamics Corp.	4,564	4,196	4,907	6,962	8,235
Raytheon Co.	6,401	6,331	5,576	6,995	7,916
United Technologies Corp.	2,368	2,072	3,373	3,607	4,548
Halliburton.......................................	658	595	428	484	3,921
General Electric Co.	1,714	1,609	1,747	1,560	2,842
Science Applications Int'l Corp.	1,358	1,522	1,748	2,075	2,616
Computer Sciences Corp.	744	1,165	819	808	2,531
Humana, Inc.	620	129	394	1,305	2,362
L-3 Communications Holding, Inc. ...	316	378	495	1,660	2,086
BAE Systems PLC	729[d]	997	865	1,116	1,928
Health Net Inc.	(a)	551	939	1,691	1,756
Carlyle Group	1,336	1,195	1,232	(a)	1,670
ITT Industries Inc.	659	554	808	994	1,235
Triwest Healthcare Alliance Co.	414	336	554	824	1,200
Honeywell International Inc.	746[f]	951	902	1,278	1,199
North American Airlines	(a)	(a)	(a)	622	1,195
Fedex Corp.	356	452	211	386	1,047
Bell Boeing Joint Program	(a)	(a)	(a)	(a)	987
Bechtel Corp.	600	695	621	1,030	910
Booz Allen & Hamilton	370	420	435	688	808
Boeing Sikorsky Comanche Team ...	296	385	528	662	799
The Titan Corporation	162	314	345	502	799
Government of the United States......	251	591	(a)	299	781
Electronic Data Systems Corp.	238	330	223	468	772
Veritas Capital Corporation	(a)	(a)	441	522	767
Exxon Mobil Corp.	208[g]	325	705	571	757
Textron Inc.	1,423	1,164	572	909	723

Source: Department of Defense, "100 Companies Receiving the Largest Dollar Volume of Prime Contract Awards" (Annually).
 a Not in top 100 companies for indicated year(s).
 b Includes awards previously reported separately as Rockwell International Corp.
 c Includes awards previously reported separately as Litton Industries Inc. and TRW Inc.
 d Includes awards previously reported as General Electric Co. PLC.
 f Includes awards previously reported as Allied Signal Inc.
 g Includes awards previously reported as Mobil Corp. and Exxon Corp.

NATIONAL AERONAUTICS AND SPACE ADMINISTRATION
MAJOR CONTRACTORS
Fiscal Years 2000–2003
Listed by rank according to net value of prime
contracts awarded during last fiscal year
(Millions of Dollars)

Company	2000	2001	2002	2003
TOTAL PROCUREMENTS	$12,504	$12,748	$13,303	$13,274
Awards to Business Firms	9,273	9,210	9,569	9,510
% of TOTAL PROCUREMENTS	74%	72%	72%	72%
United Space Alliance LLC	$ 1,609	$ 1,659	$ 1,798	$ 1,760
The Boeing Co.	1,236	952	988	898
Lockheed Martin Space Operations Co.	485	494	504	624
Lockheed Martin Corp.	710	608	611	552
Thiokol Corp.	368	378	390	396
Boeing North America	258	304	348	381
Space Gateway Support	218	261	310	297
Lockheed Martin Engrg. & Science	287	228	212	223
Science Applications Int'l Corp.	107	138	152	192
Boeing Satellite Systems	88	104	89[b]	164
Computer Sciences Corp.	143	126	149	141
QSS Group Inc.	83	126	158	136
Raytheon Information Systems Co.	130	128	132	111
Ball Aerospace & Tech. Corp.	67	81	71	110
Delta Launch Services	(a)	62	92	107
McDonnell Douglas Corp.	320	282	222	105
Boeing Space Operations Co.	(a)	(a)	9	97
Raytheon Technical Services Co.	62	86	74	91
Swales & Associates Inc.	63	116	113	79
OAO Corp.	76	37	81	74
Wyle Laboratories	55	53	55	74
Sverdrup Technology Inc.	74	70	68	73
TRW Inc.	124	83	97	73
Hamilton Sundstrand Space Systems	55	55	50	71
Honeywell Technology Solutions	67	60[c]	62	63
Science Systems Applications	20	57	61	63
Northrop Grumman Systems Corp.	(a)	(a)	51	60
Orbital Sciences Corp.	82	74	60	58
Mississippi Space Services	57	59	53	53
Dyncorp Technical Services	27	33	31	51

Source: National Aeronautics and Space Administration, "Annual Procurement Report" (Annually).
a Not in list of major contractors for indicated year(s).
b Previously reported as Hughes Aircraft Co.
c Previously reported as Allied Signal Technical Services.

DEPARTMENT OF DEFENSE PRIME CONTRACT AWARDS OVER $25,000
FOR SELECTED MAJOR MILITARY HARD GOODS
BY GEOGRAPHIC REGION
Fiscal Years 2001, 2002, and 2003

Program and Region	Millions of Dollars			Percent of Program Total		
	2001	2002	2003	2001	2002	2003
AIRCRAFT—TOTAL.......	$33,491	$34,707	$43,387	100.0%	100.0%	100.0%
New England..................	$ 3,319	$ 4,072	$ 6,687	9.9%	11.7%	15.4%
Middle Atlantic.................	2,258	2,485	3,031	6.7	7.2	7.0
East North Central...........	3,163	1,935	2,317	9.4	5.6	5.3
West North Central..........	4,560	4,210	4,659	13.6	12.1	10.7
South Atlantic	7,423	6,375	3,960	22.2	18.4	9.1
East South Central	734	406	556	2.2	1.2	1.3
West South Central	4,257	5,795	11,588	12.7	16.7	26.7
Mountain	1,888	2,360	2,409	5.6	6.8	5.6
Pacific[a]	5,889	7,070	8,179	17.6	20.4	18.9
MISSILE & SPACE SYSTEMS—TOTAL........	$ 9,347	$13,050	$14,931	100.0%	100.0%	100.0%
New England..................	$ 355	$ 609	$ 1,011	3.8%	4.7%	6.8%
Middle Atlantic.................	494	411	268	5.3	3.1	1.8
East North Central...........	61	140	146	0.7	1.1	1.0
West North Central..........	149	172	288	1.6	1.3	1.9
South Atlantic	596	1,320	1,243	6.4	10.1	8.3
East South Central	594	693	945	6.4	5.3	6.3
West South Central	416	1,464	1,062	4.4	11.2	7.1
Mountain	2,773	3,797	3,419	29.7	29.1	22.9
Pacific[a]	3,911	4,444	6,550	41.8	34.1	43.9
ELECTRONICS & COMMUNICATIONS EQUIPMENT—TOTAL ...	$13,875	$15,763	$18,134	100.0%	100.0%	100.0%
New England..................	$ 1,860	$ 1,527	$ 1,595	13.4%	9.7%	8.8%
Middle Atlantic.................	1,808	2,298	2,774	13.0	14.6	15.3
East North Central...........	887	1,061	1,080	6.4	6.7	6.0
West North Central..........	741	868	968	5.3	5.5	5.3
South Atlantic	4,433	5,481	5,854	31.9	34.8	32.3
East South Central	204	197	208	1.5	1.3	1.1
West South Central	857	977	1,356	6.2	6.2	7.5
Mountain	845	770	1,158	6.1	4.9	6.4
Pacific[a]	2,240	2,584	3,141	16.1	16.4	17.3

Source: Department of Defense, Washington Headquarters Services, Information Technology Management Directorate.
    a   Includes Alaska and Hawaii.

Aeronautics: the science and art of designing and constructing aircraft, also, the art or science of operating aircraft.

Aerospace Employment: annual average calculated as one-twelfth of sum of monthly estimates of total number of persons employed during a designated pay period by the aircraft, missile, and space industries (SICs 372 and 376) plus estimated aerospace-related employment in the communications equipment (SIC 3662), instruments (SICs 381 and 382), and in certain other industries (SICs 28, 35, 73, 89, etc.)

Aerospace Industry: the industry engaged in research, development, and manufacture of aerospace systems including: manned and unmanned aircraft; missiles; spacecraft; space launch vehicles; propulsion, guidance, and control units for all of the foregoing; and a variety of airborne and ground-based equipment essential to the test, operation, and maintenance of flight vehicles.

Aerospace Payroll: estimated on the basis of average weekly *earnings* for a given calendar year for *production workers* plus an estimated annual salary for other employees.

Aerospace Sales: the AIA estimate of *aerospace industry sales*, developed by summing: DoD expenditures for *aircraft, missiles*, and space-related *procurement* and RDT&E; NASA expenditures for *research and development* and space flight control and data communications; *outlays* for space activities by other U.S. government departments and agencies; commercial sales of space-related products; net domestic and export sales of civil aircraft, engines, and parts; *Foreign Military Sales* and commercial exports of military aircraft, missiles,

propulsion, and related parts; sales of *related products and services* including: electronics, software, and ground support equipment; and sales of *nonaerospace products* which are produced in aerospace-manufacturing *establishments* and which use technology, processes, and materials derived from the aerospace industry.

AIA: Aerospace Industries Association of America, Inc., formerly Aircraft Industries Association.

Air Carriers: the commercial system of air transportation, consisting of domestic and international scheduled and charter service.

Aircraft: all airborne vehicles supported either by buoyancy or by dynamic action. Used in this volume in a restricted sense to mean an airplane—any winged aircraft including helicopters, but excluding gliders and guided missiles.

Aircraft Agreement (Agreement on Trade in Civil Aircraft): negotiated in the Tokyo Round of the *Multilateral Trade Negotiations* and implemented January 1, 1980, providing for elimination of tariff and non-tariff trade barriers in the civil aircraft sector.

Aircraft Industry: the industry primarily engaged in the manufacture of aircraft, aircraft engines, and parts including propellers and auxiliary equipment. A sector of the *Aerospace Industry*.

Airframe: the structural components of an airplane, such as: fuselage, empennage, wings, landing gear, and engine mounts, but excluding such items as: engines, accessories, electronics, and other parts that may be replaced from time to time.

Airlines: see *Air Carriers*.

Appropriation (Federal Budget): an act of Congress authorizing an agency to incur *obligations* and make payments out of funds held by the Department of the Treasury.

Assets, Net: the sum of all recorded assets after reducing such amount by allowance of reserve for bad debts, *depreciation*, and amortization, but before deducting any liabilities, mortgages, or other indebtedness.

Astronautics: the art and science of designing, building, and operating manned or unmanned space objects.

Average Weekly Hours: average hours for which pay was received; different from standard or scheduled hours.

Avionics: communications, navigation, flight controls, and displays.

Backlog: the *sales* value of *orders* accepted (supported by legal documents) that have not yet passed through the sales account.

Budget Authority: authority provided by the Congress; mainly in the form of *Appropriations*, which allows Federal agencies to incur *obligations* to spend or lend money.

Bureau of Economic Analysis (BEA): an agency of the Department of Commerce.

Bureau of Labor Statistics (BLS): an agency of the Department of Labor.

Bureau of the Census: an agency of the Department of Commerce.

Constant Dollars: calculated by dividing current ("then-year") dollars by appropriate price *deflator* and multiplying the result by 100.

Deflator: index used to convert a price level to one comparable with the price level at a different time, offsetting the effect of inflation. The base period, which equals 100, is usually specified as either a given fiscal or calendar year.

Depreciation: the general conversion of the depreciable cost of a fixed asset into expense, spread over its remaining life. There are a number of methods, all based on a periodic charge to an expense account and a corresponding credit to a reserve account.

Development: the process or activity of working out a basic design, idea, or piece of equipment. See also *Research and Development.*

DoD: Department of Defense.

DoE: Department of Energy.

DoT: Department of Transportation.

Durable Goods Industry: comprised of major manufacturing industry groups with SIC Codes 24, 25, and 32-39. All major manufacturing industry groups in SIC Codes 20-23 and 26-31 are considered nondurable goods manufacturing industry groups.

Earnings: the actual return to the worker for a stated period of time. Irregular bonuses, retroactive items, payments of various welfare benefits, and payroll taxes paid by employers are excluded.

Average Hourly Earnings: on a "gross" basis, reflecting not only changes in basic hourly and incentive wage rates, but also such variable factors as: premium pay for overtime, late shift work, and changes in output of workers paid for an incentive plan.

Average Weekly Earnings: derived by multiplying *average weekly hours* by *average hourly earnings.*

Establishment: the basis for reporting to the Census of Manufacturers; an operating facility in a single location.

Evaluation (Department of Defense): determination of technical suitability of material, equipment, or a system. See RDT&E.

Expenditures (Federal Budget): see *Outlays.*

Export-Import Bank of the United States (Eximbank): created in 1934 and established as an independent U.S. government agency in 1945, Eximbank is designed "... to aid in financing and to facilitate *exports...*" Eximbank receives no *appropriations* from the U.S. Congress. It is directed by statute to: (1) offer financing that is competitive with that offered exporters of other countries by their official export credit institutions, (2) determine that the transactions supported provide for a reasonable assurance of repayment, (3) supplement, but not compete with private sources of export financing, and (4) take into account the effect of its activities on small business, the domestic economy, and U.S. employment.

Exports: domestic merchandise including commodities which are grown, produced, or manufactured in the United States and commodities of foreign origin which have been changed in the United States from the form in which they were imported or which have been enhanced in value by further manufacture in the United States and which are traded or sold to other nations.

FAA: Federal Aviation Administration (formerly the Federal Aviation Agency), an agency of the Department of Transportation.

Facility: a physical plant or installation including: real property, building, structures, improvements, and plant equipment.

Fiscal Year (Federal Budget): beginning October 1, 1976, the fiscal years run from October 1 through September 30 and are designated by the year in which they end.

Flyaway Value: includes the cost of the *airframe*, engines, electronics, communications, armament, and other installed equipment.

Footnotes: common to many tables throughout this edition are the following:

E	Estimate.
NA	Not available/ Not applicable.
p	Preliminary.
r	Revised.
Tr.Qtr.	*Transition Quarter.*
NOTE:	Detail may not add to totals because of rounding.

Foreign Military Sales (FMS): export *sales* to foreign governments arranged through the Department of Defense, whereby DoD recovers full purchase price and administrative costs; often mistakenly used to include foreign military aid and foreign commercial sales as well.

FY: see *Fiscal Year.*

GDP (Gross Domestic Product): the market value of goods and services produced by labor and property located in the United States.

General Agreement on Tariffs and Trade (GATT): a multilateral treaty among more than 100 governments whose primary mission is the reduction of trade barriers. The World Trade Organization was established January 1, 1995 to implement the agreement and provide a forum to discuss trade issues.

General Aviation: all civil flying except that of air *carriers.*

Helicopter: a rotary-wing *aircraft* which depends principally for its support and motion in the air upon the lift generated by one or more power-driven rotors, rotating on substantially vertical axes. A helicopter is a V/STOL.

Heliport: an area, either at ground level or elevated on a structure, that is used for the landing and take-off of helicopters and includes some or all of the various facilities useful to *helicopter* operations such as: helicopter parking, hangar, waiting room, fueling, and maintenance equipment.

Helistop: a minimum facility *heliport*, either at ground level or elevated on a structure for the landing and take-off of helicopters, but without such auxiliary facilities as: waiting room, hangar parking, etc.

ICBM: InterContinental Ballistic Missile, with a range of more than 5,000 miles.

Imports: classified as "general imports" or "imports for consumption." This volume refers generally to "imports for consumption," which are entries for immediate consumption plus merchandise withdrawn from bonded storage warehouses for consumption. Data are compiled from Import Entries filed with U.S. Customs officials and are in general based on the market value or price in the foreign country at the time of exportation of such merchandise, including the cost of containers and coverings, as well as other charges and expenses incidental to placing the merchandise in condition, packed and ready for shipment to the United States, but excluding import duties, insurance, freight, and other charges incidental to arrival of the goods in the United States. The foreign values of imported merchandise are converted into U.S. currency at the rate of exchange prevailing on the day the merchandise is shipped to the United States.

Income:

Net Operating Income: total *sales* less total operating costs.

Other Income and Expenses: includes interest income, royalty income, capital gains and losses, interest expense, cash discounts, etc.

Net Income (Before Income Taxes): *Net Operating Income* plus or minus Other Income and Expenses.

Net Income (After Income Taxes): *Net Income (Before Income Taxes)* less federal income taxes.

Lump-Sum Wage Payment: a one-time payment given in lieu of general wage increases and/or cost of living adjustments in labor settlements.

Manufacturing Industries: those *establishments* engaged in the mechanical or chemical transformation of inorganic or organic substances into new products, and usually described as plants, factories, or mills, which characteristically use power-driven machines and materials-handling equipment; also establishments engaged in assembling component parts of manufactured products if the new product is neither a structure nor other fixed improvement.

MDA: Missile Defense Agency, an agency of the Department of Defense.

Merchandise Trade Balance: the difference between the value of U.S. goods exported to other countries and foreign goods imported into this country. The trade balance is generally regarded as "favorable" when *exports* exceed *imports*—a trade surplus—and "unfavorable" when imports exceed exports—a trade deficit.

Missile: sometimes applied to space launch vehicles, but more properly connotes automated weapons of warfare, that is, a weapon which has an integral system of guidance, as opposed to the unguided rocket.

Multilateral Trade Negotiations (MTN): a forum within the GATT in which countries negotiate to overcome their trade problems. Awaiting ratification by each of the 112 nations involved in the MTN, the "Uruguay Round" seeks to strengthen the GATT and expand its disciplines to new areas such as: services, agriculture, and trade-related intellectual property rights.

NAICS (North American Industrial Classification System): a system developed by Canada, Mexico, and the U.S. government that groups *establishments* into industries based on a production-oriented concept in order to provide uniformity and comparability of statistical data and facilitate economic analyses between industries and the three North American countries.

NASA: National Aeronautics and Space Administration.

NATO: North Atlantic Treaty Organization.

New Obligational Authority (Federal Budget): see *Budget Authority.*

Non-Aerospace Products and Services: products and services other than *aircraft, missiles, space vehicles,* and related propulsion and parts, produced or performed by *establishments* whose principal business is the development and/or manufacture of aerospace products.

OASD: Office of the Assistant Secretary of Defense.

Obligations (Federal Budget): commitments made by Federal agencies to pay out money for products, services, or other purposes—as distinct from the actual payments. Obligations incurred may not be larger than *budget authority.*

Orders, Net New: the *sales* value of new orders (supported by legal documents) minus cancellations during the period.

Other Aerospace Products and Services: all conversions, modifications, site activation, other aerospace products (including drones), services, plus *research and development* under contract, defined as: *basic* and *applied research* in the sciences and in engineering and design and *development* of prototype products and processes.

Other Customers: all customers other than the U.S. government to include but not limited to: *air carriers,* private citizens and corporations, and state, local, and foreign governments.

Outlays: checks issued, interest accrued on the public debt, or other payments made, net of refunds and reimbursements.

Overtime Hours: that portion of the gross *average weekly hours* which was in excess of regular hours and for which premium payments were made.

Passenger-Mile: one passenger moved one mile.

Payroll, All Manufacturing: includes the gross *earnings* paid in the calendar year to all employees on the payroll of operating manufacturing *establishments.* Includes all forms of compensation paid directly to workers such as: salaries, wages, commissions, dismissal pay, all bonuses, vacation and sick leave pay, and compensation in kind; prior to such deductions as: employees' Social Security contributions, withholding taxes, group insurance, union dues, and savings bonds. Does not include employers' Social Security contributions or other non-payroll labor costs such as:

employees' pension plans, group insurance premiums, and workmen's compensation.

Procurement: the process whereby the executive agencies of the Federal Government acquire goods and services from enterprises other than the Federal Government.

Production Workers: includes working foremen and all non-supervisory workers (including lead-men and trainees) engaged in fabricating, processing, assembling, inspection, receiving, storage, handling, janitorial services, product development, auxiliary production for plant's own use, and recordkeeping and services closely associated with the above production operations.

RDT&E (Department of Defense): Research, Development, Test, and Evaluation.

Related Products and Services: sales of electronics, software, and ground equipment in support of aerospace products, plus sales by aerospace manufacturing *establishments* of systems and equipment which are generally derived from the industry's aerospace technological expertise in design, materials, and processes, but which are intended for applications other than flight.

Research: see *Research and Development.*

Research and Development:
  Research: systematic study directed toward fuller scientific knowledge or understanding of the subject studied. Research is classified as either basic or applied according to the objectives of the sponsoring agency.
  Applied Research: with the objective of gaining knowledge or understanding necessary for determining the means by which a recognized and specific need may be met.
  Basic Research: with the objective of gaining fuller knowledge or understanding of the fundamental aspects of phenomena and of observable facts without specific applications toward processes or products in mind.
  Development: the systematic use of scientific knowledge directed toward the production of useful materials, devices, systems, or methods including design and development of prototypes and processes.

Independent Research and Development (IR&D): a term devised by the Department of Defense and used by Federal agencies to differentiate between a contractor's research and development technical effort performed under a contract, grant, or other arrangement (R&D) and that which is self-initiated and self-funded (IR&D).

Industrial Research and Development: research and development work performed within company facilities, funded by company or Federal funds, and excluding company-financed research and development contracted to outside organizations such as: research institutions, universities and colleges, or other non-profit organizations.

Rotorcraft: an *aircraft* which, in all its usual flight attitudes, is supported in the air wholly or in part by a rotor or rotors (i.e., airfoils rotating or revolving about an axis). See *Helicopter.*

Sales: net of returns, allowances, and discounts, the dollar value of shipments, including dealer's commissions, if any, which have passed through the sales account.

Satellite: a body that revolves around a larger body, such as the Moon revolving around the Earth, or a man-made object revolving about any body such as the Sun, Earth, or Moon.

SIC (Standard Industrial Classification): a system developed by the U.S. government to define the industrial composition of the economy, facilitating comparability of statistics. See *Aerospace Industry* for explanation of SIC codes applicable to the aerospace industry.

Space Vehicle: an artificial body operating in outer space (beyond the Earth's atmosphere).

Stockholder's Equity: *assets* minus all obligations of the corporation, except those to stockholders. Annual data are average equity for the year (using four end-of-quarter figures). For details, see "*Quarterly Financial Report* for Manufacturing, Mining and Trade Corporations," compiled by the *Bureau of the Census.*

STOL: short take-off and landing *aircraft.*

Test (Department of Defense): an experiment designed to assess progress in attainment or accomplishment of *development* objectives (see RDT&E).

Thrust: the driving force exerted by an engine, particularly an *aircraft* or *missile* engine, in propelling the vehicle to which it is attached.

Ton-Mile: one ton moved one mile.

Total Obligational Authority: the sum of *budget authority* granted or requested from the Congress in a given year, plus unused budget authority from prior years.

Trade Balance: see *Merchandise Trade Balance.*

Transition Quarter (Tr. Qtr.): the three-month interval from July 1, 1976 to September 30, 1976 belonging to neither Fiscal Year 1976 nor Fiscal Year 1977. See *Fiscal Year.*

Turbine, Turbo: a mechanical device or engine that spins in reaction to a fluid flow that passes through or over it. Frequently used in "turboprop" or "turbojet."

UK: United Kingdom.

US: United States of America.

USA: United States Army, an agency of the U.S. Department of Defense.

USAF: United States Air Force, an agency of the U.S. Department of Defense.

USN: United States Navy, an agency of the U.S. Department of Defense.

Utility Aircraft: an aircraft designed for general purpose flying.

V/STOL: vertical short take-off and/or landing *aircraft.*